Praise fo

"It is rare for a book about practicing law to be so enthralling that you can't put it down. This is a such a rare book. It is inspirational, empowering, and blunt. It is not judgmental or preachy. Courtney and Theresa have been there and done that—and they are willing to share their experiences, both good and bad. The stories have a familiar ring to them, but they use them to illustrate important things about being a woman, being a trial lawyer, being a mom, being a wife, sister, friend, and all at the same time. Sometimes, these courageous women write poignantly about making almost impossible choices, feeling lonely and wrestling with guilt. They also offer valuable tips about trying cases. They offer us their whole lives with grace and with dignity. All women lawyers should read it and so should most male lawyers."

—Roxanne Barton Conlin, past president of the AAJ and member of the Inner Circle of Advocates

"This is the book women lawyers have long awaited. A *Lean In* for women attorneys, it teaches you how to speak up for yourself and the people you represent; quiet the fears that keep you from being your best; connect with the jurors, the judge and, most importantly, your true self; and start and run your own law practice. With great insight and gentle humor, Courtney and Theresa show why a woman's unique talents make her the best advocate in the courtroom. Sprinkled through with stories of their own adventures (and a few mistakes), these two young powerhouse trial lawyers will have you eagerly packing your shoulder bag for your next trial."

—Randi McGinn, past president of the Inner Circle of Advocates and author of
Changing Laws, Saving Lives: How to Take on Corporate Giants and Win

"A thoughtful, lively, and much needed book on how to be a female trial lawyer. Filled with practical advice and inspiration for women—but also for men. An important addition to any trial lawyer's library."

—Rick Friedman, past president of the Inner Circle of Advocates and coauthor of *Rules of the Road: A Plaintiff Lawyer's Guide to Proving Liability*

"It's about time! This book will be the splendid mother of a necessary progeny of great seminars, articles, workshops, and more good books from more voices we all need. I'd wanted to say that Courtney Rowley and Theresa Bowen Hatch have done a masterful job, but the lack of a feminine form of the word 'mastery' is precisely the kind of thing that makes this book so essential. And yeah, I have to admit that men better read it, too."

—David Ball, trial consultant and author of *David Ball on Damages*

"*Trial by Woman* has insightful and valuable advice for all trial lawyers. This is a book for all new lawyers and those who mentor with guidance and commonsense advice. Women who are trial lawyers need this book and men who are trial lawyers need it just as much or more."

—Paul Luvera, past president of the Inner Circle of Advocates and the Washington State Bar

"*Trial by Woman* is not lawyer with an asterisk. It is lawyer with an exclamation point. For those skeptics, check out Theresa and Courtney's trial results, take a good look at the current landscape, then get to reading this book. As zealous advocates who are deep in the trenches, trying their cases, Courtney and Theresa generously share experiences, the lessons they've learned from others and on their own, along with techniques to utilize in the practice of law and their wisdom moving forward. *Trial by Woman* is not meant to be 'read by woman' only. It's too valuable a resource for that, especially during these times. This is not about separation—it is all about empowerment."

—Artemis Malekpour, litigation partner at Malekpour & Ball Consulting and co-presenter in *Focus Groups: How to do Your Own Jury Research*

"Only when truth is openly discussed can progress be made. Theresa and Courtney candidly explore the truth of being a woman in the legal profession. As your read their story, you'll find yourself saying 'me too' as you enjoy vignettes about their journey, and through their perseverance and shared wisdom you'll be inspired."

—Jayme Simpson, member of the Consumer Attorneys of San Diego, committee chair of the New Lawyers Division of Consumer Attorneys of California, and former director of the New Lawyers Division of San Diego County Bar Association

"Rowley and Bowen Hatch remind us that we, modern women, are uniquely equipped to shape the hearts and minds of jurors through genuine connection. They challenge us to elevate our practice and ourselves. Nurturing and empowering, *Trial by Woman* is more than a book. It's a mantra."

—Ibiere N. Seck, member of the board of governors of the Consumer Attorneys Association of Los Angeles and Consumer Attorneys of California, and president of the National Black Lawyers 40-under-40

"*Trial by Woman* is a must-read book for female trial lawyers at all stages of their career and the men who mentor and support them. Together, Courtney Rowley and Theresa Bowen Hatch have called upon their years of experience as top trial lawyers to develop an innovative approach to trying cases called Trial Perspective. Using it, women can learn the skills and strategies needed to work smarter instead of harder, allowing them to use their unique talents to successfully represent their clients while also finding that always elusive work/life balance. Rowley and Bowen Hatch finally address in print what women in the trial world have been struggling with privately for decades, and they do so with grace, humor, and common sense. I intend to recommend it to all my female law students who are planning to try cases for a living."

—Susan Poehls, director of trial advocacy at Loyola Law School in Los Angeles and recipient of Stetson Law School's Lifetime Achievement Award for Excellence in Advocacy

"Are you lucky enough to have a female best friend to turn to who also happens to be a trial lawyer in a predominantly male profession going through the same experiences or hurdles that you are facing? If so, consider yourself truly fortunate. If not, this is the book for you. Crammed full of helpful insights, war stories, and advice, it is a book that reminds you that you must be good to yourself in order to be good in the courtroom for others. And most importantly, it reminds us that we are all part of a precious sisterhood that needs to be cherished. Enjoy it over a warm cup of tea or cocoa and remember: you are not alone. There is nothing we cannot accomplish together."

—Deborah Chang, selected by the *Daily Journal* as one of the Top 100 Lawyers in California, named as one of the "Elite Women of the Plaintiffs Bar" by the *National Law Journal* and ALM, recipient of the 2014 Consumer Attorney of the Year Award and 2017 Women's Caucus Women Consumer Advocate of the Year Award, and has consistently obtained some of the largest verdicts and settlements in California and Las Vegas

"As a trial lawyer and the proud father of one daughter who just became a new lawyer and another daughter who just started law school, I appreciate that Courtney Rowley and Theresa Bowen Hatch have written a book that can advise my daughters on being strong women in a demanding profession from a female perspective."

—Brian Panish, member of the Inner Circle of Advocates

"*Trial by Woman* is a brutally honest trial practice book that deals with issues confronting women in the courtroom today. It is a must read for anyone who wants to learn how to balance the demands of real-life with real law. This book should be read by every women who wants to become a better trial lawyer and any man who wants to come into the twenty-first century."

—Gary Dordick, emeritus member of the Consumer Attorneys Association of Los Angeles Board of Governors and obtained the highest jury verdict in Ventura County ($125 million) in 2016

TRIAL BY WOMAN

COURTNEY ROWLEY
AND
THERESA BOWEN HATCH

TRIAL GUIDES, LLC

Trial Guides, LLC, Portland, Oregon 97210

Copyright © 2018 by Courtney Rowley and Theresa Bowen Hatch.

All rights reserved.

TRIAL BY WOMAN is a trademark of Courtney Rowley and is used under license.

TRIAL GUIDES and logo are registered trademarks of Trial Guides, LLC.

ISBN: 978-1-941007-81-5

Library of Congress Control Number: 2018958385

These materials, or any parts or portions thereof, may not be reproduced in any form, written or mechanical, or be programmed into any electronic storage or retrieval system, without the express written permission of Trial Guides, LLC, unless such copying is expressly permitted by federal copyright law. Please direct inquiries to:

Trial Guides, LLC
Attn: Permissions
2350 NW York Street
Portland, OR 97210
(800) 309-6845
www.trialguides.com

Managing Editor: Tina Ricks

Production Editor: Travis Kremer

Copyeditor: Patricia Esposito

Proofreader: Tara Lehmann

Cover Photo: Annette Logan

Original Interior Template Design by Laura Lind Design

Interior Layout by Travis Kremer

Printed and bound in the United States of America.

Printed on acid-free paper.

To Our Children

Contents

Introduction xiii

Part 1: Our Time Is Now 1

1. Together, Women Run the World 5
2. The New Model for Practicing Law 9
3. Women Have Superpowers 23
4. We Have the Power to Create the Future We Want 43

Part 2: The Power of Being a Woman in the Law 53

5. Hold on a Minute, Let's Keep This Real 55
6. An Interview with Roxanne Barton Conlin 79

Part 3: Unexpected Ways to Increase Your Success . . . 93

7. The Power of Women Promoting Women 95
8. Finding Your Voice 107
9. The Courage to Be Feminine 115
10. How to Open Your Own Law Firm 119

Part 4: Trial Perspective and Trial Techniques 135

11. Trial Perspective 137
12. Focus Groups by Woman 145
13. Discovery by Woman 149
14. Jury Selection by Woman 163

15. Opening Statement by Woman.................................. 195

16. Direct and Cross-Examination by Woman................. 221

17. Closing by Woman... 243

18. Negotiation and Settlement by Woman..................... 267

Part 5: The Highest and Best Use of Your Time....... 279

19. The Importance of Physical, Mental, and Spiritual Health ... 281

20. On New Motherhood and Family 297

21. On Health and Healing... 317

22. Tips for Law Students... 329

Part 6: Being a Woman in the Courtroom.......... 339

23. Dressing the Part... 341

24. Minding Your Behavior.. 361

25. Calling Men to Action... 369

Epilogue.. 381

Appendix A... 385

Appendix B 387

Appendix C 389

Appendix D 393

Publisher's Note

This book is intended for practicing attorneys. It does not offer legal advice or take the place of consultation with an attorney who has appropriate expertise and experience.

Attorneys are strongly cautioned to evaluate the information, ideas, and opinions set forth in this book in light of their own research, experience, and judgment. Readers should also consult applicable rules, regulations, procedures, cases, and statutes (including those issued after the publication date of this book), and make independent decisions about whether and how to apply such information, ideas, and opinions for particular cases.

Quotations from cases, pleadings, discovery, and other sources are for illustrative purposes only and may not be suitable for use in litigation in any particular case.

The cases described in this book are actual cases, and the names and other identifying details of participants, litigants, witnesses, and counsel have not been fictionalized except where otherwise expressly stated.

All references to the trademarks of third parties are strictly informational and for the purposes of commentary. No sponsorship or endorsement by, or affiliation with, the trademark owners is claimed or implied by the authors or publisher of this book.

The authors and publisher disclaim any liability or responsibility for loss or damages resulting from the use of this book or the information, ideas, and opinions contained in this book.

Introduction

Both of us have worked for some of the top law firms in the country, and we have worked with the best trial lawyers in the country. We did what many of you are doing: paid our dues, put in long hours, struggled to manage an ever-increasing caseload with clients we barely knew, and lost any glimmer of hope for time for ourselves in the process. We hung in there because we were promised more money and more trials. Those promises fell short. And while we grew tremendously in those roles, we both had the nagging feeling that there was a better way to do things—that we could practice law, connect with our clients, but also be more plugged in to ourselves, our interests, our lives, and the people who matter most to us. So, we started our own practices. We found very few resources on starting law firms, and even fewer resources on doing it as a woman and with the balance we both yearned for.

As trial lawyers and as women, we have been each other's mentors—professionally and personally—for the better part of a decade. During the time that we came up in the profession, there weren't a lot of women trial lawyers, and there still aren't. Statistically, we're in the minority. That meant that while there were legends out there—the Randi McGinns and Roxanne Barton Conlins of the world—they were legends, and we didn't feel like they were accessible to us. When we showed up at the trial lawyer events, we were among the few women. Even the elder stateswomen—the vintage ahead of us in our own towns—the Cindy Chihaks and Ginny Nelsons in San Diego and the Debbie Changs and the Christine Spagnolis in Los Angeles—didn't seem like accessible mentors because they weren't of our generation and experiencing what we were experiencing—at least not right now. They had already fought the good fight, fought hard for their places at the trial table, and many had their own firms. But even they seemed too far removed from the everyday experiences of our lives as young, female trial lawyers working for men in an increasingly modern time.

So, we fumbled through and figured a lot of things out the hard way over the past ten years. One of us would have an experience with a male coworker getting more trial opportunities, and the other was able to empathize and relate and bring some perspective and insight to the situation. Or one of us would find out that a male colleague was making more money for doing the same job, and the other would pull out a bottle of wine, sob in the wine, and then figure out a way to ask for, and get, more money.

And, time and again, we find ourselves having the same, tired discussion about what to wear to court: *Are these heels too high? Can I wear flats? Is a dress OK? How about a skirt? Is this skirt too short when I sit down? Pantyhose or no pantyhose? Hair up or hair down? Suits are for men; why do I have to wear a man-suit costume? Isn't it my work that's important? And, please, God, can you give someone in this world the creative juices to come up with a court costume for women that makes us feel comfortable so that we don't have to think about what we're wearing? Or, in the alternative, God, could you please have the United States of America spontaneously and immediately adopt the custom of all lawyers wearing robes like the barristers of England? Please and thank you, Amen.*

Over the past ten years, we've married, had children, and looked for resources that spoke to both our roles as women raising families and women running our own businesses. And we didn't find what we needed. So, as we have done in many areas of our lives, we made it ourselves. We had to become the mentors, role models, and gurus we were searching for. We hope we can help you do the same. We offer this book as an act of service and mentorship and paying it forward to you, our trial lawyer sisters, in the hopes that it will make your journey easier, happier, and more fulfilling, and keep you in this beautiful, meaningful practice we all do called the law.

Over the years, we've had the unique opportunity to learn from, and practice with, some of the best and most successful trial lawyers in our profession, but what works for men doesn't always work for women. And so, through trial-and-error, we've taken the best approaches we learned from our male colleagues and modified them to work for us, as women. And we've developed our own methods for trial work that capitalize on the unique superpowers of women in the courtroom. You were made for this, and we'll show you how to make changes to your practice today that highlight and honor your unique feminine gifts.

By working your cases from an approach we've developed called Trial Perspective, you can advance yourself and your cases faster—and increase your value as a lawyer, along with the value of your cases. We do not believe in "paying your dues" or "waiting your turn." That model is outdated and rarely in service to our highest and best use of time. By investing in yourself through learning the trial techniques in this book and using the outside resources we suggest, you will immediately start producing better work and doing better for yourself and your clients, no matter how low or high you are on the totem pole.

This book is a compilation of research, tried and tested systems for working cases from a Trial Perspective approach, advanced trial skills, as well as encouragement and advice that we have accumulated in a decade of trying cases and growing businesses, getting married, getting unmarried, huge wins, a lot of losses, having babies, watching our babies grow into toddlers, our toddlers grow into teens, moving our kids off to college while sobbing quietly on the ride home, learning to love and take care of ourselves, and supporting one another the whole way through. The tools and advice you will find in this book are invaluable resources and insights that we have developed, use, and wish we had when we started our careers, our businesses, and our families. Take them, modify them to fit you, and use them in good health!

Whether you are just getting started and want to learn about the practice of law or you have been doing this a long time and are looking to reinvigorate your practice, we'll share with you our experiences, advice, and insights that will enhance your practice and enrich your life.

This is also a fantastic resource for any man who wants to mentor, work with, encourage, and better use the skills of the women lawyers in their lives. We have met a lot of great men who are striving to break free of the traditional law firm mold and are looking for resources and insights on how to create dynamic, diverse, supportive, and creative environments for women. Right now, at this time on the planet, we are experiencing a significant and welcome shift in the legal culture. The most successful law firms are ones with women in leadership positions. Women all over the country are starting successful, vibrant, and rapidly growing law firms that are raising the bar in the legal and business communities. Men and women are working together to reclaim and redefine what it means to be a lawyer in the twenty-first century.

Bottom line: this is a must-have resource for the modern law firm and practitioner.

In writing this book, we have three main groups in mind:

1. New lawyers, male and female, just starting out or with limited experience in litigation or running a law firm. If you are looking for a playbook that will give you the edge you need to achieve the results you are capable of—this might be the book for you. We will lay out the basics of litigating and trying cases, teach you how to work your cases from our Trial Perspective method, and show you how to do all of this while also making meaningful space for your dreams, your life, and your self-care.

2. Women of any experience level, maybe even where they think they want to be, who don't feel fulfilled. Maybe you aren't getting the results you want. Maybe you are dissatisfied with the opportunities you are being given. Maybe you are working for a great firm and have your name on the door, but you aren't getting the opportunities you want to try cases. Or you feel like you are working too much and neglecting yourself, your family, or your dreams. This book is for you.

3. Managers and owners of law firms—men and women—who have female partners and female employees and who are looking to improve the experience and maximize the value of the people in their firms.

We'll teach you the basics of how we try cases. But we'll go deeper than that; we'll have real conversations. We'll show you why women are uniquely and wonderfully suited to be trial lawyers. We'll talk about what women trial lawyers are really experiencing in the trenches and the struggles of balancing a demanding career and a full family or personal life. We'll share the strategies we both have used to build our own businesses, propel ourselves into the realm of the most successful trial lawyers in the country, and nourish thriving family and personal lives at the same time.

Above all, our goal in writing this book is to share what we've learned to help other lawyers, male and female, accomplish whatever goals they set for themselves, personally and professionally. This is a book for all women and men, from law school to the bench, that provides guidance, education, and tools to embrace the new female future: Trial by Woman.

PART ONE

Our Time Is Now

Our Time Is Now

The Matriarchal Society

In this part, we'll talk about the rapid rise of women as leaders in the law, why the old model of legal practice and paying your dues is antiquated and useless, why women are uniquely suited for trial work, and how the quality of your life tomorrow is inextricably bound to the thoughts you have and the actions you take today.

America is seeing an unprecedented shift away from the patriarchal hierarchy that has dominated our culture for millennia. The shift comes in the form of a movement which is gaining momentum at a rapid pace, driven by strong, powerful, modern women, who are redefining what it means to be women, mothers, professionals, and citizens. We are at the precipice, an opening of possibility, and we have to be vigilant, prepared, and willing to seize this opportunity for change. As professionals in law and leaders in our society, we are in a unique position to make that change and set an example for the evolution of our civilization, for the future of our world. As women, mothers, professionals, and leaders, we will succeed only if we work together, supporting one another in our work to teach and foster equality in our profession, in our workplaces, in our homes. The image and role of women in the law must dissolve and can no longer be defined by the past.

Women are becoming leaders in their careers at an unprecedented pace. The shift is happening all around us, across the country, across all major industries, without regard to race, education, or income. Each of us can choose to be part of the shift, to ride this historic wave of change and improvement. To participate and engage will take effort. It will require that we open space within our minds and our hearts to allow for change. But, more importantly, it will require us each to equip, grow, and better ourselves so that we move with the momentum.

This book is a wake-up call of sorts. It's a call to action. It's a grabbing you by the shoulders and giving you a good shake kind of delivery. And the message is this: now is the time; you have the power and the ability to raise yourself up, to make yourself more valuable and more powerful and more satisfied with your life in and out of the courtroom.

We'll walk you through specific techniques you can start using today to shift your thinking and your approach on cases. We'll show you how to use Trial Perspective methods in every part of your work, from discovery to client meetings to depositions to your interactions with opposing counsel. If you are not bringing a Trial Perspective approach to your case from the moment you begin, you are already losing.

The days of working your way up the ladder are gone. The days of waiting your turn for the position you want are gone. Access to technology, and thus to people and to information, can advance your experience and increase your value quickly and effectively, if you take advantage of it. Opening your eyes to look at what's around you in a different way, identifying where you want to be and what skills you need once you get there, and getting those skills today is what makes women leaders.

Standing in line leads you to be the next person in line. Stepping out of line and making your own way leads you to your highest and best greatness.

Look what happens when women step out of line and don't take the traditional path and wait their turn:

- Hillary Rodham Clinton (lawyer, First Lady, senator, secretary of state, 2016 Democratic Party presidential nominee)
- Mary Barra (joined General Motors when she was eighteen and has become the first woman to be CEO of a major car manufacturer)
- Danica Patrick (began Indy racing at age twenty-three, became the first woman to win the pole position at the Daytona 500)

- Oprah Winfrey (was demoted from her anchor job to be a local talk show host and later went on to have her own talk show for twenty-five years, which was the highest rated in television history, now has her own television network)
- Savannah Guthrie (lawyer who went on to become cohost of The Today Show)
- Megyn Kelly (lawyer who went on to host her own shows for Fox News and NBC News)

Your star can shine as bright as you'd like. It's 100 percent up to you and 100 percent within your control to make your life and your career whatever you want it to be. If it's your dream to work for a big-name firm, do it. If it's your dream to have your name on the door, do it. If it's your dream to work part-time and try only a case or two a year, do it. Our point is, decide where you want to be, and then figure out your own pathway to get there.

1

Together, Women Run the World

Women outnumber men in the world. Read that again, and really take it in. There are more women on this planet than there are men. Now, consider the adage that there is power in numbers. If you put those concepts together, we know for a fact that when women band together and work toward a common goal, they have insurmountable power.

Think about all of the examples in our world right now. Let's start with the #MeToo movement. When one woman makes an allegation of sexual harassment, misconduct, or abuse against a man, and the man denies the allegation, it's one voice against another voice. But when one woman stands up and says she was sexually harassed or abused by a specific man, and dozens of other women stand up and say, "Me too, I was sexually harassed or abused by that same man," now it is many voices against one. The energy shifts. Our collective psyche goes with the group. We believe them because there are more of them. If all of these women are saying a particular man did this, it's more likely true than not true. This is a prime example of the power of women united in a cause.

In the United States, there are roughly five million more women than men. Women voters outnumber male voters in America, casting between four to seven million more votes than men in recent elections. Women outnumber men in college enrollment by nearly two million as of 2015, the last year for which data is available. That enrollment gap is projected to grow to nearly three million by 2025.

Over the past twenty years, the number of women-owned businesses has grown 2.5 times faster than the national average. As of 2014, women were the primary breadwinners in 40 percent of households with children under eighteen.

The same growth exists in the law, but the momentum is not as great as it is in other parts of society. As of January 2017, 36 percent of attorneys in America were women. That's up nearly 7 percent from 2000. Yet, women were awarded 47.3 percent of JDs in 2017.

What's happening? The traditional practice of law is not working for women. The old way isn't working. Working your way up the "ladder," sitting in a room churning out law and motion documents and oppositions, waiting years to take your first deposition, having to sit second—or even third—chair in your first half-dozen trials, waiting your turn to become a "partner" and then finding out that "partner" doesn't mean the same thing as "equity partner" and, therefore, not getting the money that should come with the title, taking six to twelve weeks of maternity leave and then rushing back into the office leaking milk and looking at a picture of your baby so your milk will let down and you can pump enough to be at the office again tomorrow . . . none of it works for women anymore. Not in this modern age. Not with the state of technology and the information available to us with a few keystrokes and an internet connection. This old way is why women were leaving our profession. Those traditional ways of practicing law are coming to an end. This is a new day with a new direction and new focus that allows women to not only remain in law, but thrive and become leaders.

Women are using all of the resources available to them outside the office to skip the line, forego this ladder-climbing nonsense, and become leaders of their own firms and leaders in the law. They are trying cases, they are running their own firms, and they are having families and taking care of themselves and their families. They're doing all this while developing their physical health, emotional health, and spiritual health. Later in this book, we'll show you what these successful women are doing, how they are doing it, and how you can start doing the same thing today. You'll see that one of the big things women are doing is working with other women personally and professionally and, in doing so, magnifying their spheres of influence in and out of the courtroom. The most successful female trial lawyers have figured out that their health, wellness, mindfulness, and presence outside the courtroom directly correlate with their success inside the courtroom.

We can all increase the momentum of women as professionals and leaders in the law, which is what binds our country together and sets it apart from others. It's through working together and lifting one another up that we all work better, feel better, and are better. Confidence, courage, support, and motivation are key ingredients for all of our success. Later in this book, we'll show you how to unlock those qualities within yourself and within others. Or you can go back to the Table of Contents right now, pick a section that your heart draws you to, and dig right in.

Success is not a fixed commodity. There's not a limited amount of success to be divvied up among us all, or even an amount that has to be divvied up among women. Your personal success is limitless, and so is the personal success of each of your trial lawyer sisters. As we use the power in our numbers as women, as we come together to lift one another up, encourage one another, and help one another find fulfillment, happiness, and wellness in and out of the courtroom, a multiplier effect occurs. Two female trial lawyers working together are no longer 1+1 = 2. They are 2 squared. That's the power of women.

The best part: there are concrete actions you can start doing today to put yourself, and other women, on the path to a more fulfilling professional and personal life. Whether it's amplifying other women where you work or putting out your own shingle, we provide advice, techniques, and ideas to inspire and push you to start now. Skip to the part of the book that calls to you. When we put ourselves and other women on the path to a better life, that's when, together, women have the power to run the world.

Chapter Takeaways

- The old way of practicing law forced women out of the profession in huge numbers.
- The new way of practicing law makes it easy for women to open their own firms, work fewer hours, and make more money.
- There is enough room at the top for all of us.

2

The New Model for Practicing Law
Lessons from the #MeToo Movement

The patriarchal paradigm historically held women back, but when women learned how to merge their power and voices with the power and voices of other women, the patriarchal paradigm began to crumble. There are many lessons from the ongoing #MeToo movement that we can apply to our practices today to make them stronger, better, and more successful.

Women's Rights in Our Not-So-Distant Past

Historically, men have been the dominant gender, and women were the subordinate gender. This is the patriarchal paradigm. It started when our country was founded and is clearly illustrated in the early—and not-so-early—laws of our land.

By 1777, no woman in any state had the right to vote; every state had passed laws taking away that right. Nearly one hundred years later, in 1890, Wyoming became the first state to grant women the right to vote in all elections.

In 1848, hundreds of women, and some progressive men, signed the Declaration of Sentiments, in an effort to end discrimination against women. While this marked the first wave of the feminist movement, we know from our experiences today that the feminist movement as a whole was not 100 percent successful. Women still aren't 100 percent equal to men in all aspects of our society. Early on in our history as a nation, women were systematically subverted and discriminated against in all spheres of life, and women are still being subverted to men in some areas, including how much we make for doing the same job. Later in the book, we give you specific ways to ask for and get more money.

Did you know that in 1873, the United States Supreme Court ruled that states had the right to prevent married women from practicing law? It's all in black and white in *Bradwell v. Illinois*.[1] And it wasn't until 1938 that a minimum wage was established for men *and* women under the Fair Labor Standards Act. The minimum wage applied only to men before that.

Let's not forget, women's rights have been slow coming when it pertains to the bedroom. Shoot, up until 1964 it was still legal for men to rape their wives. In 1965 the U.S. Supreme Court finally overturned one

---

[1] *Bradwell v. Illinois* 83 U.S. 130 (1872).

of the last state laws that banned the prescription or use of contraceptives by married couples. Think about that. Adults you know—maybe you, maybe your parents—lived at a time when the government took away their choice to decide whether or not to conceive a child. And, it was in 1973—again during our lifetime or our parents' lifetimes for some of us—that a woman's right to terminate an early pregnancy was recognized in *Roe v. Wade*. But, at that time, it was still *legal* for employers to discriminate against *pregnant* women. For example, someone could choose not to hire you because you were pregnant, and that was actually legal. It wasn't until 1987 that the Pregnancy Discrimination Act banned discrimination against pregnant women.

Oh, and it's worth mentioning that it wasn't until 1981 that the Supreme Court overturned state laws designating the husband as the "head and master" of his wife and his property. Until then, the husband was basically a sovereign who had 100 percent control of property that he *jointly* owned with his wife. Even if the wife owned the property with her husband, it wasn't really hers. It wasn't until *Kirchberg v. Feenstra* that the law changed in women's favor.[2]

Women at Work

As recently as the 1980s, it was still acceptable for law firms to discriminate against women when deciding who to promote to partner. In other words, it was *legal* for a firm to promote a man who was less qualified than a woman. That funny business was finally shut down in 1984 in *Hishon v. King and Spalding*.[3] It's exhausting, right?

The patriarchal paradigm is *why* there is a history of abuse and subjugation of women. Being in a patriarchal society is why we have the numbers as women but, until now, we didn't have the power. It's why

---

[2] *Kirchberg v. Feenstra* 450 U.S. 455, 459–60 (1981).

[3] *Hishon v. King and Spalding* 467 U.S. 69 (1984).

we were and continue to be paid less than men for equal work in a shocking number of industries. Across 120 occupations, women's median earnings are lower than men's median earnings in nearly every job.[4] Women earn on average 82 percent of what men earn in identical positions for identical work.[5] Mind you: that's the *average*. When we break those numbers down by ethnicity, the gaps in pay are significantly more grim when it comes to female minorities.

This patriarchal paradigm that governed our society for so long is why women hold fewer of the top power positions in the work world. Only thirty-two CEOs of Fortune 500 companies are women. That's less than 6.5 percent.[6] It's also why we are underrepresented in politics. Only 19.8 percent of our U.S. Congress are women.[7] And, globally, the picture is the same. Only 38 percent of the 146 nations studied by the World Economic Forum had female government leaders for at least one year in the past half-century.[8]

But here's the good news: all of this is changing. And it's changing fast. In the law, for example, more and more women are opening their own firms, advocating for and getting higher pay, and establishing

---

[4] Ariane Hegewisch and Emma Williams-Baron, *The Gender Wage Gap by Occupation 2016 and by Race and Ethnicity* (Washington, DC: Institute for Women's Policy Research, April 4, 2017), https://iwpr.org/wp-content/uploads/2017/04/C456.pdf.

[5] Nikki Graf, Anna Brown, and Eileen Patten, *The Narrowing, but Persistent, Gender Gap in Pay* (Washington, DC: Pew Research Center, April 9, 2018), http://www.pewresearch.org/fact-tank/2018/04/09/gender-pay-gap-facts/.

[6] Fortune Editors, "These Are the Women CEOs Leading Fortune 500 Companies," *Fortune*, June 7, 2017, http://fortune.com/2017/06/07/fortune-500-women-ceos/.

[7] Center for American Women and Politics, *Women in the U.S. Congress 2018* (New Brunswick, NJ: Eagleton Institute of Politics, Rutgers University, 2018), http://www.cawp.rutgers.edu/women-us-congress-2018.

[8] Abigail Geiger and Lauren Kent, *Number of Women Leaders around the World Has Grown, but They're Still a Small Group* (Washinton, DC: Pew Research Institute, March 8, 2017), http://www.pewresearch.org/fact-tank/2017/03/08/women-leaders-around-the-world/.

professional boundaries that allow their personal lives to flourish. And the most successful of these women have figured out that the way to get on the fast track to these achievements is to work with like-minded women. They have figured out that there is strength in numbers. Much of this momentum is being fueled by the energy leading up to the ongoing #MeToo movement.

The #MeToo Movement

There is a tremendous rise in women putting men on trial, and unlike previous times, women are being heard, listened to, believed, and vindicated. And men are facing real consequences.

On October 5, 2017, the *New York Times* published an article by female journalists Jodi Kantor and Megan Twohey, blowing the lid off nearly thirty years of sexual misconduct allegations against movie mogul and Miramax films head Harvey Weinstein, supported by evidence of financial settlements tied to strict confidentiality requirements.[9] Brave women—some actresses, some models, and some otherwise unknown employees—spoke to these trailblazing journalists on the record and off the record. According to the article, dozens of Mr. Weinstein's current and former employees said they knew of Mr. Weinstein's inappropriate conduct, but few had spoken out. Employment contracts apparently prohibited criticism of Weinstein or the Weinstein Company.

According to the article, civil rights attorney Lisa Bloom, known for representing victims of sexual harassment, had been advising Mr. Weinstein on "gender and power dynamics." She was quoted in the article as calling her client "an old dinosaur learning new ways."

Shortly after the New York Times article was published, #MeToo became a movement on social media for victims of sexual harassment

---

[9] Jodi Kantor and Megan Twohey, "Harvey Weinstein Paid Off Sexual Harassment Accusers for Decades," *New York Times*, October 5, 2017, https://www.nytimes.com/2017/10/05/us/harvey-weinstein-harassment-allegations.html.

and assault to show solidarity and support. By April 2018, there were more than one million #MeToo posts on Instagram alone and counting.

Weinstein was fired from the film company he founded and is currently facing criminal charges. Around the same time, numerous other powerful men were accused by women of inappropriate sexual behavior and misconduct:

- American's dad and star of *The Cosby Show* Bill Cosby
- Fox News anchor Bill O'Reilly
- Forty-five-year journalist Charlie Rose
- *New York Times* reporter Glenn Thrush
- Senator Al Franken
- Longtime *Today Show* anchor Matt Lauer
- USA Gymnastics physician Larry Nasser, who is now a convicted serial child molester sentenced to forty to one hundred seventy-five years in prison

Anita Hill and the Clarence Thomas Hearings

This wasn't the first time in recent history that women have accused powerful men of sexual harassment.

We look back at Anita Hill, a young black woman who in 1991 testified in detail before the Senate Judiciary Committee where she publicly accused United States Supreme Court justice nominee Clarence Thomas of sexually harassing her. Ms. Hill had been a personal assistant to Clarence Thomas for two years and accused him of trying to date her and engage her in conversation about sex and pornography. She testified about specific sexual remarks she said Thomas had made to her and references to specific pornographic actors she said he made to her, including Long Dong Silver.

The confirmation hearings were televised, and the public was enraptured with Hill's testimony, as well as Thomas's denial. Thomas supporters were furiously attacking Hill and the hearing process as a whole, calling it, in essence, a modern-day lynching. And they weren't alone. Public opinion polls at the time showed that a plurality of Americans *did not believe* Hill's allegations. Thomas's nomination was confirmed, by a vote of 52 to 48.

He may have been confirmed, but the ordeal woke us up. At the time this was going on, we didn't even have a word for what happened to her. That's right; because of Anita Hill, we now have the words *sexual harassment*. What does that matter? We are language based—we need to name something in order to act on it. And that's what happened: only a month after Anita Hill testified, Congress passed the Civil Rights Act of 1991, giving sexual harassment victims the right to sue their employers for damages and back pay—giving women a vehicle for protection and recourse in the workplace, and giving us, attorneys, the power to represent those victims and demand justice on their behalf. An onslaught of sexual harassment at the workplace lawsuits were filed. And guess what? In the years that followed, sexual harassment in the workplace decreased—significantly.

Hill is now a lawyer and law professor and has spoken about the lack of public support she received. Despite the fact that Thomas was confirmed and most Americans largely disbelieved Hill, this was a defining moment in our society, when people began talking about sexual harassment and gave it a name.

Anita Hill had the courage to speak even when it brought her before our government and our nation to be asked difficult questions of a sexual nature in a very public forum. Anita Hill's journey and her fortitude shed light on sexual harassment in the workplace in an unprecedented way. Government agencies and businesses almost without exception in our country now have policies against sexual harassment in the workplace, and some have training in place to prevent sexual harassment in the workplace. It's no longer commonplace or acceptable for men to grope anyone at work, thanks primarily to Anita Hill, in our view. As modern women, we would be shocked to be groped at work. But there was a time that many women still remember when that was not abnormal. (Heck, in well-known law firms in Los Angeles, secretaries were asked to jump out of birthday cakes up until the nineties.) And if a modern woman is groped or otherwise sexually harassed at work in this day and age, there are laws on the books in every state to protect her. Thank you, Ms. Anita Hill, we say, for having the courage to speak and to stay the course. Your bravery changed history.

In stark contrast to Anita Hill's experience, in 2017, when women came forward and told their stories and accused very powerful men of sexual harassment, for the first time, the walls came tumbling down. Other women had the drive and the fortitude to come forward and tell their own stories. They came forward in droves. And they were believed. Whereas our culture historically disbelieved women who made sexual harassment claims against powerful men, that culture is gone. Instead, we seem to have shifted to a default position of believing accusers, rather than disbelieving them.

Female Lawyers, Female Jurors

As trial lawyers, we're interested in the beliefs jurors bring to the courtroom. What we're seeing and hearing, anecdotally, is that the collective community has also shifted to a place of believing, rather than disbelieving. We're now seeing cases won and lost based on whether there are women trial lawyers connecting with jurors. In other words, we're seeing female jurors connect with female lawyers in an unprecedented way. If the female juror and the female lawyer connect in voir dire, a bond is formed between the women that appears to impact how the female juror decides the case.

The Aquarian Age

Why is this happening? Because the time is ripe for the forging of women bonds on a much larger scale. We're moving from the religious- and patriarchy-based Piscean age into the egalitarian- and matriarchy-based Aquarian age, which is about reclaiming power.

Whether or not astrology is your thing, it's one way of putting words to concepts, in this case, our collective consciousness and the shifts therein. We are always looking for ways to articulate ideas—to help us verbalize and conceptualize our role in change and momentum. Whichever lens you choose, there are beautiful things happening at this time on the planet, things which deserve to be recognized, celebrated, and catalyzed for good.

The best description we've seen of the Aquarian age is by Guru Jagat, founder of Ra Ma Kundalini yoga:

> *The Aquarian Age*, or Golden Age, is about the ascension of thought, action, experience, and the reclaiming of human goodness, compassion, creativity, and kindness. The Tibetan Buddhists call it Shambala or the creation of Enlightened Society, where the heavy veil of competition, lack, violence, and human suffering becomes transparent and we as humans walk into a much more Human Beingness through our continued discovery of our own spiritual depth (who we truly are) and our desire to see that depth and beauty in others.[10]

The Aquarian age represents a rise of feminine leadership. Feminine. Not female. Just being female doesn't get you there.

---

[10] Guru Jagat, "No, Really: It IS the Dawning of the Age of Aquarius: There's a New Sheriff in Town, Planet Earth, and It's Called the Aquarian Age," Wanderlust.com, June 17, 2015, https://wanderlust.com/journal/no-really-dawning-age-aquarius.

Tap into Your Feminine

Feminine means graceful, in tune, soft, sensitive, tender, aware, and engaged. Want to tap into power? Choose to be a woman and embrace what that means to you. To the extent we have any rough, nonfeminine edges, any harshness or bitterness, any male qualities, now is the time to release those. They take away from all that you really are. They reduce the incredible power inherent in your femininity. You are a lawyer. You are not an mixed martial arts fighter. You are not a boxer or football player. You are not trying to physically keep up with men. Every step you take to defeminize yourself robs you of power in the courtroom and in life. You are a woman. You are graceful. You are aware of the energy in a room. You are aware of what people need. You are a caretaker. You are strong beyond your wildest dreams.

It is you, mama, who tends the sick child all night. It is you, mama, who tends the sick parent. It is you, mama, who sows the seeds of the family, creating Christmas, Easter, Ramadan, Passover, and whatever other celebrations are meaningful in your family. But for you and your femininity, your intuition, your deep knowing of what people need and how to provide comfort and how to turn four walls into a home and how to create memories, but for you and all of these things you innately do, there is a house, but no home. There is food but no meal. There are hugs but no tenderness. It is your feminine energy that allows you to communicate without words and to know what people really need most. Imagine what you could do in the courtroom by embracing, rather than hiding, this beautiful gift of femininity. This is what the Aquarian Age is about.

We're not saying you should suppress competitiveness if that's part of your personality. That's not what embracing your femininity is about.

The wolf mother is fierce and unyielding when it comes to the protection of her pack. Your loyalty and generosity is not in conflict with your lust for competition. There is a reason that justice, morality, and ethos have been represented by the feminine from ancient Egyptians to Romans to the lady we see in courthouses today: women are able to combine intensity with humanity. This benefits our clients, our families, our societies. When we deny pieces of ourselves, we diminish this power and we find ourselves dissatisfied, incomplete.

Here's the other thing: not all of us are competitive. Some of us are equalizers, seekers of fairness and justice on principle. We're not looking for the hunt or the kill. We're not keeping a tally of our performance or trying to meet quotas. We're standing in our role as officers of the court and using the channels of justice to right a wrong—one client at a time. And there's space for that personality type too. We are fighting for the just outcome and for accountability. Those of us who identify this way view this process less through the lens of wins and losses and more through the lens of balance and achieving equality where equality won't come on its own. It's similar to the way we as women intervene in conflicts between our children, between our siblings, between our own mother and sister, between two friends. Some of us are ever searching for stasis in humanity.

Whatever your gifts are, there is space for them. It's about sharing your gifts with others. It's why we've written this book, as an act of service to women who haven't found their way or haven't found their true voice, who still feel they are struggling in a man's world. The secret, dear sister, is that this isn't a man's world unless you believe it is. It's a woman's world. You are a woman practicing law in a woman's world. All of the discomfort you feel, all of the uneasiness and feeling out of place and playing second fiddle is because you still think it's a man's world. When your mindset shifts, the world around you will shift too. Become a woman practicing law in a woman's world, and you will find fulfillment and joy in what you do. You won't be contemplating giving it all up to teach yoga or tend bar or work at Pottery Barn. You'll be happier, healthier, and whole.

So, why is it *now* that women have the courage to come forward and make public allegations of sexual misconduct? The energy has shifted, and, as a society, we've created a container within which these conversations can happen without fear of retribution. The container is an energetic space. It was created by Ashley Judd, Gwyneth Paltrow, Reese Witherspoon, Mira Sorvino, Christy Turlington, and other famous and widely respected celebrities. Their willingness to stand up and say, "This happened to me, and it was wrong," created an energetic container for sharing. In other words, they created a safe space. They may not have intended it, and they probably didn't realize they did it. But the combination of who they are and what they have accomplished and the grace with which they shared their experiences made it safe and acceptable for others to share. These women, these celebrities, have been around for decades. We've seen them in movies. We feel like we know them. That's why they are able to create this energetic container within which others feel safe to share.

So, what we've learned from the #MeToo movement is that we, as women, have the power to create energetic containers that make people feel safe. How does that translate to your practice? You, with your beautiful, God-given feminine energy, can create a space within which people feel safe to share—potential jurors, clients, witnesses, even judges. You can create a space where people can connect. Where people *want* to connect. And if you know how and are willing to open yourself up to that feminine energy within you, you can create the space they need. We'll talk more about exactly how to do that in part 4, "Trial Perspective and Trial Techniques," later in this book.

Chapter Takeaways

- Learning from our past as women helps us see where we want to go in the future.
- There is power in our collective voices.
- Female jurors are connecting with female trial lawyers in an unprecedented way.
- Women have the power to create energetic containers that make people feel safe.

3

Women Have Superpowers
We Are Abundantly Suited to Be Trial Lawyers

Connection is building a rapport between two people. Connection is uniting, linking, bonding. Some people call it interacting, but it's much more meaningful than that. Connection is seeing someone and being seen. It's a knowing and a caring between two humans, even between strangers. Connection is life, and a life without connection is a lonely prospect.

Connection isn't just conversation. It's conversation with emotional content, whether that emotional content is spoken or unspoken. For example, when a woman asks, "How was your day?" she wants to hear about, and identify with, the emotional experiences of the day—the joy of watching a child accomplish something new, the heartache of finding out that a parent is sick, the stress of an uncomfortable interaction with someone. That's the connection: when we identify with an underlying emotion.

If, on the other hand, a woman asks, "How was your day?" and gets a list of activities, there's no connection because there's no emotional content.

It's easy to shift a conversation from surface level to connecting. "How was your day?" becomes, "What was the best part of your day?" or, "What was the worst part of your day?"

Connection doesn't end with phrasing a question a certain way to get an answer with emotional content. To be connection, the answer must be received. For there to be a true connection, the person speaking must feel heard. You know how it feels when someone asks you a question and you're answering and you can tell the person isn't really listening to what you're saying. She's waiting for her turn to talk again! It feels crappy. No connection there.

On the other hand, when you speak, and someone is looking into your eyes and really listening to what you're saying and really trying to understand your perspective, you feel seen *and* heard. You feel like you matter. That's connection.

It doesn't take a lot of time to connect. And there are lots of ways to connect. You can connect with someone by making *real* eye contact. By really *seeing* someone and by letting them really see you. You can connect by saying, "Thank you," or, "How are you?" and *really* meaning the words as they come out of your mouth. How can you show someone that you're really listening, really hearing what they're saying, really seeing them? Rephrase what they just told you. Be a mirror and reflect the emotional content of what they just told you. *That must have been scary. That must have been really painful. That must have been an exciting surprise. You were really proud. That hurt you.* Putting words to the emotion that you're relating to creates a connection. Your hearts relate. Connecting is about caring.

Theresa:

I was walking one afternoon in Hawaii along a narrow beachside neighborhood road. Up ahead, I saw a small car parked in front of a little house. The trunk was open. I also saw a kitchen chair sitting behind the car. As I got closer, a little, old lady walked out of the front door of the house, down the path to the street, and stood behind the car, looking at the car and the chair. She was dressed in a crisp, white blouse. She had freshly pressed pants on and lovely silver hair. She couldn't have been more than five feet tall. As I walked by, I stopped and said, "Hello. Could I help you with that?" She didn't have to answer because the look in her eyes said everything. This woman was deeply, profoundly, appreciative. She didn't know how she was going to lift that chair into her car. I don't know her name. She doesn't know mine. We don't know anything about one another. But we *connected*.

Do you ever ask the bank teller what she has planned for the weekend? If you're really curious and interested in the answer, the other person *feels* that energy, and you connect.

Has it ever happened when you're checking out at the grocery store that you walk up to the counter and the clerk says, "How are you today?" but never makes eye contact with you? She's already scanning your food and never looks at you. You can feel that she's asking you because she has to and she's not really interested in how you are.

Women are made to connect. Think about it. Between you and your significant other, who is the one who knows your child's teacher and whether or not he or she is married? Who is the one who knows which neighbor is about to put their house on the market? Who is the one who knows which friends are planning a vacation to Hawaii this summer? Who knows that a mutual friend is having relationship issues? Who knows the best doctor, dentist, hair stylist, gardener, and so on in town? The woman does! Because connection is one of a woman's great superpowers.

Women Working with Women

Women connect in person and online, with friends and with strangers. It's the superpower of connection that allows women to build *lasting* relationships with one another. This is why women working with other women is also so powerful. If you want to immediately multiply your success, start working with other women now.

What happens when women work with other women? Well, take us, for example. Way back when, before we met, we knew of each other. We were introduced. And it could have ended there, but it didn't. We *connected*. And it just so happens that we're both introverts and deep connectors and much prefer to go down the rabbit hole and have a one-on-one, deep, meaningful conversation with someone—even someone we've just met—than to have surface level chitchat. We both find chitchat stressful and draining and boring. But get us in front of someone who's willing to go deep, and we're energized and charged up and can talk, hypothesize, and solve the world's problems all night long. And so, when we met, we immediately picked up on this energy from each other, connected, went deep, and we're still going. As the years pass, we go deeper with each conversation, it seems. We didn't start working together right away, but when we did, we knew it would be a perfect fit. We understand, love, care for, and want the best for each other. We communicate. When one needs slack, the other picks it up and vice versa. When one feels sensitive and gets rubbed the wrong way, we discuss it, resolve it, and it's over. While we're similar in many ways, we're different in ways too. We have different strengths in the litigation and trial process, but we don't box each other in. We lift each other up, and we balance each other out, and we push each other to be better. Better trial lawyers, better wives, better mothers, better friends, better women. This core connection makes our partnership in the law unshakable.

We are more successful together than apart. The whole is greater than the sum of its parts. And this, dear sisters, is what we want for you too. We view this book as something we wish we'd had when we were trying to figure things out. We've reached a place in our careers where we know enough and have experienced enough that we feel we can and should give back, and we believe that the highest and best use of our experience is to share with other women what has worked for us in the hopes that you will find your own path a little easier.

Courtney:

Theresa and I were invited to a ladies dinner during the annual Iowa Association of Justice trial lawyers conference in Des Moines. The dinner was hosted by Roxanne Barton Conlin, a trial legend and powerful political organizer, a philanthropist and firm owner, not to mention an outright fox. If you ever fear aging, go visit Roxanne. More on her when Theresa interviews her for the book, but suffice to say we were out of our league and nervous to be at a party of women we didn't know. Let's be honest, we've done this before: women's legal networking. Women sit around and drink cheap wine and either cheer one another on for lackluster accomplishments or bash men and bond over mutual victimhood. We all go home in the same positions we came. Meanwhile, men are eating at fine restaurants drinking the good stuff and making million-dollar deals.

Long story short: this was something entirely different. When we walked in the door, we were greeted by Roxanne. She stood at the door to welcome each woman, shake her hand, make her feel special and wanted. We were offered a drink; someone took our coats. Standing in her grand, impeccably decorated (stunning reds and golds and books and delicious antiques, yes please) entry, we were introduced to other women casually as appetizers were passed.

When it was time to eat, we sat at a round table. Everyone with an equal seat. Roxanne welcomed us all and invited us to introduce ourselves, and then we got down to brass tacks. What we do, what we want to do, and what experiences we've had relating to #MeToo. (It had just exploded in the media that week.) Roxanne went first, shared first, and set the tone with her leadership and courage. The stories around the table were profound, each one unique but inextricably connected in its emotion and urgency. In less than two hours, we were connected, profoundly, to one another, because of the supportive, safe, and protective environment our hostess built for us. And yes, we left with two new cases to boot. But the point I wanted to make was that it was Roxanne's spirit of encouragement, of solidarity, of genuine encouragement of each of the women in the room, that set this apart from anything I had experienced before.

If I can encourage you to do one thing this month, host a dinner for women in your community. That means women lawyers, women professionals, or even just women. It's up to you. It can be simple. But make it special. Put out some fresh flowers, stand at the door, and set the tone for the night with your grace and your welcoming heart. Building these connections will propel us into the next phase of our lives, our careers, our civilization. Also, they make you live longer (and, apparently, look better), so what's not to like?

Because we're always thinking about other people, we're thinking about how we can connect other people to meet needs. *Sarah is converting her spare bedroom into an office and selling her headboard. Ashley has been looking for a headboard and would love Sarah's style.* Connect. *Paige is going back to work part-time and needs someone to watch her daughter on Monday afternoons. Rachel doesn't use her nanny on Monday afternoons, and they live in the same area.* Connect. *Jennifer wants to launch her catering company. Kristin is a web designer.* Connect.

As women, we do this all the time without even thinking about it. We're connectors and problem solvers. What we need to be doing is expanding that skill to our law practices. *Kimberly is a personal injury lawyer who specializes in bicycle cases and has more work than she can handle. Amy is a lawyer who wants to learn how to litigate bicycle cases.* Connect.

Now, here's the important part to understand: This connection doesn't take money out of Kimberly's pocket. It *adds* money to Kimberly's pocket. Kimberly will share her fee with Amy, and, in exchange, she will get Amy's hard work. Kimberly will show Amy exactly how bicycle cases are to be worked up and tried. So, in essence, Kimberly has cloned herself. Now, because of Amy's work, Kimberly can take on cases she wouldn't have otherwise had the resources to handle, thereby putting more money in Kimberly's pocket and more money in Amy's pocket. And it doesn't stop there. As it turns out, Amy takes a liking to civil rights cases. Amy teaches Kimberly to litigate these civil rights cases. They split the fee on those cases too. Now, they have both expanded their practice areas, they are sharing costs on cases, and they are both making more money than they could have made on their own. That's the magic of the multiplier.

And all of this connecting we do as women makes us feel really good. Turns out, our brains release oxytocin, the so-called love drug, when we connect. The production of oxytocin can be stimulated by bonding and creating lasting friendships.[1]

---

[1] Rita Watson, MPH, "Oxytocin: The Love and Trust Hormone Can Be Deceptive," Psychologytoday.com, October 14, 2013, https://www.psychologytoday.com/us/blog/love-and-gratitude/201310/oxytocin-the-love-and-trust-hormone-can-be-deceptive?amp.

Connection in the Courtroom

Connection doesn't end with us as women lawyers interacting with one another and growing our businesses. Connection can, and should, happen in a courtroom. But I've only got thirty minutes for voir dire, you say. No judge in my jurisdiction will let me talk about really personal stuff with potential jurors, you say. I don't have enough time to connect with each person on my panel of potential jurors, you say. Doesn't matter. None of that is what you need to connect.

It Doesn't Take Much Time

First, it doesn't take much time at all to connect. There are three simple steps:

1. Be genuinely interested in the person you're talking to.
2. Phrase your questions to get to the emotional content.
3. Listen with your eyes, ears, and heart.

    Having a list of questions and blasting through as many questions as you can with each potential juror does not create connection. It turns people off. You'll accomplish much more by spending time with a few potential jurors, making a true connection and then using a technique we call *folding in* for other members of the group. We talk more about *folding in* in part 4, "Trial Perspective and Trial Techniques," but it's where you simply ask another potential juror how he feels about what this juror just said. Does he feel the same? A little different? You fold them into the group conversation.

    You can't fake this stuff. And you shouldn't have to. These are the people who are going to decide your client's case. Be interested in what they think, what they feel, who they are.

When you talk to them, phrase your questions to get to the emotional content. For example, instead of asking, "How do you feel about gun control?" you might try, "When I say the words 'gun control' what feelings does that stir up in you?" That's going to give you a lot of good information and get to the heart of the matter.

"Sir, we've been talking about a kid riding a bike without a helmet. Does that bring anything up for you?" Sometimes, you don't even need words to connect. You might ask one potential juror how she feels about what another juror just said. After listening to the answer, really taking it in, you can make eye contact with another potential juror and even with a raising of your chin or a tilt of your head, ask them what they think without using words. Some may just nod in agreement with the prior potential juror. And that may be enough, depending on the circumstances of your questioning, your voir dire, and your case.

You Don't Have to Connect with Everyone

Second, you don't have to connect with every person in the group. When you're in a courtroom picking a jury, you have the stage. When you have the stage and you connect with this person, then that person, and then another person in the group, every other member of the group sees that. That opens them to connecting with you. The result is you connect with those observers more quickly when you do speak with them, and many of them will connect with you even though you never speak with them. There is a one-sided intimacy that develops. They see you acknowledging, respecting, seeing, and connecting with others in the group. If they have the same opinions or feelings or emotional connections that others are discussing, they connect with you just as their fellow potential juror did, even though you have never spoken directly. You have created a group, and each of these people are part of the group.

Finally, ask yourself if you're *really* listening to what these people are saying. Are you having a one-on-one conversation; or are you checking boxes, looking at your notes, thinking about what you're going to say next, or thinking about who you're going to question next? If it's not authentic, people can feel it. They know. And no one likes it. Here's where it gets worse: just as easily as you can connect with people without talking to them, you can disconnect from people without talking to them. If members of your *venire* see you not really listening, not really paying attention to or caring about what people are saying, they will close up before you even have a chance to talk to them. And when you do talk to them, they won't connect with you. That door will be closed. Make eye contact when you're listening. Listen with your ears, but also listen with your eyes, and, most importantly, listen with your heart. Focus only on what's in front of you, what that person is saying, and you will connect. You will feel it, they will feel it, and the group will feel it.

You can do it because this is one of your womanly superpowers.

Use Your Intuition

As women lawyers, we don't want to be seen as emotional, sensitive, moody, dramatic, or illogical. It's the law, right? We're supposed to be thinking with our heads and not our hearts, right? Wrong. The most powerful tool you have is your intuition. Your gut. That little voice that says something's not right. Or that little voice that says, yes, this is it. Some of us already know this voice. Some of us have become really good at making that little voice go away. The quicker you find that voice and listen to it at all costs, the quicker you'll be going in the right direction, even if it's not always easy.

It's difficult to describe the power of intuition. It's instinct. When we make decisions based on intuition, often, we can't explain why or how we made the decision. We just *knew* it was right.

Well, intuition is a real thing. It exists in men and women. But you should know that *women's intuition* is a real thing too. In some cases, it's heightened. According to a 2011 *Psychology Today* article, women are better at reading facial expressions and more likely to pick up on subtle emotional messages.[2]

A June 16, 2017, article in the *New York Post* cites a study where ninety thousand people were shown photos of people's eyes and asked to interpret their moods from the photographs.[3] Women were consistently more accurate, and Katrina Grasby of Australia's Berghofer Medical Research Institute in Queensland was quoted as saying the study results showed "significant differences" between men and women.

Your intuition is a gift. It's your ability to process nonverbal and verbal evidence and energy and run it through that amazing brain of yours that scientists and doctors still don't fully understand. The result is a sense or a knowing, sometimes without any evidentiary basis. People who have long followed their intuition will say it's never wrong. People who ignore their intuition often say they regret doing so.

Your gift, your intuition, is a powerful tool to use in trial.

In trial, your intuition is a valuable tool that you should not ignore or leave as an afterthought. If you really tune in, you can get a sense of what's happening with opposing counsel, with your judge, with your potential jurors, with your client, and with yourself.

For example, intuition is what gives you the power to go off script. Going off script is where you take it to the next level. We don't go to

---

[2] *See* William Ickles, *Everyday Mind Reading: Understanding What People Think and Feel* (New York: Prometheus Books, 2003); David G. Myers, *Intuition: Its Powers and Perils* (New Haven: Yale University Press, 2003); and Ronald E. Riggio, *The Charisma Quotient: What It Is, How to Get It, How to Use It* (New York: Dodd Mead, 1988).

[3] *See* Ashleigh Austen, "Science Confirms Women's Intuition Is a Real Thing," *New York Post*, June 16, 2017, https://nypost.com/2017/06/16/science-confirms-womens-intuition-is-a-real-thing; and V. Warrier et al., "Genome-Wide Meta-Analysis of Cognitive Empathy: Heritability, and Correlates with Sex, Neuropsychiatric Conditions and Cognition," *Molecular Psychiatry* 23 (2018), 1402–1409, https://doi.org/10.1038/mp.2017.122.

trial with a script. We go to trial with points we need to make. Let's look at how this comes together. Let's say you're examining a witness on direct. You have points that you need to make with this witness, and the points need to resonate with your jury. Use your intuition. Make sure you don't have tunnel vision between you and the witness.

Put yourself in your jurors' shoes:

- What do they need?
- What do they want to know that you aren't asking?
- What were you going to cover with this witness that the jury no longer needs to hear?

Always remember what it feels like to be a juror. They don't get paid. OK, they get money, but in most courthouses, it doesn't cover parking and lunch. They're herded through the courthouse like cattle and made to wear name tags that poke holes in their clothes. They can't use the restroom when they need to. They can't eat when they're hungry. In many, many courthouses, they're forced to sit in a room without windows and listen to lawyers drone on for hours on end, day after day. Boring. So:

- Always make it quick.
- Don't repeat what doesn't need to be repeated.
- Tune in to your jurors.
- Switch places with them in your mind.
- Are they getting what you want them to get?
- Can you cut it short with this witness?
- Do you need the next witness to prove your case?

With rare exception, we always drop witnesses during trial. We build our trial presentation and our proof and our story before trial, but we are always tuned in to our jury during trial so we can give the jurors what they need.

Courtney:

> We were trying a case in Long Beach, California, a brain and back injury of a mother of twelve kids. We had most of the kids listed as witnesses. It is our firm belief that the more your client's damages story can be told by people other than your client, the better. As the trial went on, our momentum kept building, and we kept crossing witnesses off the list. Not because the kids weren't wonderful or endearing or helpful, but because the jury got it. We wanted to move the thing along and respect their time, and we did that by trusting them and trusting our intuition: we don't need more, so we can stop.

We see overkill a lot. We see it in depositions. We see it in trial. Overkill always means the lawyer lacks confidence. Overkill looks like this:

- Calling multiple witnesses who say the same thing (Yes, there's a place for repetition in some cases, but there is a difference between repetition and cumulative, boring evidence.)
- Calling witnesses to make collateral or unimportant points
- Giving extensive coverage of a witness's background (Other than experts, we just need to know who this person is and what this person knows.)

Get in the courtroom, tune in to your jury, and get the evidence out there that they need. That's what a confident and intuitive lawyer does.

Intuition before Trial

Here's the thing: intuition is even more valuable *before* trial. Your intuition is something you can plug into to help build your case. Your intuition is what takes you out of lawyer-land and puts you in the shoes of your jurors.

We were talking about a brain injury case recently, and there was one piece of evidence that made us both feel like something was fishy—not about the case, but *about that evidence.* Imaging of the woman's head was read as negative in the emergency room, negative by the treating doctor, and negative by our own retained expert. Our expert even testified in deposition that the imaging didn't show any injury. But then, sometime after his deposition, our expert looked at the imaging again while he was preparing a PowerPoint slide for his trial presentation, and he saw a skull fracture for the first time. It didn't make sense to either of us. How could all of these people, including our own expert, look at these pictures and say there was no fracture and then, right before trial, change his mind? There are lots of explanations for how it happened in that case and how it could happen in any case. But that's not the point. The point is that the feeling in your gut that something doesn't make sense—that's your intuition.

Our natural inclination as lawyers, at that point, is to explain that feeling away, find the reasonable explanation for why all these people missed this evidence for so long and to make this evidence work for trial because it's good evidence! But, if you skip right to that step, if you skip right to the explaining, you're missing out on a lot of valuable insight.

If these feelings and thoughts are coming up for you when you hear about evidence, then more likely than not, your jurors are going to have those same feeling and questions. And your jurors don't have lawyer minds that can skip straight to the reasonable legal explanation.

Your intuition is your insight into the minds of your jurors. That's why it's such a magical and powerful tool. And that's why you have to sit with that fishy feeling and roll it around a little bit and explore it. Because that's what your jurors will be doing.

We handle those fishy feelings by putting together a focus group. Take a look at part 4, "Trial Perspective and Trial Techniques," for a more thorough discussion of focus groups, but for now, it bears repeating that focus groups don't have to be expensive. You can post an ad on your city's Craigslist page and hire ten people at $35 per person—the current going rate—to come and sit down for two hours and roll around in your fishy feeling about this evidence. It doesn't require anyone to do an opening statement or present evidence or anything like that. You don't have to have a consultant—do it yourself if that's what you have available. Don't get discouraged because you don't have a bunch of resources or experience. Do it cheap and dirty—you're still going to get a ton of benefit. It could be as simple as standing in front of those ten people (probably only seven or eight will show up from a Craigslist ad, even if they've confirmed) and saying something like this:

> A woman was walking on the sidewalk and was hit in the head by the side mirror of a transit bus. Her head and body were then thrown into a stop sign. Both sides agree that she was diagnosed with several broken vertebrae and later had surgery. Both sides agree that the emergency room doctor found a lump on her head and evidence that she had bleeding on her brain. One side claims she has a permanent brain injury as a result of the head trauma. The other side claims she does not now, and never did, have a brain injury. Both sides have experts to support their claims. All of the imaging—the pictures—taken at the hospital were read by a radiologist and the radiologist did not find any skull fractures. Experts hired by both sides testified under oath that the imaging didn't show any skull fractures. After his deposition, while preparing a PowerPoint slide for trial, one of the experts saw a skull fracture on the imaging for the first time. I'm going to step out of the room, and I'd like you to discuss the evidence.

If you don't have a one-way glass mirror, you can literally take a chair outside of the room, leave the door wide open, and listen from the hallway. You'll find out if they have that fishy feeling too. If they do, you'll hear lots of counterarguments, arming yourself for trial. And you'll get a lot of other nuggets that will make your case better. We recommend anything by Malcolm Gladwell on the subject, as well as David Ball. Hector Lanz has a great YouTube video on focus groups to give you some background.[4] You can even run online focus groups—we haven't tried it yet but have heard great things about FocusVision.

Plugging into your intuition plugs you into your jury. It's getting out of the lawyer brain and into a real human being's with the same types of thoughts and reactions as other human beings. And, as lawyers and women, that's a superpower.

Empathy

Empathy is the ability to identify with another person's feelings. Creating empathy, in ourselves and in others, is very powerful. And empathizing is another superpower that women have. Research shows that from the time we are born, women are better empathizers than men.[5]

In general, according to the research, women are better at "decoding nonverbal communications, picking up subtle nuances from tone of voice or facial expression, or judging a person's character." That's a superpower.

---

[4] Hector Lanz, "How Do Focus Groups Work?" TEDEd, accessed August 1, 2018, https://ed.ted.com/lessons/how-do-focus-groups-work-hector-lanz.

[5] *See* Liraz Margalit, PhD, "Men Systemize. Women Empathize," Psychologytoday.com, July 17, 2015, https://www.psychologytoday.com/us/blog/behind-online-behavior/201507/men-systemize-women-empathize; and Maria V. Mestre et al., "Are women more empathetic than men? A longitudinal study in adolescence," *Spanish Journal of Psychology* 12, no 1. (May, 2009), 76–83.

We can create empathy in less than a minute. All it takes is creating space for people's feelings/points of view/experiences to be expressed; putting yourself in others' shoes and feeling what they must have felt in that scenario; and then validating that feeling or offering the words they need to hear. It's your ability to feel what another person is feeling that creates empathy in you. Reflecting that back to the other person is what then connects the two of you. And that empathetic connection opens the floodgates of communication and trust.

When you're showing empathy, you're treating people the way they want and need to be treated. It's not about what you think people want or need. It's about putting yourself in the shoes of others and figuring out, from that perspective, what they want or need. You are seeing things through their eyes. You're feeling things as though you are them. A lot of times, it's as simple as naming the feelings people are having and validating those feelings.

The ability to empathize creates deeper bonds in our friendships, heals conflicts in our marriages, and gives our own experience greater depth and meaning.

Cultivating Energy

Everything in life is energy. The Earth we're all spinning around on is energy. The cells of our body are energy. The food we eat is energy. Our words carry energy. Even our bodies, as we sit still and quiet, have and communicate an energy. We want our energy to be as high as possible because like attracts like. That is, the higher our energetic vibration, the more good things we attract. That's what we believe, and that's what we practice. And while the metaphysical underpinnings of this concept are beyond the scope of this book, we can say without a doubt that this practice has worked for both of us.

In the simplest terms, the way to build your energy and lift your vibration is through slow and steady breath and positive thoughts.

You have an aura around you that is made up of energy. That's why when someone is giving off a bad vibe, you can tell. If your partner is mad at you, you can tell. When you meet a good person, you know. And, most of the time, when you come across a bad person, your gut knows. That's all because of the energy we give off as human beings.

Have you heard of the three Cs? Guru Jagat says when we *complain*, *compare*, or *compete*, we are lowering our precious, good energy by a third. Did you just complain to your friend how late you had to work tonight? Kaboom! One third of your gorgeous light energy is gone. You robbed yourself. Did you just think about how much you wish you had someone else's house or car or job or life because it all looks so much better than what you have? Kaboom again! Robbed again. And if we really pay attention, the truth is, we know it doesn't make us feel better to do those things. Don't you actually feel worse afterward? That's because it isn't good for you, and your body knows it!

We are all working hard and managing a lot of things in our lives. None of our lives on the inside is identical to what it looks like on the outside. That's especially true if we look at social media, which is mostly a lie. Let's remind ourselves of that and be gentle with ourselves and be gentle with one another. Let's not let one of the three Cs take away our energy.

There is some energy we do want to get rid of, though, and that's stress and negative energy. That energy does not serve us and gets in the way of our good energy flowing through and making all areas of our lives brighter and softer and prettier and better.

The easiest way to manage your stress or negative energy and start building up your positive energy is to start a practice like Kundalini yoga or meditation today. That's what we do. We found that when we really committed to those practices, we saw big results in all areas of our lives. We were calmer and more patient with our husbands and children, had more clarity, were more efficient and effective when working our cases, and we were generally happier, more relaxed, and felt more balanced. These types of practices will shift your thinking, open your mind to new possibilities, and maybe even change your life.

There's scientific evidence that changing your thoughts can change your brain. By repeating new thoughts, you create new neural pathways in your brain. That's why we say, if you believe it, you can achieve it.

The best way to train your mind? ==Meditate. So, clear out the cobwebs, decide what you want, see it in your mind, raise up your energy, and go get it.==

Courtney:

I was trying a case in northeast Iowa about a mother of small children who was killed by medical malpractice. Maybe it was the content of the case or the fact that we were in a really tough venue, or maybe it was just that this was our third case in three months, but my nervous system was shot and I had really, really high anxiety. So, I did what I always do when my world is spinning out of control and I have decided it will never go back together again: I called Theresa crying at 7:00 in the morning. After allowing me to bumble my way through all of my anxieties and failures and life declarations (yes, that was me she was referring to who threatens to leave the practice and tend bar and teach yoga when the going gets rough), she said, "Meditate."

(I imagine her seated quietly in her light-filled kitchen with hot tea in front of her, calmly advising the crackpot on the other end of the line.) But she didn't stop there, because Theresa is practical and direct and never gives me a way out.

"Twenty minutes, every morning. Put on your headphones, shut your eyes, and don't listen to anyone else. Download something."

And I did. Like it was my job. Eyes squeezed shut, my arms wrapped around my body, boom. Twenty minutes. By the time I drove to the courthouse each day, I wasn't just a different person, I was the person I love the most: the real me. I was calm, focused, empowered, and proud of myself. Hey—one thing I was supposed to do this morning and already nailed it! With my junk cleared, I was ready to be that channel between the jury and my clients, and I did a phenomenal job.

Something so simple can have such a profound impact on who we are with ourselves and in the world, with so little effort. I like the Insight Meditation app and the Headspace app,[6] any mantra sung by White Sun,[7] or even just a silent timer. Through this book, we hope that, when you get spastic and frazzled, you hear us calling out to you, with love and with gentle understanding and rose petals, yelling, "GET IT TOGETHER, WOMAN. MEDITATE!" Remember, the science out there is clear: five minutes is all it takes to make a difference. In some cases, two minutes. Whatever space you can carve out will change your brain and change your energy and lift you up. Just do it.

Chapter Takeaways

- Learn to see, harness, and appreciate your own superpowers.
- A woman's three main superpowers are connection, intuition, and empathy.
- You can build your own energy reserves to make these innate powers even stronger.

---

[6] These apps are available on iTunes, Google Play, or online at https://insighttimer.com and https://www.headspace.com.

[7] Look up White Sun on YouTube, SoundCloud, other music services, or at http://www.whitesun.com. This is a vocal music group featuring sung mantras and the sound of gongs. It's beautiful.

4

We Have the Power to Create the Future We Want

Each of us has the power to create our own present and our own future. There is nothing that is out of reach for you if you believe you can achieve it. We tend to box ourselves in with the word "because." *I can't work part-time because . . . I can't have my own firm because . . . I can't switch from practicing this type of law to that type of law because . . . I don't have time to work out because . . . I don't have time to eat a healthy breakfast because . . . I don't have time for a good night's sleep because . . .* The other limiting word we hear is "until." *I can't work part-time until . . . I can't quit this job until . . . I can't buy a house until . . . I can't start a family until . . .*

Sometimes these limitations are real—we have to use our maturity, experience, and instincts to make the best decisions for us. Other times, though, these stipulations can be fake—conditions we made up in our minds that prevent us from getting what we want. It's up to you to take a hard look at the things you think are stopping you. Check in with yourself and get honest. It can be easy to confuse excuses for facts. How do we know? Because there was a time that we said those things to ourselves too. And the second we stopped saying and believing those things, everything changed. Everything can change for you too, if you just believe it can.

You have to get creative in your planning to make the changes you want in your life. That's true for all of us. If you're a single parent whose child has a health condition and you need a certain caliber of health insurance, of course you can't throw caution to the wind and wish your way to a brighter future. But you can make a plan. Heck, make several plans; we do. They key is to decide what you want, believe you can make it happen, figure out all of the ways to get from A to B, and start taking concrete steps to get there. You make your own future. What better time to get started than now?

Thoughts Become Things

Our thoughts become things. In other words, what we focus our thoughts and energy on gets bigger and comes into our lives—good things *and* bad things. If you think you don't have enough time in the day, you won't have enough time in the day. If you don't think you'll ever find the right partner, lose the weight, be able to buy a house, and so on, you won't. Your negative thoughts can block things. Another way of saying it is that focusing on the absence of something gives power and energy to the lack. We find that by focusing on gratitude for what we have in our lives and who we have in our lives, more good things and good people come.

Here's a slightly less "woo-woo" way to look at it: In this time of, in some ways, unprecedented societal upheaval, women and men, Democrat and Republican, view all of these well-publicized sexual misconduct allegations as symptomatic of widespread societal problems.[1] That means something is broken and needs to be fixed. And that means there is an opportunity. The opportunity is for women to ride this momentum, shift the existing paradigm, and assume positions of power in our homes and our workplaces. Shift your thinking. Stop thinking yourself into a box. Sit down, quiet your mind, and then ask yourself what you really, really want.

Once you figure out what you want, make a plan to make it happen now. You want to open your own firm, but think you don't have enough experience? We promise you, people with less experience than you have opened their own firms, and those firms are still open. You think you don't have the money to run a business? It doesn't cost much, as we'll discuss later in this book.

The point is, the power to be more, to do more, to give more, is all within you. We have the power to advance ourselves. No one is going to take you by the hand and lead you to where you want to go. Only you can do it.

A Word on Losing

There is another important and practical reason to develop those goals and mantras and dreams and values and repeat and repeat until you change your neurochemistry for good: at some point, you're going to lose. Faith isn't for when you are winning, friends. You have to build that positive energy and develop your abilities and deepen your self-practice so that you have the fortitude you need when the shit hits the fan. And it does. Anyone who isn't losing cases isn't trying cases.

---

[1] John Gramlich, *10 Things We Learned about Gender Issues in the U.S. in 2017* (Washington, DC: Pew Research Center, December 28, 2017), http://www.pewresearch.org/fact-tank/2017/12/28/10-things-we-learned-about-gender-issues-in-the-u-s-in-2017.

Courtney:

Look, I started out this thing trying criminal cases. Criminal defense is like waking up every morning, lacing up your shoes, and then walking straight into a bus. But I was lucky; my mentor—a generous, even-keeled, eccentric friend of my mother's, who practiced mostly gang work in Ventura County—knew I needed to learn how to lose. So he threw me in. He told me the only way to learn is to do it (that's some ultimate truth—it's hard to learn how to give an opening from a back room summarizing depositions), so there I was. Started in misdemeanors, quickly escalated to felonies. For the most part, I got my ass handed to me. He would process with me, tell me where I went wrong, and then he would send me right back in. I didn't have a choice. He didn't give me one, and for that I'll always be grateful. I started to win some, and I kept losing a lot, but I was learning to work with the fear, to invite it to my table and give it the best seat but not to let it dominate the conversation. I learned to lose.

One of the most painful losses was a trial I did with my husband, Nick Rowley, in San Diego. It was a medical malpractice case where a father was killed when hospital staff incorrectly intubated him before helicopter transport. The medicine was intricate and complicated, and we were trying the case with an empty chair—the referring lawyer had let the hospital out before we came into the case. (More on that another time, but if you ever think you want to try a case with an empty chair, you should first sign yourself up for an ultramarathon with one hand and one foot tied behind your back. And be sure it's your dominant hand. Just sayin'.)

When the doctor was on the stand, to illustrate how impossible it was for him to practice careful medicine, he stood up, put his hand to his brow, and looked off in one direction and then the other, saying, "not another hospital for miles." Apparently this guy was practicing at the fucking Alamo. I did one of the best cross-examinations of my life. I know I did. But aside from having hands and feet tied behind us, we made other mistakes. We had an ex-defense lawyer on the jury whose mind we thought we could change (you read that right). Did I mention she's now a pastor at a very strict church and does not believe in judging others? No biggie. Sometimes you have to do the thing to learn the thing, even when you think you already know the thing. Sorry.

Devastation, shame, humiliation, disgust, sadness, depression. That is how I feel failure. In my chest, in my hands, in my jaw. Failures bubble up and float in front of me months, years, decades later. Cases, relationships, lies, betrayals, shame. These are inevitable and part of being a human being on this planet.

Sadly, we dwell on the losses, and we quickly move past the wins. I do it, and the lawyers I know do it, and it breaks my heart. I hope that changes, for both sides, the more women infiltrate and influence how law is practiced.

Theresa:

I do it too. I carry my losses with me, and I barely remember the wins. I remember the look on the defense lawyer's face. I remember the feeling of the wind being knocked out of me. Not being able to make eye contact with the jury. Dragging myself into the hallway to talk to them but not really hearing anything that would have made a difference. It's easy for me to see the uselessness of this approach as an outsider looking at someone else's loss.

> I remember getting a call late one night from a friend. I could barely recognize his voice, it was so distraught. From the sound of his voice, I thought there had been an accident or someone was dead. "What? What's going on?" I kept asking.
>
> "I lost."
>
> Well, the truth is, I knew the case, and it would have been a miracle if my friend had won. A pure, 100 percent, no-doubt-about-it miracle. But I know it sticks with him, as my losses do with me. But maybe we can remember how it feels to look at it objectively, from the outside, and give ourselves a little bit of the love and kindness we'd give our friends when the losses come.

The bottom line is that we have to learn to use our losses as fuel for our next steps, our next growth, our next accomplishments. The way we learn how to lose is by nourishing and creating our vision for ourselves so that we know where we are going, what we want, and why we want it. Taking the time and energy to develop our goals and identify the things that light us up gives us the strength and faith we need to get back up and keep going.

Using Technology to Move the Needle

Our access to technology is unprecedented and continues to grow. Trial Guides, the publisher of this book, has free videos online with some of the best lawyers in the country telling you what they do and explaining to you, step by step, how they do it.

To be a great trial lawyer, though, you need to think outside of the legal field. There's a website called masterclass.com, for example, that offers online courses for a minimal fee. These classes have nothing to do with the law, but many of them have a lot to do with being a trial lawyer. You could take a singing class with Christina Aguilera and learn all about breathing and tone and pitch. It's probably not as great as hiring a voice coach who is also a singing teacher, which we've also done, but think of it as a way to tread into the waters and start learning about how you can make your voice better. Your voice is one of the most powerful tools you have as a trial lawyer. Take the jury on a journey with your voice. Move them through the story with the volume of your voice—quiet here, louder there; with your tempo—holding back, building momentum; and with your word choice—allowing your empathy for your client to come through in your words. The energy in your delivery of your client's story is something that everyone in the courtroom will feel if you do your job right. They don't teach you how to do that in law school. So, invest in yourself. Take a class with a master. Work with a voice coach.

What about your body language in court? You can take acting classes with Helen Mirren and Samuel L. Jackson and learn how to present and deliver a story. Learn how your body can enhance and emphasize your words and the emotional content of your words.

You can take writing classes with some of the great authors and screenwriters of our time. You can take a photography class with Annie Leibovitz, a true master. Imagine what you'll learn about how pictures tell stories. You are a trial lawyer, a storyteller. You could take an investigative journalism class with Bob Woodward. These types of resources are pure gold to you.

Some of you are thinking, "I don't have time to add anything else to my plate." Yes, you do, and we'll teach you how to better manage your time in part 5, "The Highest and Best Use of Your Time." You can't afford to miss these learning opportunities. When we actually carved out time to dedicate to reading all of those trial books we had bought and watching the Trial Guides videos and taking the Master Classes (by the way, most are broken into multiple classes that are only ten minutes each)—Coursera and Skillshare are great too—engaging our minds and hearts had a multiplier effect on our performance in litigation, in trial, and in life.[2]

The path from where you are to where you want to be is not linear. We don't practice in a time where you go from law clerk to associate to partner. We don't even practice in a time where you go straight from college to law school. People have vibrant and interesting careers before they become lawyers. Many people go to law school at night now. Some people don't even go to law school until after their kids are raised up and out of the house.

This is your time. Invest in yourself. Practice yoga to learn to control your breath. Take unconventional classes. Expand your thinking and your experiences beyond the law. Know where you're headed and how you're going to get there. Don't choose the traditional route. Energize and fuel your wind horse.[3] You're going to need it when you skip the line.

Chapter Takeaways

- Our thoughts can become things—so real to us that we start organizing our lives around them. Learn to see what is real and what are your own self-imposed limitations.
- Learn to lose. It will help you learn to be a better lawyer and to be willing to take risks.
- Learn to take advantage of legal resources and resources in other industries to improve yourself fast.

---

[2] https://www.coursera.org; https://www.skillshare.com

[3] In Tibetan theology, this strategy is called *riding the wind horse*.

PART TWO

The Power of Being a Woman in the Law

The Power of Being a Woman in the Law

In this section we dive a little deeper into what it means to practice law as women. We talk about why women are uniquely suited to be successful and effective lawyers. And we provide tools for how to navigate the realities of being a female lawyer and how to effectively handle situations where we are underpaid, underrepresented, sexually propositioned, not given credit, interrupted, or the recipient of sexist remarks.

5

Hold on a Minute, Let's Keep This Real

*What It's Really Like to
Be a Female Trial Lawyer*

When you get to part 4, "Trial Perspective and Trial Techniques," you'll see one of the techniques we developed and use on direct examination is called, "Hold On a Minute, Let's Keep This Real." It's where we embrace all of the flaws of our case, and we don't hide from them. When we have nothing to hide, we have nothing to fear. To truly thrive as women lawyers, we have to apply the same approach to looking at our own profession and our role in it.

So, let's talk candidly about the realities of being a female lawyer. As women in the law, many of us are treated in ways that we shouldn't be. Our intent here is not to complain or compare. It's to shed light on the fact that these behaviors are still happening, to give female lawyers tools for how to handle these situations with grace and authority, and to learn how to stop the behavior once and for all, for all women.

Sexism Is Real

First, let's identify the inappropriate behavior. Female lawyers still face gender bias in the workplace. It's sexism. Sexism is discrimination. It's illegal. Even when it's implicit. And it still happens in our profession. Let's put a stop to it.

We have been mistaken for the secretary; we have been mistaken for the court reporter. We have been asked for a cup of coffee, "dear" or "honey." And then thanked and called "sweetheart." We have been disrespected by opposing counsel. We have been publicly demeaned by our coworkers. We have had coworkers take credit for our ideas. We have shared ideas in meetings and then had coworkers restate the same idea and be praised for it. We've been interrupted and spoken over. We've been hit on. We've been flirted with. We've been sexually propositioned by colleagues and superiors. We've been made to feel like trial law is an old boys' club and that we are trespassers or interlopers.

However, this is not our experience anymore. And if it is, it's rare. It's not our experience anymore because we don't accept the behavior, and, most importantly, we *correct* the behavior immediately.

But before we get to that, hear this loud and clear: there was a long, long time when we didn't stand up for ourselves. We thought keeping quiet was required. We thought we had to grin and bear it to keep climbing the ladder and to earn a seat at the trial table. We were wrong. All wrong.

Theresa:

When I was a relatively new lawyer, I was in trial, and there was an older, male lawyer on the other side. He was friendly. I hadn't had any issues with him during the litigation. We were four days or so into trial. I had worn my hair tied back for the first few days. Then, one morning, I showed up with my hair down. I was in the courtroom as soon as it opened. He walked in a few minutes later. We made eye contact, and I said, "Good morning."

He said, "Good morning, Theresa. Your hair is different today. How do you decide how to wear your hair every day?"

I can still feel the emotions of being in that moment:

Why is he noticing my hair? I spent too much time on my hair. I didn't spend enough time on my hair. Why is he asking about my hair? I'm not being taken seriously here. I must have really screwed up yesterday. What am I doing here? This is a man's job. I'm not qualified to be doing this. The proof that I'm not qualified to be doing this is that this man is talking to me about my hair. He isn't taking me seriously at all. I bet the judge isn't taking me seriously. I bet the jury isn't taking me seriously. Was I supposed to wear my hair the same every day of trial? Is that a trial technique that no one told me about? No one ever mentioned that in law school, and I was on the trial team. Why didn't anyone talk about this? Is what I look like distracting? Am I going to lose now?

With all of these thoughts coming at rapid-fire speed, all I could muster in response was a forced smile and to mumble something about not knowing how I decide how to wear my hair every day.

This is not a comment that a male lawyer would make to another male lawyer. Never. It will not happen.

Courtney:

During law school I interned at a district attorney's office over a summer. It was an exciting, fast-paced office. I got certified quickly so I could get into court. About midway through the summer, I got assigned to the big-deal post, where I would get to do preliminary hearings. That meant I got to put on mini trials. (This is a total over-exaggeration, but it was big-deal stuff for a law student, and I was over the moon.) Of course, they don't let some law student just walk into a courtroom and go nuts, so I was assigned to a prosecutor who would be my mentor. He was a nice guy; people seemed to like him; his dad was a judge. I didn't understand the hierarchy yet, but it was clear he was much higher up on the totem pole than I was.

We were sent down for the prelim on a domestic abuse case, and I was to take the lead. I was nervous, but I had on my Nana's blazer and the confidence (adrenaline) started moving up my spine. I had all my notes out on the table like a lawyer.

Prosecutor guy leaned over and tapped me on my shoulder. He had his phone out. "This is a photo of my wife."

OK. Strange way to connect, but maybe he was trying to make me feel comfortable? It's amazing how we immediately start explaining and making excuses for the inappropriate behavior of men. I continued, for the next ten years, to make excuses, ignore, explain away, and blame myself, for the transgressions of men who had more power than me.

"She's hot, right?"

"Um. Yep. Hot."

That's polite, right? It's important to be polite. Good job, Courtney.

The judge took the bench. He was fumbling with the livestream from the court reporter. He was about to ask for appearances, something I was especially ready for. My heart was pounding. I was so nervous.

Prosecutor guy leans closer and whispers to me. "My wife likes women. She would like you."

At this point I was standing to introduce myself to the court.

What. The. Fuck.

I don't think I have to tell you that I had no idea what to do other than keep going. The spotlight was on me, and the judge's son was being welcomed by the judge on the bench, who was "happy" to see him, chuckles and smiles all around. Over the next hour, in between witnesses, I received proposition after proposition, in escalating specificity and detail. I disassociated so hard I must have looked like a mannequin. When it was over, I went straight out to my car, climbed in the back, put my head down, and cried. I quit the next day. I didn't give a reason. I came off as a complete flake. I never said a word about what happened. I wish I had.

Sexism Isn't Always Clear

Sometimes it's easy to recognize that we're victims of sexism. Other times, it's not crystal clear. In those scenarios, we give men the benefit of the doubt and second-guess ourselves. Hold on, let's keep this real: a *lot* of times, we give men the benefit of the doubt and second-guess ourselves even when the situation *is* crystal clear.

We know in our guts, from our intuition, when we're being treated differently than our male colleagues. We know in our guts when someone makes sexist statements to us. Every time a man called us "honey," "dear," "sweetheart," and we forced a smile in response, that hurt us, lowered our energy, took away from our spirits, and put us in a class of women who accepted being treated as "less than."

We have support, by the way. In 2016, the American Bar Association (ABA) amended its professional code of conduct to prohibit women from being referred to as "darling," "dear," "sweetheart," or "honey." It's discrimination, and it's not acceptable.

Scripts for Correcting Sexism

Every single example we've written above is something that happened to us. And in every single one of those instances, we did nothing to *correct* the behavior. And by not correcting the behavior, we endorsed and accepted it, and, thus, it continued. It's embarrassing to admit that. But this is what's important and why we're willing to admit it: *correcting* the behavior immediately eliminates the behavior, unless you're dealing with someone who has a mental illness.

If you've let these waves of sexist remarks wash over you, it may be hard to change your response. But we did it, and you can do it too.

When Someone Makes a Sexist Remark

Take a deep breath in, feel your ribs expand, breathe out. Inhale again, ribs expand, make eye contact, and then speak these words. Here's your response:

> *"That's not an appropriate question for you to ask."*

Or

> *"That's not an appropriate statement. Now, let's move on."*

Imagine the words coming out of your navel and traveling to the other person, hitting him right in the brow. Then stop talking. No more words. The delivery is not coy, kind, demure, girlish, or bitchy. It is firm, deliberate, and factual.

When a Coworker Makes a Sexist Remark

If the offender is a supervisor or coworker, here's your response:

> *"That's not an appropriate question for you to ask."*

Or

> *"That's not an appropriate statement. I am filing a report with Human Resources."*

This is not a threat; you actually do it.

"Now, let's move on."

That is the end of the conversation. It's important to know and understand that you have not done anything wrong. You are not inviting this behavior by being a woman lawyer.

When You're Interrupted

How about when you're interrupted? How do you handle that? Here's your response:

"Bob, I am not finished speaking."

The delivery is the same as above—firm, deliberate, and factual, with eye contact, and with words coming from your navel and landing right on his brow. If you're sitting, some women find it effective to stand up as they speak those words. Take up space. Hold court. You are speaking, and what you are saying is an important contribution.

When a Colleague Takes Credit

How do you handle it when a colleague takes credit for your idea and is then praised for it? Here's your script:

You: [stating your idea]

Colleagues: [nothing]

Male Coworker: [restates your idea as though it is his own]

Bob: Great idea, Male Coworker. You are brilliant, Male Coworker, and will surely save our asses in this case, save the legal profession, and save the world.

You: Actually, Bob, Male Coworker just restated my idea. Yes, it is the best solution in this situation, and here's why. [You go on to give context and depth to your idea.]

Your delivery is the same as the other examples above: firm, deliberate, and factual, keeping eye contact, while envisioning the words coming from your navel and landing at his brow. Notice that you are not talking to the person who stole your idea and claimed it as his own. You could absolutely change the script and speak directly to the idea thief. But we'd classify that as an advanced skill. We don't recommend that approach until you have mastered your breath work, voice, tone, and pitch. Skip ahead to chapter 8, "Finding Your Voice," if you need to. If you haven't mastered these things and you speak directly to the idea thief, you may unintentionally come across as complaining, childish, or petty. And you are not! You are a grown woman correcting the behavior of a grown man who is discriminating against you because of your gender.

When Someone Sexually Propositions You

And, finally, what if you are sexually propositioned or hit on? Here's your script for that:

"No. That's not an appropriate thing for you to say. I am filing a report with Human Resources."

Again, this is not a threat. You actually do it.

"Let's move on."

Again, your delivery is firm, deliberate, factual, and powered by the breath from your navel to his brow. No man who chooses this behavior gets a pass. It is 100 percent illegal 100 percent of the time, and the behavior must be corrected immediately.

Standing up isn't easy. Sometimes it isn't practical. But sometimes, we have to recognize when we are in a position where we can stand up and embrace that responsibility.

Courtney:

> I remember practicing in a courtroom, when I first started, with a standing order that women were not allowed to wear pants. I was a first-year lawyer. I didn't argue. I wish I had, but I thought I was already out of my league as a certified law clerk. I certainly didn't bring it up to the other lawyers in the courthouse, male or female. Yes—there were women who had been practicing in that courtroom every day for years! But man, sitting here now, if that order was standing, I'd pack a toothbrush and some culottes and take the next case on the calendar!
>
> It goes beyond clothes, though. I wish I had a script or someone to talk to when I first started practicing law. For the most part, the people I learned from and was mentored by were men. There were many times, when men I respected greatly hit on me, spoke to me in a way that was devastating, grabbed, and even kissed me without my permission. In most of those situations, I did nothing, and that still haunts me. It's those experiences and regrets and emotions that fuel my courage today and help me do the uncomfortable, sometimes scary thing: the right thing.

We are protected by the law, but our culture is slow and it takes time to change behavior.

Courtney:

I practice with my husband; sometimes we each have a plaintiff or plaintiffs. I have had more than one judge question whether or not we were "allowed" to represent separate plaintiffs as a married couple. In Los Angeles, a judge went on to say, in open court, that though my husband and co-counsel could have their separate opening and represent separate plaintiffs, I could not do either because—chuckle, patronizing side smile down to the silly little girl at counsel table—"we all know there's no real separation. Everyone knows about pillow talk."

Luckily, both the California State Bar Standing Committee on Professional Ethics and California courts addressed this issue (as late as 2004, mind you) when they ruled that in order to make sure women were encouraged and supported in the practice of law, there was a clear distinction between lawyers regardless of whether they were romantically involved, let alone married. In both opinions, there was lengthy discussion about the importance of encouraging women to practice law. Even with the law on my side, though, I felt pretty awful. I was embarrassed, afraid that I had done something wrong, and angry to be the butt of a judge's joke. I don't like admitting it, but I still get insecure when I first walk into a courtroom when my husband and I both represent plaintiffs. I feel like I have to prove that I'm allowed to be there, even though of course I don't.[1]

---

[1] *DCH Health Services Corp. v. Waite* (2002) 95 Cal.App.4th 829.

Women in Law Are Still Underpaid

Women lawyers still earn significantly less than their male counterparts. For example, a female attorney earns only 89.7 percent of a male attorney's weekly salary.[2] Female equity partners in the two hundred largest firms earn only 80 percent of their male counterparts' compensation.[3]

The American Bar Association's Commission on Women in the Profession has a Gender Equality Task Force with resources and publications aimed at achieving equal pay for women. One publication, *Closing the Gap: A Road Map for Achieving Pay Equity in Law Firm Partner Compensation*, brings to light a shocking reality.[4] The pay disparity between men and women actually increases as women gain seniority within law firms and the leaders of these law firms (that is, men) decide bonus amounts and the bases of profit sharing, business origination compensation, and the like. Yet, an ABA survey dating back to 1983 found that male attorneys believe their female counterparts are "harder working, more dedicated, conscientious and serious."[5] The conclusion for us to draw, then, is that there is an inherent gender bias against women. Let's change that. We'll teach you how to talk about money and how to negotiate and advocate for yourself.

---

[2] American Bar Association, *A Current Glance at Women in the Law* (Chicago: American Bar Association, Commission on Women in the Profession, January 2017), https://www.americanbar.org/content/dam/aba/marketing/women/current_glance_statistics_january2017.authcheckdam.pdf.

[3] *Id.*

[4] Lauren Stiller Rikleen, *Closing the Gap: A Road Map for Achieving Pay Equity in Law Firm Partner Compensation* (American Bar Association, Commission on Women in the Profession, 2013), https://www.americanbar.org/content/dam/aba/administrative/women/closing_the_gap.authcheckdam.pdf.

[5] Bill Winter, "Survey: Women Lawyers Work Harder, Are Paid Less, But They're Happy," *American Bar Association Journal* 69 (October, 1983): 1384.

But, first, let's start at the beginning. The truth is, as a brand new lawyer, you don't have much leverage in negotiating your salary because you don't have experience. As law clerks and as inexperienced lawyers working for law firms, we were happy to have jobs. Whatever they were paying was more than we were earning before; so, we took it.

But as our skill level increased, so did the amount of money we earned for our respective employers. That meant our value increased. We have always tracked the amount of profit we've generated for employers so we had that information ready at a moment's notice.

We practice in an area of law that is 100 percent contingency-fee based. That means our risk is high. If we lose a case, we lose all of our money that we put in, and we don't get paid for any of the time we put into the case, which can be years of work. Sometimes, we get less money from a case than we anticipated. In those situations, when we look at the amount of time we invested versus the amount we earned, we can see in retrospect that we made a poor business decision.

Many of us find ourselves negotiating with men for our money. That's hard because men, generally, are more comfortable talking about money and asking for money. Immediately, that puts us at a disadvantage. What do we do?

Well, there are plenty of publications available with mainstream advice for negotiating pay as a female attorney, including resources by the American Bar Association. Here are a few we like:

- *Lean In* by Sheryl Sandberg is a great resource.[6]
- *Women Don't Ask: Negotiation and the Gender Divide* by Linda Babcock and Sara Laschever is another resource we really like.[7]

---

[6] Sheryl Sandberg, *Lean In: Women, Work, and the Will to Lead* (New York: Alfred A. Knopf, 2013).

[7] Linda Babcock and Sara Laschever, *Women Don't Ask: Negotiation and the Gender Divide* (Princeton: Princeton University Press, 2003).

- *Feminist Fight Club* by Jessica Bennett is hilarious, soothing, and very helpful if you are looking for some empathy as well as some solid advice on negotiation.[8]
- A few articles in *New York* magazine's *The Cut*, including "How to Negotiate a Salary According to 25 Famous Women" by Julie Ma, provide great jumping off points for salary negotiation.[9]

Because those resources are available, we're not going to address how to research what other lawyers get paid, how to assess the compensation structure if you're at a large firm or government institution, or any other such basics.

How to Negotiate for Money

We're diving in and talking about what to do when you're ready to negotiate.

First, be ready for the conversation. Make sure you are strong physically, spiritually, and emotionally. Breathe in, and feel your ribs expand. Tap into your resonant voice (see chapter 8, "Finding Your Voice," if you're not familiar with resonant voice). Speak from your navel and aim your words to land on his brow.

Negotiating If You're an Employee

Here are specific tips for negotiating your salary or a raise if you're an employee:

---

[8] Jessica Bennett, *Feminist Fight Club: An Office Survival Manual for a Sexist Workplace* (New York: HarperCollins, 2016).

[9] Julie Ma, "How to Negotiate A Salary, According to 25 Famous Women," *The Cut* (March 15, 2018), https://www.thecut.com/2018/03/25-famous-women-on-how-to-negotiate-salary.html.

1. **Money and benefits are separate and should be negotiated separately.** It's like buying a car: the price of the car is a negotiation and has no bearing on how much money you are given for your trade-in.
2. **Enlist advocates in advance.** Find people who are willing to advocate for you before you ask for a raise or negotiate a salary. Your best advocates are opposing counsel. You read that correctly. Your best advocates are the people you litigate against. Why? Because when your legal adversaries reach out to your superiors or future potential employer and say something good about you, that means you are making your current firm look good, which makes your superiors very happy, and it means that you will make your future employer look good. Humans are egocentric beings by nature, made to look first for what's in their own best interest. Your second-best advocate is a male coworker willing to advocate for you. If your male coworker compliments your work on a particular deposition or on handling a client or a trial, say, "Thank you. That means a lot. It would also mean a lot if you'd share that with my supervisor."
3. **Ask for what you want, and be specific.** "I would like a raise of X amount."
4. **Advocate for yourself.** "Here's why a raise of X amount is justified and reasonable . . ." Then present your evidence. Make it compelling. How much income have you generated for the firm? What percentage of that is your current salary? If you are given your requested raise, what percentage is that of the funds you've generated for the firm? The amount you're asking for may sound like a lot. But it may not sound like a lot when put in the perspective of your profit generation. *Note*: Some people find it helpful to pretend they are actually advocating for a client.

Sharing Fees

Courtney:

I was asked to come in to try a case with a man I met through the Trial Lawyers College. I participated in numerous focus groups, and then a two-week-long trial. It was a lot of work. One night during trial, watching *American Idol*, after checking my (negative) bank account online, I asked about fees. Let's be clear: I didn't do a good job asking—I didn't know how to talk about money and up until that point had relied on the men I worked with to do it for me. Seeing that, knowing that, this man told me that he was glad I accepted the opportunity he had offered me to come and learn from him, and depending on outcome, I might get paid. He was still working out percentages, but five percent sounded fair. Didn't I agree?

You know what I did? Do you think I said, "Hold on, buddy, you've been calling this a job for the last month, I have put everything else on hold, and I am making a significant contribution to this case, so you can eat my shorts!" like I did in my head for the next weeks and months to follow? Nope. In the moment, I said, "You're right. Thank you." Then I proceeded to explain, make excuses for, and justify this man's response. And when it was all over, guess how much I got paid on that one?

Negotiating Fee-Sharing Agreements

Here are specific tips for negotiating your fee if you are sharing fees with another attorney or law firm:

1. **Discuss the fee split immediately:** The subject of fees is not taboo. We work in exchange for compensation. It's that simple. When you are approached to partner on a case, evaluate the case, discuss your role, and then explain what fee split would be acceptable under the circumstances. The lawyer who has approached you can accept, decline, or negotiate. Your responsibility is to decide in advance whether you are willing to negotiate. The same is true if you approach another lawyer and ask her to partner on a case.
2. **Do not accept less than the value of what you are contributing to the case:** Your contribution to a case may be your knowledge of a particular type of case or client, your work product, your money, your mentorship, and so on. Know your value and know the value of what you are contributing.

Courtney:

I got a call from a friend who wanted my help on some really impressive cases, a group of them. They were cases that had to do with a cause I believed in, and they were guaranteed to be high profile, interesting, and lucrative. When it came to the low fee, though, he wouldn't budge. It was really hard to turn him down, but I had to be true to my value, to my time, and to what I needed in order to feel appreciated. It's taken a lot of time and a lot of growing up to understand that I need to stand up for my value even if it means letting someone down or giving up potential work. It doesn't always feel good in the moment, but it does feel right.

3. **Fee splits can and should be determined on a case-by-case basis:** One size does not fit all. That's why a thoughtful assessment of the case and your contribution, along with open communication, is important from the outset.
4. **Memorialize the fee split in writing:** Some jurisdictions require the fee split to be disclosed in writing and approved in writing by the client. I thought it made me "cooler" to not have my fee splits in writing. It sure did. Cooler and poorer. I could start a girls' school with the amount of money I've lost because I didn't get it in writing—maybe two. Get it in writing at the beginning, keep it clean, and then it's done and everyone is clear and on the same page.

Advocating for the pay you deserve is your responsibility. And it's a responsibility that you hold for all women. Every woman who advocates for the money she deserves sets a precedent for herself and for all those who follow her. We owe it to ourselves, and we owe it to all women to ask for and get the money that we deserve.

We are owed under the law the amount of money that fully compensates us for the work we perform. That's fair trade value, and that's what we all deserve. See appendix B for samples of fee-sharing agreements.

Women in Law Hold Fewer High-Ranking Positions

Here are the most recent statistics. In 2017, of the women attorneys in private practice, about 20 percent were partners, only 18 percent were equity partners, 45 percent were associates, and nearly 49 percent were summer associates.[10] Fewer than 25 percent of all general counsel in Fortune 500 companies were women.[11] The picture on the bench isn't much different. Women held only about 27 percent of state and federal judgeships.[12] This picture of women in the law is slowly changing, however, and we're giving you the information and understanding necessary to accelerate that change.

We both used to fit squarely within those statistics. Fortunately, we didn't know the statistics existed. And though it never occurred to us to be limited by whatever the statistics said, we knew we weren't getting what we were promised. The pitch from those in charge at our firms, the deal we'd been sold, it wasn't panning out. Promises of more trials, more money, and more autonomy weren't bearing out. We wanted what we were promised. In some ways, we figured if it was promised to us, then it was possible, and it was out there. It just wasn't being given to us. So, we had a choice to make: play it safe or take a chance.

We both decided we could have whatever life and whatever kind of law practice we wanted. Then we kicked it up a notch and decided we could work the days we wanted, the hours we wanted, earn what we wanted, choose only the clients we wanted, really connect with our clients, feel fulfilled, and feel like what we were doing really mattered.

---

[10] American Bar Association, *A Current Glance at Women in the Law* (Chicago: American Bar Association, Commission on Women in the Profession, January 2017), https://www.americanbar.org/content/dam/aba/marketing/women/current_glance_statistics_january2017.authcheckdam.pdf.

[11] *Id.*

[12] *Id.*

Opening our own firms is the best professional decision we've ever made. It made us accountable to ourselves and even to our clients in some ways we weren't before. It made us decisive. It made us businesswomen and entrepreneurs, neither of which we had ever planned to be. It accelerated our trial skills dramatically. And now, it has given us the ability to share what we fumbled through and figured out the hard way in hopes of making the way easier for those that come after us.

Women in Law Are Underrepresented

In the face of sexism, lower pay, fewer advancement opportunities, and an inequitable division of child-rearing and household responsibilities, it's not surprising that women decide not to stay in law. The numbers of women leaving the profession, historically, are astonishing and distressing, if taken at face value.

Women make up more than half of current law school graduates. Yet ABA Market Research 2016 shows 64 percent of attorneys in the country are male and 36 percent are female. Where are we all going? It's unclear. The solution isn't as black-and-white as we've been led to believe—women don't only leave to "have families"—we believe there are a lot of reasons, many of which relate to the fact that practicing law in the patriarchal paradigm can, frankly, suck.

Courtney:

> A few years ago, I got a call from a good friend to try a case for him. The injury had to do with a woman's vagina, so this lawyer thought this was a "ladies case." I have tried multiple penis cases, despite my anatomy, but I didn't argue with him

as he was clearly uncomfortable with the case. The case was difficult, and not because of its content. Every day, my performance was critiqued. I got a good "mansplaining" each afternoon before returning home to frantically feed my kids, feed myself, and start preparing for the next day. For me, trial can be quite energizing. Not this one. I felt unappreciated, undervalued, and patronized. Luckily, I'm at a point in my career where I can choose my cases, because the truth is, I would chop up my bar card before I would work under those conditions again. This was not the first time I've felt this way. Over the years, the patronizing, being "shorted" or simply excluded from fees, being hit on by men I considered mentors, and the constant feeling of having to claw my way to get to baseline has been exhausting, demotivating, and in many ways, unsustainable. I considered leaving the practice many, many times. Luckily, I was blessed. I caught enough breaks when I needed them that it was worth my while to stay.

We are not blaming men. This is not that book. But we do want to acknowledge that the system and lifestyle of practicing law is very difficult for women to sustain, and a significant number of women continue to leave the practice, even after reaching partner in their firms. However, from our perspective, and in our experience with our own practices and interacting with female trial lawyers across the country, times are changing, and these numbers are already shifting noticeably as we all ride this wave of change for women.

Let's take a look at what's happening.

Don't Give Up Law to Be a Bartender Yet

There were times we wanted to quit being lawyers. The hours were brutal. The stress was off the charts. We felt like we had no time to exercise or take care of ourselves. We were slaving away. For what? We talked about quitting—being a yoga teacher, tending bar, working at Pottery Barn, walking dogs. Doing something where it was over and off your mind when you left work and you weren't worrying about what you didn't finish and what you had to do tomorrow in order to be recognized or even just accepted by your bosses or the firm. Then there's the structural inequity, inherent sexism, and the myriad of other inequities that can wear us down. We've heard from countless other women lawyers, especially trial lawyers, that they've felt the same at times.

We want to give you another option. Another model. We want you to see how many dynamic, successful women trial lawyers are changing the way they practice law so that the practice is fulfilling and provides space for self-care, spiritual and emotional exploration and nurturing, creating and supporting a family, and spending time with the people who bring them joy. Many, many women have made these changes, and they are making the practice work for them. Throughout this book, we'll offer you ways to, first, decide what you want your life and your practice to look like and, second, make what you want a reality. Feel free to skip ahead to any chapter that your heart gravitates toward. And start there.

Chapter Takeaways

- Sexism is real—you can combat sexist behavior by knowing what to say.
- Women are underpaid—you can learn how to negotiate for yourself.
- Fee-sharing requires more than a handshake—you can learn to create and negotiate a fee-sharing agreement that is fair to you.
- Staying in the law is difficult—don't take off just yet. We can make this better.

6

An Interview with Roxanne Barton Conlin
You Aren't Alone

Roxanne Barton Conlin runs her own law firm in Des Moines, Iowa. She's a civil lawyer who represents only plaintiffs. We have the pleasure of knowing Roxanne, although not nearly as well as we'd like to, and, my, is she an amazing woman. She is truly one of the women who made it possible for us, and for you, to be doing what we all do today.

Here's a little taste of who Roxanne is for those who may not know her. Roxanne enrolled at Drake University in 1961, when she was only sixteen, and graduated from law school with honors five years later at the age of twenty-one. From 1969 to 1976, she was an assistant attorney general for Iowa, where she was head of the Iowa Civil Rights section and fought race and sex discrimination. She also rewrote Iowa's inheritance laws, toughened the state's assault laws, and blocked a merger of two major utilities that would have hurt consumers. She left the Attorney General's Office to become a consultant to the United States Department of State for International Women's Year.

In 1977, she became one of the first two women ever to be a United States attorney. Roxanne put heroin dealers behind bars and prosecuted white-collar crimes and corruption in public office. She also served as president of the Federal Executive Council, which is composed of the heads of all seventy federal agencies.

Roxanne founded and was the first chair of the Iowa Women's Political Caucus and was president and general counsel of the NOW Legal Defense and Education Fund. She has been named by the *National Law Journal* as one of the fifty most influential women lawyers in America, one of the one hundred most influential lawyers in America, and one of the top ten litigators. She has been inducted into the Iowa Women's Hall of Fame, was selected in 1975 as one of the 44 Women Who Could Save America and in 1976 as one of 44 Women Qualified for a Cabinet Position. In June of 1982, Roxanne won a three-way primary and became the Democratic nominee for governor of Iowa. She was narrowly defeated in her effort to become the state's first Democratic governor in fourteen years, and its first woman governor. And she has had many other firsts. She was the first woman president of the Association of Trial Lawyers of America, a sixty-thousand-member organization of consumer attorneys. She was the first woman to chair the Roscoe Pound Foundation, a trial lawyers think tank. She was the founder and first chair of the Civil Justice Foundation, which provides direct support to grassroots organizations and disabled individuals. In 1995, she was inducted into the Inner Circle of Advocates.

Roxanne has been married to her husband for more than fifty-four years; they have raised four children and have five grandchildren.

We are both Iowa lawyers and were honored to be guests at Roxanne's home recently with a small group of influential and accomplished female trial lawyers. After that magical evening, we begged Roxanne to sit down with us.

Roxanne: So I'm fifteen; I'm in an all-girls Catholic school. Sister Mary Katrine was my sophomore homeroom nun's name, and I was going to be a movie star. She said, no, you have to get your education. You have to become an educated person, and then go be a movie star. And so, she said, be a lawyer. Use your brain and your flare for the dramatic. I said—OK, I will do that. And I'm absolutely certain—because I talked to her many times after that—that she had no idea what it would be like for me in law school. None, not any idea at all.

Theresa: To say nothing of the practice. Just law school.

Roxanne: Law school itself was a very great challenge. There were three women in my class. And we were one, two, and three. Seriously, that tells you that it wasn't easy. The Dean of the law school—

Theresa: And which one were you?

Roxanne: I was, I was variously one or two. The semesters that I had morning sickness I dropped a little bit, because the women's restroom was half a mile away.

Theresa: I've heard stories like that.

Roxanne: It was really something. And the professors were openly hostile to me. My classmates were openly hostile to me. I started law school when I was nineteen. There were a lot of reasons I didn't belong there as far as they were all concerned. I got married in my second semester of my freshman year to James Conlin, in part because of the rumors that I was sleeping with all the seniors, all the professors, and everyone in my environment. This was a different time, in terms of sex. You didn't say it out loud. I was hurt by that. I was a good girl.

Theresa: From the Catholic school.

Roxanne: That's right. So I thought getting married would solve that problem. It did not. It made me an adulterer.

Theresa: Yeah. You added a label.

Roxanne: Every day was a new challenge of some kind that I did not anticipate when I was pregnant. The semester that I was hugely pregnant, the Dean took my scholarships away from me. Three days before school started.

Theresa: Oh my gosh.

Roxanne: All summer long, I kept calling and talking to the secretary saying, "I don't seem to have my scholarship papers yet." She said, "Well, they should be along." I don't think she had any idea what he was going do to. Three days before school started, she said, "I'm afraid you're not going to get any scholarships." I said, "What?"

Theresa: What'd you do?

Roxanne: I hocked my engagement ring, which was about a point six carat diamond. I think I got fifty dollars for it, but there was a man in the financial aid office of the university who gave me a national student defense loan. For a thousand dollars. And I showed up on the first day of class and, and went into the dean's office and said, "I'm here."

Theresa: What moxie.

Roxanne: Yeah, yeah. The asshole. He was a horrifying person. A blatant, sexist pig who said openly, "women do not belong in law school."

Theresa: Amazing. How did you keep going back every day? Especially—and this is why I'm curious—because it wasn't something you were passionate about. It wasn't your goal, right?

Roxanne: Well, it became my goal.

Theresa: Tell me more about that.

Roxanne: In law school, I learned that women are not fairly treated by the law. They didn't expect to teach me that. I'm sure they didn't set out to teach me that, but you can't help but learn that in law school. And so, I learned that in law school, and I thought that maybe I should try to change that. So, that's what I've been doing.

Theresa: So, then we move forward to your career and, oh my gosh, all the things you've done, but you were always forging the way. I mean, the trend never stopped. Right? What's that like?

Roxanne: Oh, it's fun. God, it's fun. It's challenging; it's exciting. You feel like you're doing something that is worthwhile, that matters, that, in the long run, will be helpful to the people about whom you care. I've certainly lost cases that I very much wanted to win. I have been trying to change Iowa law, to make the Iowa Constitution provide a remedy in damages to individuals whose rights the government tramples on. I think I've spent about twenty years doing it. I won last summer.

Theresa: Well, that's what strikes me. You know, the times that we've spent together and, and that we've discussed cases and this and that, for me, my takeaway from our conversations is always your focus on the law and how it should be, and how we, as practitioners, can reshape the law and make it as it should be. And that really seems to be a big part of your driving force.

Roxanne: It absolutely is, always has been, always will be. I want to abolish the statute of limitations for child sexual abuse.

Theresa: As it should be.

Roxanne: Yeah. Because, as I said to the Supreme Court, I want pedophiles, sexual abusers of children, to wonder all of their lives when the sheriff is going to be standing on their doorstep. They should never get over that because their victims will never get over it. I still lost.

Theresa: And sometimes we do.

Roxanne: I know that's a part of it. It isn't my favorite part of it. Boy, I hate to lose.

Theresa: I think it's hard for people to dig out of the day-to-day and have a vision and a goal for effecting real change. Because you're not effecting change in the industry, you're effecting change in the community, in the state, and, to some extent, the ripple effect in the world. So how do you give people the tools to do that? How do you give people the tools to look past the pile of papers on their desks right now and, and think a little bit more broadly? Maybe you don't. Maybe it's just in people to think more broadly.

Roxanne: I don't know. But I think you're quite right that people don't see the forest for the trees. I have a limited ability to represent people, and I take cases that I like. That I think are worthy cases. It doesn't matter to me whether there's any money there or not. I just think people ought to get justice. So we file a lot of cases that other people won't file. But then we can't take the cases that have monetary damages. I think everybody should have access to good lawyers. One of our firm's missions is passing the torch. We have six law clerks. We hire people at the beginning of their second year.

Usually I really like to have people who are going to be with me for eighteen months or two years and that lets me give them cases. They have a caseload. They're responsible for that caseload. They're responsible for drafting a petition, drafting a civil rights complaint, the discovery, sitting in on the depositions. Just responsible for all of it. And when we go to trial, we all go to trial. I need a lot of bodies. The intent is to let them go out into the world and do good.

Theresa: I think that component, true training in law clerks, is missing from most firms.

Roxanne: I think so too. I think a lot of firms don't understand. There are a couple of things that I would like to see change. One of them is for plaintiffs' law firms to mentor law students and new lawyers, to teach them what it's about. Of course, they may run screaming; some of them do.

Theresa: Better to do it early.

Roxanne: Exactly. And better to do it with the supervision necessary so they don't screw up somebody's life. The other thing that I think is really important is babies in law offices.

Theresa: Tell me about that.

Roxanne: Well, we started, Michelle Feldman was a legal assistant and got pregnant. And she asked if she could bring her baby to work. Michael Galligan and I were partners at the time. This was back in the eighties. And we said, let's just see how this works. It worked fine. She brought the baby. She nursed the baby. She could type with one hand; she could answer the phone. She could do everything that she was supposed to do with the baby in her lap. We thought it was great. So, I can't even remember how many babies we ultimately had in the office. One woman had twins. And then when I moved over to my husband's building, I encouraged women in law school who were wanting to have children to do so. I said, you'll never have as much time as you do in law school, and we love babies, bring them with you.

Theresa: Don't you think it's good for the mammas to have their babies—

Roxanne: Oh, my God, yes. You know, we pretend to be a society that's child centered. We're just not. I just think it's terribly important. So important. That bonding is irreplaceable. You've just got that short period of time.

Theresa: Can we talk about what to wear to court?

Roxanne: Yes. I love that dress.

Theresa: Thank you for the compliment on my dress.

Roxanne: I do love that. That's what you always think. Could I wear that to court? Yes. You could.

Theresa: Rachel Parcell. She does lovely, lovely work.

Roxanne: Do you usually wear a dress to court?

Theresa: I do. I wouldn't say I usually do, but I do. And I never know if I'm doing the right thing. My background is in journalism. I was a television news reporter before I went to law school, before I became an attorney. And so, there were no grays and blacks, but it was the pink blazer and the blue blazer and the green blazer. It was important to have color, you know, visually. And it's the opposite in court. And, so, I want to be unremarkable—

Roxanne: Yes.

Theresa: What do you do? It's challenging. I grew up in Maryland, and in the county where I grew up, it was, as late as 1995, which is when I graduated from high school, the female attorneys in that county were required to wear skirts and dresses, panty hose.

Roxanne: When I'm trying a case before a jury, I still only wear skirts.

Theresa: Is that right?

Roxanne: Yes. It probably isn't even necessary anymore. That's my wardrobe, my trial wardrobe is really dull skirts. Dull, brown, beige, gray, navy. You know, inconspicuous. Is there some seventy-year-old man who thinks that a woman shouldn't wear pants? So, don't want to offend the jury.

Theresa: And you just want to be unremarkable, right?

Roxanne: And it is tricky. What feels right to me is just sort of no thinking about it. But why should we have to worry about that?

Theresa: And that's the thing. Right. That, that's the question. And Courtney and I discuss that. And, and we'll go back and forth. Why should I care? Aren't I just here to do my job? Well, but if my clothes are distracting from the job that I'm doing, am I doing my job?

Roxanne: There's no answer to that.

Theresa: So, what do you tell the young women who come through your office these days, either law clerks or young attorneys? What do you tell them about the practice and what it's like? You have all this experience and all of this perspective in the law and being a woman in, in the law. Particularly a trial lawyer. Things have changed so much since you've started. So what do you tell them these days?

Roxanne: They should, I think, open their own law firms and, and just do what they want to do.

Theresa: You make your own rules.

Roxanne: Yeah.

Theresa: You make your own life. You make your own practice.

Roxanne: Yeah.

Theresa: You make the practice yours.

Roxanne: Yes. And you only pick the cases that appeal to you. That you want to try. That you can believe in and that may make a difference. But it is hard for people to do that. Very hard.

Theresa: What do you think we can do? What's the message that we can get out to plaintiffs' law firms about the best way to mentor young women as trial lawyers?

Roxanne: Well, give them some cases. They don't have to cross-examine the expert. But you do have to let them, maybe, do the direct examination of the plaintiff. Just get them in there and get them doing something.

Roxanne: I certainly know plaintiffs' law firms that are hostile environments for young women attorneys. And that really distresses me to learn about that. I'm perfectly willing to sue them. But for most women that's not really an option. It is a shame. And it's amazing to me. But we really have made enormous progress. Women who were secretaries were expected to sleep with their bosses. It was the thing to do. It is amazing to me how far we have come. But I think we still have a long ways to go.

Theresa: Do you do philanthropic work?

Roxanne: Yes.

Theresa: Tell me about it.

Roxanne: We have two foundations that we concentrate on helping people to meet their basic needs. With the money we have in the foundations. And nobody gave it to us. We earned that money. But outside my foundation, I give more. I've established a scholarship at Drake Law School. Again, for meeting people's basic needs. A student at Drake Law School might have to quit in his or her second semester of their junior year if some tragedy befell them. Not anymore. And then I also provide forty scholarships a year to the victims of domestic violence. I come from a very poor family, and I know what it's like to be one paycheck away from homelessness. I'm the oldest of six children. My father was an alcoholic. He was also a vicious, violent man. So I know what that feels like, and I know how insecure that can make the whole family.

Theresa: What are your final thoughts on being a woman trial lawyer?

Roxanne: It might be the best way to change the world. I went to law school to change the world. That was the whole goal. I can look at my life and see change, and see what, with the help of a willing client, I could accomplish. My best piece of advice?

Theresa: Please.

Roxanne: Wise choice of life partner. You can't do it alone. And you have to have somebody who loves you, who supports you. As I've said of my own husband, whatever crazy thing I want to do, he says, well, just go ahead and do that. And sometimes it's just nuts. He has been an amazing person. I hope he thinks the same of me because I've tried to be, to him, who he is to me, and . . . and it's been a very successful unit.

Theresa: You're right. I've had the same experience with my husband, especially running my own business, having two small babies, being a trial lawyer, being a friend, being a mother, being a wife, being all these things. And for my husband to get up in the morning and empty the dishwasher, or get up in the morning and fix the kids breakfast, or to say, "Leave your job and your salary and open your own firm." You need that, and it makes all the difference in the world.

Roxanne: I think that they have to have good mothers. They have to have something in them that permits them not to be threatened by who we are and what we want from our lives. They have to be able to adjust to all of our craziness. But that's my best advice.

PART THREE

Unexpected Ways to Increase Your Success

Unexpected Ways to Increase Your Success

In this section of the book, we'll talk about ways to capitalize on opportunities that the law doesn't often focus on, to increase your success. We're going beyond CLEs, seminars, and trial techniques. The focus is on helping others to help yourself; contributing to the success and growth of others to reap the benefits of success and growth for yourself; and understanding that there is infinite success available. One lawyer's success does not dim the light of another's potential for success.

Victory comes when you focus on your own path, not when you are constantly comparing yourself to others. Investing in yourself yields the highest returns. This chapter is about increasing your own value while also elevating the people around you.

7

The Power of Women Promoting Women

One of the most effective ways women can raise the bar and significantly change their positions is by promoting one another. The patriarchal paradigm has benefited from the myths that women are "catty" or in competition with one another. These ideas are outdated and untrue. Not only are women supporting one another, but they are learning from one another, making money with one another, and deconstructing the misconceptions that shortchange us all. This support system has led to positive, tangible, lasting results. In this chapter, we give you practical tips you can start using today to support other women in a way that improves your success and improves the success of the women you support.

Women Seek Out Relationships with Other Women

We have been socialized to believe that women are biologically programmed to be jealous or wary of one another. In fact, the opposite is true. Our neurons are programmed for community, specifically the community of other women.

In a landmark 2000 study out of UCLA, researchers found that women react to stress not by going into "fight or flight" mode but, rather, by going into "tend and befriend" mode.[1] In other words, when stress chemicals are released into a woman's bloodstream, she has a *behavioral* response. That behavior is to nurture herself and her family to keep them safe and happy, and she does this by nurturing social relationships with other women. The best, most successful response to stress for women has been passed down from generation to generation: connect with social groups and friends. Ample research teaches us that one of the key differences between men and women is women's strong tendency to seek out social support when coping with stress. By and large, women require the support of other women. Across their lifetimes, women who seek out support from other women, report more satisfaction, better coping skills, and less codependency in intimate relationships.[2] Studies have found that women who are consistently supportive of one another tend to achieve greater success across all life areas, including in the face of economic problems, work problems, interpersonal problems, death, and health problems.[3]

---

[1] Shelley E. Taylor et al., "Biobehavioral Responses to Stress in Females: Tend-and-Befriend, Not Fight-or-Flight," *Psychological Review* 107, No. 3 (February 29, 2000): 411-429.

[2] *Id.*

[3] *Id.*

Our neurons, the brain cells that process and transmit information in the brain and body, are most connected between the two sides of the brain.[4] This means the greatest exchange of information in a woman's brain is happening between the left and right hemispheres. That means women's brains are wired for social skills, memories, intuitive thinking, and emotional engagement—the foundations of community. Men's brains were more connected from the front to back, within each hemisphere, rather than between hemispheres, making them more adept at perception and coordination skills, according to the study.

This is scientific evidence that women are made to support one another. Doing so reduces our stress, extends our lifespans, and makes us better human beings. Choosing to accept contrary and divisive myths causes all women to suffer greatly. This suffering hurts our souls because we miss out on the healing and comfort of holding space for one another. When we deny ourselves our natural tendency to come together and nurture one another, we marginalize ourselves and abdicate the power of our equality.

---

[4] Madhura Ingalhalikar et al., "Sex Differences in the Structural Connectome of the Human Brain," *Proceedings of the National Academy of Sciences of the United States of America* 111, No. 2 (January 14, 2014), https://doi.org/10.1073/pnas.1316909110.

When Women Don't Support One Another

Courtney:

I remember working in a law firm with about twenty or so lawyers, three of whom were female. My first assumption was that they were friends, allies. The odds were against them, so they probably decided right from the start to stick together? Nope. All three were quite capable attorneys. But one was "too pretty" according to the intelligent one, the other was a "workaholic" according to the one who had a family, and the last one made the fatal error of having an affair with one of the male attorneys; so, she was excommunicated and warranted little more than the occasional eye-roll. Meanwhile, all three were earning significantly less than male attorneys junior to them in performance and experience. All three were struggling to accommodate their second jobs as wives, mothers, and daughters; and they were trying to hide it all so that they would be "one of the guys," for fear of losing respect. I remember a few months after leaving the firm, seeing these three women profiled in the "women lawyer" section of some legal publication, standing together arm-in-arm in power suits, appearing to be unified and connected.

Look, just because we have the same anatomy doesn't mean we have to get along. But in order to seize the opportunities of the shifts that are happening, we have to put ourselves on trial as well. We have to really look at what we are doing to promote one another, but also what we do day to day to shoot ourselves in the foot.

When We Bond and Support, Everyone Benefits

Theresa:

For a number of years, I've been part of a lady lawyers dinner group. We get together once a month, usually at one of our homes. We are all trial lawyers—plaintiffs' personal injury lawyers, employment lawyers, sexual harassment lawyers, criminal defense lawyers, elder abuse lawyers, business lawyers. We work, and many of us have families, but we carve out a few hours a month to talk, have a meal, ask each other about our cases, get advice, and connect. What those few hours can do for my soul is profound. We also have our own email list that we use to refer cases to one another, ask for help covering hearings, recommend business vendors, and discuss legal issues.

This group is evidence of what women supporting women can accomplish. When we started having our dinners, only a few of us had our own firms. Many of the women in our dinner group were associates at law firms. Only a few years later, almost all of the women have their own firms. And I am so proud of all of them.

What they did took courage. They left secure jobs. They left consistent incomes. They went from being associates to being business owners, running their own law firms. And they are all successful.

What happened in our group is this: we showed these women that they could have what they wanted. We didn't just stand as role models. We all stood together, supporting one another with information, inspiration, and love. Those of us who had our own firms already are no less successful today. In fact, we are more successful, personally and professionally, because of what we gave to the group and the women in it.

Courtney:

I was teaching a seminar on Lummi Island, Washington, not long ago, and met some pretty incredible women. One of the women had a case outside of her area of expertise and was talking about it at lunch. She needed help funding and working the case. I pointed at the other lawyer at the table, an employment lawyer who was looking to try more cases. "Try it together," I said. "And share the fees."

Many times, women I work with or meet are uncomfortable with the money side of the relationship. Time and time again I see women "networking" over lunches or dinners and then referring their cases to men.

These two Lummi ladies ended up trying that case together. My husband was trying a case across the hall and got to go watch pieces of their trial. They kicked ass. They took a pretty good case, put their heads together, and tried the hell out of it. And together, they got an eight-figure verdict.

Women Amplifying Women

As women, we hold back. We don't feel comfortable talking about ourselves and about our accomplishments. This is particularly evident in the legal field. We see successful men standing up and listing off their accomplishments proudly. We don't see women doing the same. While we aren't critical of men when they talk about their achievements, we hold ourselves to a different standard. We think talking about our own achievements is bragging, arrogant, or conceited. And what about receiving compliments? We see men in our industry accept compliments with grace and little fanfare. What do you see when a woman is complimented?

"Thank you, but . . ." Or, "Oh, it was nothing." Or we make some other statement that minimizes ourselves. We have to let go of that. We have to honor ourselves. There is grace and power in simply saying, "Thank you."

Complimenting others increases the success of both the person giving the compliment and the person receiving the compliment. Increasing how often we compliment other women has a direct correlation with elevating their success as well as our own.

Amplification in Obama's White House

A group of industrious women working in the White House during the Obama administration decided to intentionally promote one another using a technique they called *amplification*. According to an article published in the *Washington Post*, at the beginning of the Obama administration, two-thirds of Obama aides were men. Women struggled to get into important meetings. If they managed to get into the meetings, they complained that they were ignored, or if they shared an idea, a man would claim credit for that idea.[5] The women's amplification strategy consisted of one woman making a point, and then another woman repeating the point and attributing it to the woman who made it. What they found is, over time, the president noticed. He began calling more women and junior aides to top-level meetings.[6]

Let's take a lesson from these women in the White House. Commit to amplifying the women in your life, starting today. Openly compliment other women, tout their achievements, and give them credit for their contributions. When we make an effort to promote ourselves and one another, we foster our success and others' success.

Let's take a lesson from these women in the White House. Commit to amplifying the women in your life, starting today. Openly compliment other women, tout their achievements, and give them credit for their contributions. When we make an effort to promote ourselves and one another, we foster our success and others' success.

What Men Can Do to Promote Women

Men can have a substantial impact on the advancement of equality of women, and men can stand to benefit significantly from the empowerment and promotion of women at work and in the world. We talk more about this and other pragmatic tools for men in a later section, but for now, here are some specific ways men can start promoting women today.

---

[5] Juliet Eilperin, "White House Women Want to Be in the Room Where It Happens," *Washington Post*, September 13, 2016.

[6] *Id.*

Make a Woman Your Trial Partner

Whether you are a man or a woman, if you are heading to trial, ask a woman to sit at counsel table and try the case with you. Not as a token, as a trial partner. Help her, teach her, and give her as many chances to get up in front of the jury as possible. And then, regardless of the outcome, *do it again*. Actively engage in the development and training of women trial lawyers.

A handful of federal judges in Brooklyn are urging women to take a more active role in court. One judge, the Hon. Jack B. Weinstein, age ninety-six, issued a court rule "urging a more visible and substantive role for young female lawyers working on cases" before them. Judge Weinstein said that it was "particularly important because we have so few trials these days so some of the youngsters don't get the same training they used to. It's important for everyone, and for the litigation process, that the upcoming generation understands the fundamentals and just gets up on their feet."[7] The judge had informally encouraged more female involvement over the years, but he instituted this rule after a New York State Bar Association report "found that female lawyers appear in court less frequently and that when they do, they are less likely to have a prominent role."[8] He encouraged law firms to have their younger lawyers and women argue the motions and get involved in the courtroom.

This isn't a situation that is specific to New York's bar. Women are underrepresented in lead trial roles across America. Those lawyers who do have lead roles, including both men and women, can help shift those statistics.

---

[7] Alan Feuer, "A Judge Wants a Bigger Role for Female Lawyers. So He Made a Rule," *New York Times*, August 23, 2017.

[8] *Id.*

Compliment a Woman's Work to Other People

Just as the White House women amplified one another, men can amplify women. Repeat their points and ideas and give them credit. When you see a woman do something well, tell *someone else* about it. It doesn't have to be something extraordinary, simply something done well. Sometimes we tend to compliment the person herself, but that isn't enough. It's great to tell women when you think they've done something well (that's good management), but you can have an even greater impact by telling the people around you. Studies have shown that men tend to give more credence to other men. That means you have tremendous power to make a difference in a woman's career and in her perceived value in the workplace.

Give Female Attorneys Meaningful Litigation Work

If you are a law firm owner, partner, or lead lawyer on a case, introduce women to the clients as well as men. Send women to depositions and appearances as often as men. Keep track. Equalize the court time for motions and appearances. Put women on trial teams.

And start paying women equally. Put women in leadership positions. Publish your numbers. Show everyone that you pay men and women equally. Set an example for others to follow.

Success Begets Success

The big secret is that we all benefit when someone succeeds. This is more true than ever when we talk about women succeeding. Sometimes we forget that the universe isn't a pie with some predetermined limit of pieces. The truly powerful people in this world are the ones who understand that the universe is infinite, that energy is infinite, and that success and money are energy and, therefore, are infinite. That means we can all be successful without taking away from anyone else's success.

The physics of success isn't complicated. The more you give, the more you get in return. We have to make a conscious effort to reach out to one another and raise each other up. Women are capable of being each other's biggest source of support, encouragement, and inspiration. When we share our ideas, dreams, and struggles, we find community. In that community, we find strength. We do it by celebrating each other and ourselves.

When we decide to take a hard look at our own behavior and cut out the divisiveness that has been an integral part of the patriarchal paradigm, we become unstoppable and our potential soars. Instead of cutting one another down, women can raise each other up. A lot. Women can make a lot of money together. Women should be doing business with women and growing their practices and businesses together. The good-old-boys-club isn't a coffee club. It's how business owners, entrepreneurs, and professionals, across all fields, have been networking and growing their empires for centuries. It's time for us to do the same.

Supporting one another benefits women and men, and not just in the legal profession. By making room for equality and mutual respect in our profession, we are setting an example for women who don't have the power and access to resources that we do. And that makes the world a better place.

The legal profession, and each of us as officers of the court, is in service to the U.S. Constitution, our legal justice system, and all of the souls who are affected by the laws of our nation. We are also leaders, setting the tone for what the next century is going to look like. If we are role models of support, we will shift our society back to what we are hardwired to do: tend and befriend by nurturing ourselves, our children, and our relationships with other women. In doing so, we raise the caliber of everyone around us.

Chapter Takeaways

- Successful women amplify the women around them.
- Successful women work together, bonding with and supporting one another.
- Successful men work with women—supporting their efforts and encouraging them.

8

Finding Your Voice

To embrace your feminine authority, especially in the law, you must master public speaking. As trial lawyers, we're asking a jury of strangers to understand something and do something for our clients. Public speaking is how we communicate with our juries, but it's also how we present ourselves to our clients, our colleagues, judges, and witnesses. On a personal level, improving your public speaking will improve your confidence and enrich your relationships. Professionally, improving your public speaking will increase your ability to negotiate better pay, elevate your professional reputation, and improve your writing skills. Here, we'll give you tips we've learned and currently use for harnessing the power of your speech and voice.

Your Presentation

Hold on a minute, let's keep things real here: it can be hard to be a woman in court. We're usually alone, up against a man, in front of a judge who sometimes won't let us finish our thoughts, and we're wearing a costume that leaves us feeling less than confident (more on that later, or you can skip to chapter 23, "Dressing the Part"). And we've been conditioned to believe that court is still a man's domain. After all, it wasn't until a couple decades ago that women were allowed to enroll in law schools in some parts of this country.

This is what we see most commonly in court and in the legal profession in general:

1. Women trying to emulate men

Or

2. Women acting submissive and spiritless

Both groups of women are wearing their fear like armor, just different ways. So, how should you act? Be you. Don't try to be someone else. And don't be afraid to be you. You are good enough to do this job.

There are a lot of great resources to teach you how to carry yourself and how to communicate so that your message is heard. We've both had the privilege of studying with the inimitable Joshua Karton. His recent book, *Theater for Trial*, is a great read and valuable resource.[1] His background is in theater, and he takes those theater skills of connecting and projection and shows lawyers how to do those things in the courtroom. He has a fantastically effective exercise that teaches you to really speak to jurors and connect with them rather than keeping your eyes constantly moving from juror to juror and not really connecting with

---

[1] David Ball and Joshua Karton, *Theater for Trial* (Portland: Trial Guides, 2017).

any of them. In his exercise, you use a mock jury and essentially communicate one thought or sentence to a single juror, while maintaining eye contact, before moving on to another juror. Josh has a beautiful way of having you link hands with each juror while you speak so that you see and experience the physical element of the connection between yourself and that person. It's pretty neat. More importantly, it's a great technique to learn how to speak to your juries.[2]

If you have the chance to work with Joshua or someone like him, take it. And if you can't work with Joshua, take the time to find other resources to hone your presentation skills. Enroll in a local acting class, get up at an open mic, start a book club.

As a practical matter, public speaking is a skill that's best learned by doing. How do you do that if you've never been to trial or if there aren't a bunch of trials on the near horizon for you? In the office, start covering all hearings in person. Get dressed, go down to the courthouse, and make your appearance in court. Case management conferences, trial setting conferences, hearings on demurrers, motions to strike, and any other hearing you can get to. Just get there, be there, and practice appearing in court.

Outside of the courtroom, there are great programs, including *Toastmasters*, where members of the general public get together and practice their public speaking skills. You'll encounter all kinds of people. Most importantly, you'll get feedback from real people—not lawyers—about your presentation skills.

Another place to practice outside of the courtroom is in focus groups. Fast-forward to chapter 12, "Focus Groups by Woman," if you need to. The gist is that you can put an ad on Craigslist and pay five people to come to your office for an hour while you practice voir dire, opening, closing, or even arguing motions *in limine* on them.

---

[2] *Id.*, 176.

Again, you'll pick regular people who are not lawyers, and you'll get their feedback.

Between focus groups and *Toastmasters* or a similar program, you're getting feedback from would-be jurors on how well or how poorly you're communicating. That's valuable stuff.

How to Appear in Court

If you have to be in court tomorrow and you need a quick and dirty how-to, here it is:

1. Cross the bar.
2. Walk to counsel's table.
3. Put your purse or bag in the seat of the chair next to you or on the floor.
4. Put your yellow pad and pen down on the table in front of you.
5. Take control of the physical space you're occupying.
    » Stand tall.
    » Put your shoulders down and back.
    » Lift your chin slightly, opening the throat so the air can flow, powering your beautiful voice.

6. Remain standing until the judge invites you to sit.
7. Wait. *You will be given an opportunity to speak.*
    » Do not pick up your pen.
    » Do not interrupt or jump in.
    » Do not raise your hand.
    » Just listen and wait until you're called on to speak.

8. Now, turn your entire body to face the judge.
9. Breathe in.
10. Speak clearly and slowly with a resonant voice.

11. Speak in short, declarative statements.
    » No "um," "uh," "like," "I think," or "I believe."
    » One complete sentence after the other:

    > *Your Honor, this motion must be denied for three separate reasons. Any one of the reasons requires the motion to be denied. I'll list the three reasons. Then, I'll explain each reason briefly. First, the motion is not an evidentiary motion and therefore not a true motion in limine. Second, granting the motion would violate my client's constitutional rights. Third, granting the motion would be an abuse of discretion. Now, I'll briefly explain each reason the motion must be denied...*

12. Do not read from your legal pad. You are having a conversation, and it is your turn to speak. If you know that you absolutely cannot remember the three points you need to make, write them in advance on your legal pad, numbered 1, 2, 3. Don't write your analysis on the legal pad—only the three points that you need to make.
13. Once you've made your three points and given the judge your analysis, say, "Thank you," and stop talking.

This should go without saying, but just in case: We take the high road. No personal attacks on your opponent ever; no suggesting that your opponent is a bad lawyer, lazy lawyer, lousy lawyer, sneaky lawyer, ever. Address your remarks and responses to the judge, not to your opposing counsel. You can do this.

Your Voice

The way we speak is a fundamental part of our identity. Our voice impacts how others perceive, trust, and treat us. Numerous studies have found that the feminine voice is perceived as less capable, less secure, and less confident.[3]

That means your voice matters, especially in court. The question we are asked most often is whether a woman should lower the pitch of, or deepen, her voice. Of course, that's impossible to answer in a vacuum. A woman who speaks with a voice that's artificially high, as compared to her natural voice, should lower her pitch. However, a woman who speaks with a voice that's artificially low as compared to her natural voice, should raise her pitch.[4]

Resonance and Pitch

The goal is to speak within the pitch range that's natural for you and to make that pitch resonant. Let's talk about resonance and pitch.

Resonance is the richness and quality of your voice—not how high or low your voice is. To create that richness, we want the voice to reverberate throughout the head. The three main areas where the voice reverberates are the nose, throat, and mouth. Resonance allows your voice to carry without you having to be louder.

---

[3] Sei Jin Ko, Charles M. Judd, and Diederik A. Stapel, "Stereotyping Based on Voice in the Presence of Individuating Information: Vocal Femininity Affects Perceived Competence but Not Warmth," *Personality Social Psychology Bulletin* 35, no. 2 (February 2009):198-211, https://doi.org/10.1177/0146167208326477.

[4] Rindy C. Anderson et al., "Vocal Fry May Undermine the Success of Young Women in the Labor Market," *PLoS ONE* 9, no. 5 (May 28, 2014), https://doi.org/10.1371/journal.pone.0097506.

If you close your mouth and make an "mmmm" sound, you'll feel tingling in your face around your nose and upper lip. That's the air causing your voice to resonate in your facial cavities. From that "mmmm" sound, try saying, "my" or "me," keeping that tingling feeling going. That's your resonant voice, and that should also be about the midpoint of your pitch.

Pitch is how high or low your voice is. We all have a range accessible in our individual voices. To know whether or not you're speaking in your natural pitch, compare how your voice sounds when you do the "mmmm" exercise above with how your voice sounds when you spontaneously say, "mmm-hmm." What you sound like with the "mmmm" exercise should be the midpoint of your vocal range.

Breath

The most important part of your voice is your breath. Without breath, there is no voice. We have worked with a magnificent voice coach, Dory Kafoure, who is also a speech language pathologist. From her, we learned the monumental impact your breathing has on your voice.

- Our number one tip: breathe air into your belly, not into your chest, and speak from your belly, not from your chest. When you do it correctly, you'll feel your ribs expand.
- Our number two tip: Find a voice coach who can teach you how to best use your voice; it's well worth the minimal cost investment.

You Are a Public Speaker

You are a public speaker. Your voice and your body are your instrument. Any investment you make to improve your communication skills will pay off big-time. You'll have a professional and independent third party evaluate your speaking voice and the effectiveness of your communication and give you tools to improve both. That exercise alone will dramatically increase your confidence, and couldn't we all use a little confidence boost?

Chapter Takeaways

- Work with your own voice to master your resonance and keep your pitch natural.
- Hire a voice coach to help you improve.
- Use online resources if you can't afford or find a voice coach.

9

The Courage to Be Feminine

There is power in your femininity. We're not talking about dresses and perfume and beguiling behavior. That's not what we mean by femininity. We're talking about softness instead of hard edges, grace in the face of a challenge, empathy instead of coldness, and connection instead of disconnection.

A Seat at the Table

Most of us have come up believing that the law was a man's industry that made room for women. And many of us had that belief reinforced as we practiced. Some of us developed some harsher edges, dialed back our grace and empathy, and fought against our inherent ability to connect so that we would fit into the space that was made for us in this profession. In other words, some of us adapted in the ways we thought we had to, or in the only ways that allowed us to persevere and possibly succeed in this profoundly man's world.

The feminist movement told us women were equal and could do any job a man could do, and laws were passed to reflect and allow that. But the feminist movement certainly didn't provide any guidance for how to behave in a historically male profession.

Think about the law and the female pioneers in it:

- What must it have felt like to be them?
- What must they have felt they had to do to earn the space that was created for them?
- What must they have felt they had to do to prove themselves?
- What must they have had to do to keep their jobs, particularly in an era where the laws protecting women in the workforce were still evolving?

Many of them emulated men so they would cause the least amount of disruption possible and draw the least amount of attention to the fact that they were women. It was a coping mechanism of sorts, and a good one.

- Men wore dark, boring suits; so, women wore the same color and same style suit in a smaller size.
- Men were direct and blunt and somewhat abrupt in their speech; so, women became direct and blunt and somewhat abrupt in their speech.
- Men didn't express emotion or make emotional connections with clients; so, women didn't either.
- Women were essentially conditioned to give up their femininity to earn respect.

We Can Keep Our Femininity

Today, we're past that. We don't have to give up our femininity to earn respect. In fact, if we have the courage to embrace our femininity—our softness, our empathy, our compassion, our ability to connect with people, our grace—we are more powerful and more authoritative. We stand in our own strength as feminine women, and that is a true gift.

When we embrace the feminine—what's authentic for each of us—we can stand taller, be ourselves, and still be professional, graceful, successful female trial lawyers. Women have an innate capacity for love, compassion, empathy, guidance, and caring. The energy we're putting out is consistent with who we truly are. The converse is we walk into court and put on this show for days on end, suppressing our natural tendencies and acting like someone we're not. It takes too much energy to be anyone other than ourselves. And people can tell when we're not being ourselves. When we're not being authentic and true to who we really are and what we value, we are not trustworthy.

Courage, Femininity, and Fear

It takes courage to embrace your femininity. But most things take courage. One thing we've learned as mothers is that children are born with courage. Our children run around the yard, naked as jaybirds and barefoot, making silly sounds, playing silly games they make up, digging in the dirt, and laughing until their bellies ache. They don't think about what they look like, who's watching, or what someone else might be thinking. They live 100 percent in the present moment, and they are pure courage.

We were all once pure courage too. Somewhere along the line we learned fear. When we are out in the world, trying to navigate our way through our careers, our lives, and the myriad of demands on our time and attention, we can lose faith. We can start to think we are alone, but we are not. Fear is something everyone experiences, and it has nothing to do with whether we are women, men, the most successful lawyers in the profession, or people still searching for themselves and their calling. We make mistakes, we lose cases, and we experience the inevitable failures that are part of doing big things in the world. We have had to learn how to fail in order to face the fear head-on.

Instead of being an obstacle to achieving our goals, we can reframe fear and change it into a motivator. When we learn to celebrate the small victories, we shift our focus to what is going right instead of what is going wrong. By making that small shift, we generate positive, creative energy, instead of the destructive energy that keeps us from reaching our potential.

When we reframe fear, it becomes courage. Sometimes, it's a practice we have to begin anew each day. But if we look at our children, we can see the pure bliss in being courageous. We can also see that no one is judging them; we're all marveling at them. Can you see the parallel? Dig down, pull up the courage, and live without fear. Be yourself—a feminine woman with all of your beautiful gifts. They are not judging you; they are marveling at your courage and the blissful energy that surrounds you.

Chapter Takeaways

- There is power in embracing your femininity.
- Reframe your fear as courage.
- The law isn't just for men; it's for all of us.

10

How to Open Your Own Law Firm

Running your own business or law firm changes your life:

- You decide whom you want to work with.
- You decide whom you want to represent.
- You decide how often you want to work.
- You decide what days of the week you want to work.
- You decide what hours of the day you want to work.
- You decide where you want to work.
- You decide whom you want to work with.
- You decide how much money you make.

It's all up to you. Your power and control are limitless.

We could devote an entire book to the subject of opening and running a law firm. The type of trial law you practice will dictate in many ways how your day-to-day operations will run. For example, the criminal defense lawyer will most often be paid by the hour or the job, while the civil plaintiffs' lawyer will be paid on contingency. This difference in the method of compensation alone will drive where and how you get your clients, issues of case funding and funding overhead, and the types of co-counseling relationships you may choose to enter into. Our goal here is to give you the nuts and bolts on how to open a law firm and some practical tips to help run your practice, regardless of the type of cases you try.

Women are uniquely suited to run their own firms. Women are leaders. We're learning now that the most effective leaders are people who have an ability to connect with other people and make them feel happy and positive. In other words, it's social intelligence that makes great leaders, and women are masters of social intelligence.[1]

It takes courage to open your own law firm. No doubt. But opening a law firm is not difficult, and it does not have to be expensive, and *you are qualified* to open your own firm and run your own practice. You can do this, and we're going to show you how. Stick with us. Some of this stuff is dense. When you're ready to do it, just go step by step. If you're not ready yet, just skim it and know it's do-able.

Business Formation

Choose a Type of Entity

First, decide what kind of business entity your law firm will be. Depending on your state and whether you're practicing alone or have partners, you could have a sole proprietorship, a corporation, an S corporation, an LLC, or an LLP, for example. Certain entities can protect

---

[1] Daniel Goleman and Richard E. Boyatzis, "Social Intelligence and the Biology of Leadership," *Harvard Business Review* (September 2008).

your assets. Others cannot. Research the law in your state and decide which entity will best protect you and your assets. Even if you don't have any assets now, you will in the future!

Understand How Income Is Taxed

Research the law in your state to make sure you understand how the income earned by your firm flows to you, that is, by payroll, as dividends, as shareholder distributions, and so on. Check with a tax advisor to understand how the income will be taxed at the business level and how you will personally be taxed. That information will help you choose a business entity.

Hire a Certified Public Accountant (CPA)

A qualified, trustworthy accountant who can guide you through your new tax status as a business (and handle your personal taxes) is a godsend. This is the person who will explain how to organize your books and expenses in case you are ever audited, which expenses are deductible and which aren't, and how much to pay yourself as an employee of your company. The list goes on and on. CPAs can actually work with you on tax planning, which means they look at your books, talk to you, and forecast your tax obligations for the upcoming year. Make sure to get an accountant who regularly works with small businesses in your state, county, and city. There are a myriad of small local rules that your accountant will help you stay on the right side of.

In our experience, this generally costs about $1,500. It's a bargain because you can make some very expensive mistakes without proper advice. It's like going to court without a lawyer—people do it, but it usually doesn't turn out very well.

Understand Registration Requirements

Check with your state bar, your Secretary of State, and your city and county about business registration requirements for law firms. Some cities require you to get a business license. Others don't. Some states require that you file a form with the Secretary of State. Others don't.

Choose a Name for Your Firm

Choose a name for your firm. Once you have the name and you've decided what type of entity it will be, you can use a service like Legal Zoom to form your business entity. It's reasonably priced, and they create and file all of the paperwork necessary to establish your business.

Get an EIN from the IRS

An EIN is an Employer Identification Number for your business, and it's like a Social Security number. It uniquely identifies your business to all kinds of government entities and banks. Once you have your EIN and you've formed your entity, you can open a business checking account, a business credit card, and an Interest on Lawyers Trust Account (IOLTA) to hold funds that clients have any interest in. You can set up an IOLTA with your bank, based on your state's requirements. Almost all state bars have help pages, contact information, and ethics hotlines.

Set Up Bank Accounts

Once you have your EIN and you've formed your entity, open a business checking account in the name of your business, a business credit card in the name of your business, and an IOLTA client trust account, based on your state's requirements.

Order Checks

Once you have your bank accounts set up, order checks. You can order through the bank or use a company like Vista Print. There are lots of other check printing companies. See which one has the best price and can best meet your needs. In our experience, the bank is typically more expensive, but some banks offer special account incentives that include free checks.

Buy Malpractice Insurance

Purchase errors and omission insurance, that is, malpractice insurance. There are a lot of different vendors. Most local bar associations have relationships with vendors; so you can get recommendations by going to your local bar association's website. If you don't have a lot of start-up cash, many brokers will allow you to set up a payment plan for your premium so you can spread it out across the year. There are also discounts available if you are a member of certain groups, if you have good credit, and if you practice law part-time.

That's it! This is all that's really necessary to legally set up your business. Once you've formed your firm, there are a few more things you need to do to get the business fully up and running.

Choose an Office

There are a lot of options when it comes to deciding where you'll work. You can rent an office of your own. You can share office space with someone else. There are plenty of small firms with an extra office they would like to rent out, and you get to use their kitchen, conference room, and oftentimes their copier and other equipment as part of your rental agreement. You can rent a room in an executive suite through companies like Regus and have access to their common areas and office equipment. You can rent a virtual office through companies like Davinci that collect your mail, answer your calls, and give you access to conference room space when you need it for less than $100 per month. You can even work from home—for free. If you work from home, get a separate physical address, such as a P.O. box or a mail-forwarding service, so you don't have your home address listed in your business information. And your CPA will tell you there can be tax benefits to working from home if you have the right setup. In some cases, if you have a designated office, you can pay yourself rent from your business's pretax income.

Get a Phone Number and a Fax Number

You'll need a phone number and a fax number for your business. If you choose not to have a secretary, there are a lot of call-answering services that will answer your business line and forward the calls to you immediately wherever you are or email a message to you immediately.

Here are some examples of those services:

- Answer One
- Ruby Receptionists
- Davinci Virtual
- Flat Rate Answering Service

The specific services offered vary, but can range in cost from about $20 per month to about $300 per month. These aren't the only answering services available, and you'll have to do your research to find out which answering service works best for you. But the point is you don't have to hire a receptionist to run a successful law firm.

Case Management

You'll need a software-based or cloud-based case management system so you can track your cases, your deadlines, your costs, your hours, and your invoices. Some popular systems are Amicus Attorney, AbacusLaw, and MyCase. The cloud-based systems allow you to access your case information and calendar from anywhere. Most of them have low monthly fees and don't require that you have a server set up in your office.

Branding, Stationery, and Business Cards

There are companies that will help design your firm logo, stationery, and business cards for a few hundred dollars, as opposed to hiring a graphic designer for several thousand dollars. Some of these companies are 99designs, DesignCrowd, and Crowdspring.

Website and Email

Getting a website and email can also be inexpensive and easy. You don't have to hire a web designer for thousands of dollars. You can buy your domain name through a company like GoDaddy (godaddy.com), HostGator (hostgator.com), or Gandi (gandi.net), for example. Then you can go to a site like squarespace.com, weebly.com, or wordpress.com and set up your web page. Lots of sites like this have templates you can choose from; so all you have to do is choose the color scheme you want and customize your site. These sites can also set up company email addresses with your domain name.

The Paperless Office

Regardless of whether you work in an office or whether you work remotely, there are great services that let you go paperless. To manage your files, you can use cloud-based services like Dropbox (dropbox.com) or Box (box.com) or any secure cloud-based service. To manage your mail, you can use a service like Earthclassmail (earthclassmail.com), which will scan and email your paper mail to you and even deposit your checks. There are a lot of electronic services you can subscribe to that will email your faxes to you as soon as they come in, such as Efax (efax.com). Services like these are revolutionizing the way we can practice law.

Courtney travels for most of the year, including extensive travel overseas, and never has to go to an office. Theresa works 100 percent remotely and also makes extended travel plans, and never has to go to an office.

Financing

If you practice in an area that requires you to carry cases' costs, for example, contingency fee work, you don't need to have money saved up to cover costs. There are several options for you.

- One, co-counsel your case with another attorney who is willing to cover costs.
- Two, take out a business line of credit associated with your business banking.
- Three, take advantage of companies that will loan money to law firms to cover case costs and operational expenses.

Financing should not be a barrier to opening your own firm.

Getting Business

There are lots of different ways to get clients. You can hire a company to optimize your website so that your firm comes up near the top of an internet search. You can take out an ad on a billboard or a bus bench. You can pay to subscribe to a lead-generation service that will send you a certain number of a certain type of potential cases. The most effective way, in our experience, to get cases as a trial lawyer, is to let other lawyers know that you try cases. That's how we get all of our work.

Even among trial lawyers, not everyone wants to try cases. Lots of trial lawyers are more comfortable settling cases. Some want to try cases, but something is holding them back, whether it be fear, risk aversion, finances, or other. To be a trial lawyer who actually tries cases is less common than you might think. Join practice-specific Listservs and let other lawyers know you try cases. Go to practice-specific events and let people know you try cases.

Connect with lawyers who have busy practices and not enough help. A lot of times in our experience, they'll be willing to hire you to do contract work (that is, to work on a case or cases for an hourly fee) or even pay you a percentage of their fee to work on cases.

If you have a lot of experience in a particular area—for example, a criminal lawyer who has done a lot of DUI defense, a civil lawyer who has done a lot of bicycle cases, or a family law attorney who has done a lot of custody cases, let people know! There are lawyers in your area of practice who have these cases and could use your help. They can learn from you, and you can work with them on future cases. Connect with people. You'll find your place.

What the Day-to-Day Looks Like

We don't work 9 to 5, 8 to 6, 6 to 9, or any other set or crazy hours anymore. We don't work every day Monday through Friday. We don't go to an office. All of that stopped when we opened our own firms.

We work on cases. We get them ready for trial, and we try them. We spend our time on what matters: getting to know our clients and understanding their stories; envisioning and planning how we'll present our case at trial; doing focus groups.

Sometimes we work a case from start to finish. Other times we're brought in right before trial. That means some weeks we're working every day. Other weeks, we don't work any days.

This isn't a special or privileged lifestyle that was given to us. This is what we intended and created when we started our own firms. If you want this type of lifestyle, you can have it to. Or maybe you want something different. The point is you can create whatever type of practice you want. Be intentional about setting goals before you open your practice. How many cases do you want to carry at any one time? How much money do you need for operating costs each month? How much money do you want to net each year? How many days per week do you want to work? How many cases do you want to try each year? Create a plan for yourself, use the tips we've given you here as a starting point, and then reach out to another woman who is where you want to be. Mentor and help one another. That's what we've done for one another, and, through this book, we're hoping to do that for you and to encourage you to do it for other women.

Stumbling Blocks

Yes, it's easy to open your own firm. But we've noticed a few stumbling blocks along the way—things we wish we would have known about, been prepared for, and had a plan for in advance.

The Fear of No Work

The biggest stumbling block is the fear that the cases, the work, and the money—that is, your livelihood—will dry up. Yes, this is a possibility. But lots of things are possible. It's possible that people will stop shopping on Amazon, stop obsessively buying iPhones, call it quits on grocery stores, and start farming in their own backyards. All real possibilities, but not probable, statistically speaking.

We work in a field that has existed for a *long* time. That's because people need lawyers. Think about this: the clients who hire us don't actually want us, but they need us. Someone sued them; someone hurt them in a car crash; they got a DUI; they're getting a divorce; a business deal went bad. The legal system is the place that people go to fix problems, and the lawyers are the only people who are competent and qualified to work within the legal system. So, first, work with the probabilities, not the possibilities. Then, think about how you're going to manage what's in front of you.

What we've found from time to time is that when the fear of failure and famine ratchets up, our instinct is to take any and every case that comes our way. Let's keep it real here for a second—can you think of a case that you regret taking? We can. Plenty of them. There was a point, usually at the beginning, that you likely knew the case wasn't good, or wasn't good for you. That's your intuition. And when you ignore it, that's when trouble starts.

Theresa:

> I had a case years ago that I knew I shouldn't take. I heard the little voice. My intuition. But I ignored that little voice inside because, on paper, it was a "good" case. A great case, actually. Let me make this short: I was verbally abused and threatened, the jury didn't believe the client, the judge didn't believe the client, the bailiff didn't believe the client, and the client ultimately placed a curse on me and my family. I can assure you that if you take the money I made on that case and divided it by the amount of hours I spent working the case—not to mention the abuse and the family curse—it was not worth my while. All cases take time. All cases take energy. But some cases take more time and more energy, and if we really pay attention, we know from the outset which cases those are.
>
> The point here is don't panic and grab every case you can get your hands on. When you scale back your caseload, you can put more meaningful time into a case. And what does that do? Increases the value of the case. So, you can make more money on fewer cases. That's a lesson we learned early on. The more value you add to the case in front of you, the fewer cases you have to take on.

Ideas and Action Items

- Refer a case to another woman.
- Try a case with another woman.
- Start a monthly dinner group with women lawyers.
- Start a monthly phone call/zoom call with women lawyers.
- Find a mentor and get guidance in opening your own firm.
- Join the Forum, Trial By Woman's Listserve, at www.trialbywoman.com.

Books We Read

- David Allen and James Fallows, *Getting Things Done: The Art of Stress-Free Productivity* (New York: Penguin, 2015).
- Timothy Ferriss, *The 4-Hour Work Week: Escape 9–5, Live Anywhere, and Join the New Rich* (New York: Harmony, 2009).
- John C. Maxwell, *No Limits: Blow the CAP Off Your Capacity* (New York: Center Street, 2017).
- John Morgan, *You Can't Teach Hungry: Creating the Multimillion Dollar Law Firm* (Portland, OR: Trial Guides, 2015).
- Tom Wheelwright, *Tax-Free Wealth: How to Build Massive Wealth by Permanently Lowering Your Taxes* (Scottsdale, AZ: RDA Press, 2015).

Chapter Takeaways

- Your bar card is a license to run a business, and you're qualified to do it.
- Follow our step-by-step guide in this chapter to open your own law firm.

PART FOUR

Trial Perspective and Trial Techniques

Trial Perspective and Trial Techniques

Teaching you how to try a case from beginning to end is beyond the scope of this book. To go deeper, we recommend anything you can get your hands on. We love these:

- Nick Rowley's *Trial by Human*
- David Ball's *David Ball on Damages*
- The Trial Guides LIVE: Fireside Chats series
- Gerry Spence's *How to Argue and Win Every Time*
- Keith Mitnik's podcast *Mitnik's Monthly Brushstroke* on iTunes

Instead, we'll get right to the good stuff. We'll cover the basics for those who haven't tried a case or need a refresher, and then we'll dive right into the way we try cases. We'll highlight some of the specific techniques and approaches that we use so that you'll have tips you can start using today to make your practice better. Though these are technically trial techniques, they are also tools you can start using today—in and out of trial—to improve your cases. Take what fits for you, and modify or forget about what doesn't. Above all else, be true to you.

11

Trial Perspective

Taking a *Trial Perspective approach* doesn't mean trial preparation. Trial Perspective means knowing how all of the evidence will come in and how that evidence will be seen through the eyes of a jury during trial. Trial Perspective is knowing how this whole show will play out in front of a jury and what factors will increase or decrease the value of your case *in trial*.

Use a Trial Perspective Approach from the Beginning

You can and should use all of the trial techniques that we talk about in this section of the book *before* trial—in meetings with your client, in written discovery, and even in depositions.

Using a Trial Perspective approach from the beginning increases the value of your case. It's how your opposition is evaluating your case.

We were taught as young lawyers to go into a mediation or a settlement conference with a list of jury verdicts and reported settlements to support the "value" of our cases. But there's so much critical information that's not encapsulated in those numbers. Let's look beyond the numbers and examine what is really done to prepare big verdict cases and big settlement cases. Big numbers happen when you use Trial Perspective techniques from the beginning. That means you should do the following:

- Understand the nature and extent of your client's injuries in a civil injury case by spending quality time with your client on her turf.
- Explore liability, damages, and evidentiary issues with focus groups even before cases are filed and certainly before discovery.
- Have your experts' preliminary opinions.

We do these things as soon as we get a case.

There are people who say, "I'm working this case to settle," suggesting that they would work a case up differently if they were going to try it. If you don't work a case *expecting* and *intending* that it will go to trial, you are losing value on your case.

Using a Trial Perspective approach isn't the easiest route. Or the cheapest. It takes more time, and it can cost more money. But the payoff for those investments is substantial. We owe it to our clients to do our best work and not give them short shrift because we plan on settling.

Let's take a look at some of the reasons, other than case value, that we all need to use Trial Perspective methods when we work our cases.

Your Opponent Tosses Grenades

Here's an example. Your opponent or opposing witnesses toss grenades casually during depositions all the time. These grenades are *designed* to explode at trial. If you don't recognize the grenade, you've lost case value as soon as your opponent tosses it.

That's why, if you are in law school, if you've never tried a case, if you're a young woman in a midlevel position at a law firm where your job is to respond to written discovery and take depositions and you haven't made it into a courtroom for trial yet, you need Trial Perspective techniques as part of your training. If you're taking depositions and responding to discovery, you're creating evidence that will be used at trial. Therefore, you need to be able to recognize grenades. And you need to be able to toss a few grenades of your own.

Following a Trial Perspective approach is a way to enrich and add value to yourself as a lawyer and move yourself up quickly. Understanding what trial is and how all of the evidence created along the way plays out at trial directly affects how you build and develop your case. Trial Perspective strategies apply whether or not you're going to trial tomorrow, going to a deposition tomorrow, or responding to discovery tomorrow.

Think of a trial like a car manufacturing plant. All of the work that's done in litigation is like assembly-line work. Someone makes sure there's a frame to support the car, and someone else puts the doors on. Another person makes sure there's an axle so the car can be steered, and another person puts the tires on.

And the trial lawyer drives the car. She gets into the finished product, finds the ignition, adjusts the mirrors and seat, looks down to see if she'll be driving an automatic or a stick shift, plans her route, puts it in gear, and goes.

If you're the woman whose job is to put the tires on the cars—car after car, tire after tire, day in and day out—you need to know how to drive the car. That way, you can see if something is wrong on your assembly line and, more importantly, contribute your insight, perspective, and understanding to make the car work better once it hits the road. If you're just looking at one or two pieces of the car in isolation, the end result won't be as good as it could be, you won't be as satisfied, and you'll be less likely to grow out of that assembly-line role.

With a Trial Perspective outlook, you can eliminate avoidable consequences. For example, we are referred personal injury cases and, quite often, the referring lawyer has chosen to informally order the client's medical records using a signed authorization and a check for $15 rather than signing on to the legal subpoena issued by opposing counsel and paying $50 plus the cost of records. That means you don't have all of the records your opponent has, and neither does your retained expert. There are records out there that neither of you know about. Let's say you have a neck injury case, and your client told a doctor her neck hurt ten years earlier. It has been ten years and seems to have been an isolated complaint; so, understandably, the client doesn't remember, doesn't tell you, doesn't tell any of her doctors, and doesn't tell any of the experts about it. Fast-forward to the deposition.

First, your client is asked if she ever had neck pain before this, and says, "No." She will now be impeached at trial with the medical record you don't have.

Second, your retained expert is deposed and offers all of the opinions he intends to give at the time of trial and identifies everything he has relied on in forming those opinions. Your expert offers his opinions without even considering that there was prior neck pain. There likely won't be any hoopla or fanfare about it during deposition. It will be very straightforward.

Your opponent will say, "Doctor, did you see in any of the medical records whether Ms. Smith had neck pain before this?"

And your expert will say, "I did not see a prior complaint of neck pain in the records."

This is a grenade waiting to explode at trial. When your expert is cross-examined at trial, this medical record will be projected on a screen and much will be made of the fact that your expert didn't even consider that she had this complaint of neck pain before. Your opponent will raise questions about what other medical records he chose not to consider.

At that point, your expert will most likely say, "Those records were not given to me."

Your opponent will perk up. "Ms. Smith's lawyer didn't give you those records?" he will ask with disbelief. And you will look like a sneaky lawyer with something to hide, and your case will unravel from there. You need to recognize these grenades so that you can defuse them before it's too late.

Courtney:

As I mentioned earlier, I started my practice doing criminal defense. The criminal world is fast; there are no depositions, and you have to roll with the punches. In civil, there is a lot more time for strategy and preparation. A lot of what I do is trying cases for other lawyers, coming in before trial, picking up the file, and going to court. The winnability of the case is directly correlated with whether or not it was worked up using Trial Perspective methods. I have walked into court on a wrongful death case where we have zero photographs of the decedent. I have had experts excluded entirely on the first day of trial because they were not asked the proper questions at deposition. I have seen huge amounts of damages excluded simply because someone forgot to respond to discovery requests. Without Trial Perspective strategies, instead of rolling with punches, you are taking them right in the face. It doesn't have to be that way. With the proper work-up, you can set yourself and your case up for success.

What Trial Perspective Is

Trial Perspective is understanding the facts that are important to the jury—not the facts that are important to lawyers. We'll show you how to figure out the difference between the two later in this book when we talk about focus groups.

Trial Perspective is knowing what questions to ask your own client in deposition. If you're not asking your own client a question or two in deposition, you are not using a Trial Perspective approach.

A lot of lawyers believe that if they do not do trial work, then they don't need to learn about trial skills and trial strategy. They are wrong. Without Trial Perspective, you are working your cases without context, and you are losing value. Worse, you limit yourself to whatever role you are in now.

It's next to impossible to use Trial Perspective if you've never tried a case or haven't watched cases being tried. But you can fix that starting today!

If you've never tried a case or you haven't tried a lot of cases, the first thing you should do is go to court, find a trial, sit down, and watch. It doesn't matter what kind of case it is, what venue it is, who the judge is, how good the lawyers are, how good the case is. What matters is that you sit through enough trials to begin to understand how the facts you establish today will play out in front of a jury tomorrow.

Many venues have expedited jury trials. That's a great place to start. You can see an entire jury trial in a day, sometimes less. Once you do that a few times, then carve out time to watch a longer jury trial with lawyers you admire. Maybe you're thinking, *my desk is piled high with discovery and motions I need to respond to, my inbox has over one hundred emails, and I have five depositions this week. I don't have time for this!*

We totally get it. We've been there. But a critical part of understanding Trial Perspective is carving out time to better yourself. If you can't make time to improve your practice, how can you grow? How can you move from the job you have to the job you want? How can you become the lawyer you want to be? That's all part of the Trial Perspective approach—making time for your own growth. There are still days that we're buried in a case, buried in trial—just buried. What we've found, time after time, is when we make the time for growth, we actually *grow*, and, as a result, everything else that was bearing down on us gets easier. We're reinvigorated. We're excited that we've learned something new, and we're looking for new ways to apply it. After a small investment of time, suddenly that discovery sitting on our desk isn't so intimidating because we understand what it needs to say *at trial*. And we have a fresh idea about how we're going to oppose the motion that's waiting on our desk. Expanding our minds using Trial Perspective methods, making room for fresh and useful thoughts, makes things easier.

Working a case with Trial Perspective techniques will increase the value of your work, the value of your cases, and your value as a lawyer. And you may stumble across something that makes you a happier woman!

Chapter Takeaways

- The Trial Perspective approach increases your value and the value of your case.
- Trial Perspective is most important for law students, for lawyers who haven't tried a lot of cases, and for midlevel lawyers who respond to discovery and take depositions but don't have a lot of trial experience.

12

Focus Groups by Woman

Focus groups are a great place to hone your Trial Perspective techniques. If you want to find out what people think about your case, what they think about different pieces of evidence, what they think about your client, and what they think about you, a focus group is the most efficient, reliable, and enjoyable way to find out. The biggest mistake we see people making is not doing focus groups at all or not doing a focus group until shortly before trial, when it's too late to get more evidence.

If you look back over this book and you look forward into this section on trial techniques, you'll notice we talk about focus groups a lot. We use them throughout our process, sometimes even in case selection. Whenever we have a question or are worried about something, whether it's analyzing a piece of evidence, worrying about a witness's credibility, or testing an opening statement, we run a focus group. They don't have to be big, expensive, or complicated, and you don't need a consultant.

Run Focus Groups Early and Often

Ideally, run a focus group as soon as you get a case. When we need to, we use it in case selection. Put your bad facts out there, and put your good facts out there. Figure out what people care about and what they don't care about. ==If your bad facts really are bad facts, a focus group will help you figure how bad they are and whether and how to embrace them. When you learn how to embrace even the bad facts, you acquire the confidence to embrace your whole case==.

Sometimes, we run focus groups to evaluate a single piece of evidence. Sometimes, we run focus groups to get feedback on how our client presents when she talks about a certain subject. Sometimes, we run contested focus groups together, where we each take a side and give a very argumentative opening statement. Then we sit down and listen to the deliberations. An important note, in our experience (which is a lot when it comes to focus groups), the groups are really great for themes, evaluating evidence, and giving you new perspectives and arguments you wouldn't have come up with on your own. However, we rarely if ever rely on focus groups when it comes to the number. In terms of damages, a focus-group jury is helpful in gauging the overall reaction to your case, but not relevant in terms of predicting what you will get in trial. David Ball (and others with Trial Guides) have done a lot of great work on this subject if you are looking for more information.

Focus groups don't have to be expensive. We love to run one-hour lunchtime focus groups downtown. We post an ad on Craigslist, serve sandwiches, and get access to people who wouldn't otherwise be able to show up during business hours. The last focus group we ran together cost a couple hundred dollars for three hours of valuable information. We put an ad on Craigslist, rented a conference room in the venue where our case was being tried, and got three hours' worth of feedback on our evidence and our client. Early on, when Courtney was doing criminal defense (and had less than no money), she would buy "Two-Buck Chuck" from Trader Joe's and host focus groups with her Nana's church group. Focus groups do not have to be expensive to be effective.

Of course, once you get going in the world of focus groups, like anything, there are plenty of options. On bigger or more complex cases, we have run focus groups with three groups simultaneously deliberating. That means the evidence is presented to a large group, and then that group gets broken up into three different groups for deliberations. This yields higher statistical significance and basically packs three rounds of feedback into one sitting. We usually do these with companies that specialize in focus groups and have facilities with one-way glass, video, microphones, and so on.

Things You Can Do Today

Bottom line: Focus groups aren't a luxury for trial lawyers; they're a necessity. You should factor them into the amount of costs you'll spend on a case. Focus groups are free voir dire experience. You're out in the world interacting with people and honing your skills. The more focus groups you do, the better your Trial Perspective techniques will be and the quicker you'll develop your Trial Perspective approach; so, get out there and run one today!

What's bothering you about your current cases? What thorny questions keep you up at night? It might be something you can get some insight on from a cheap focus group that you can run in a conference room with a Craigslist ad.

Chapter Takeaways

- Don't save focus groups for trial prep—do them even during case selection.
- You can do focus groups inexpensively, and you don't need a consultant.
- Do focus groups early and often, to answer all kinds of questions about your cases.

13

Discovery by Woman

The key to increasing your success in your cases is preparation. The way to get the best results is to do the best case work-up. A top-notch case work-up will get you a top-notch result every single time. There's no substitute for doing the work. Women can be particularly great at working up a case because women tend to be very detail oriented. We're not saying all women are detail oriented. One of us is and one of us isn't as much, and that's OK. The important thing is to know your own strengths. If discovery is part of your job, you can get organized and detail oriented enough to make it through or to kick it up a notch.

Assume *Every* Case Goes to Trial

Here's how we do it.

Trial begins with case preparation. We *expect* every case to go to trial, and we *prepare* as though every case is going to trial. Unless we have reached a settlement agreement, we prepare for trial—even if we've been asked to mediate, even if we think the case will settle, even if we think we're close to settling. This mindset puts us ahead of our opposition every time.

In fact, there have been dozens of cases that we *wanted* to take to trial, but because we had prepared the cases so well, we were paid the full insurance policy limits before trial.

By the time of trial, we've prepared so thoroughly that we've lived our client's story and the story of the case, and we're ready to share that story with a jury. Here's how we do it in six simple steps.

Step 1: Connect with Your Client

Connection is a two-way street. It's you and your client getting to know *each other*, understanding *each other*, and creating a real bond with *each other*. If you can authentically create this relationship with your client, you will get the best result.

Authentically creating this connection takes effort and time. It doesn't happen during an intake meeting, going over discovery responses, or preparing for deposition or other testimony—when the lawyer is giving directions or asking questions that aren't open ended.

It happens just like any other relationship—over time. But there are ways to get there faster.

The fastest way to connect with your client is to "date" them. Not really, of course, but as if you were. ==Spend time together and be interested, inquisitive, and engaged, just as you would be if you were dating someone you were really interested in.==

We go to clients' homes. We bring food. We sit, we talk, we cook together, and we share meals with our clients, their families, and anyone else who is important to them, and important to helping us understand our clients' stories.

More importantly, we bring our clients to our homes. They meet our husbands, they see where we live, they watch our children run around, and they meet our friends. We share ourselves with our clients. That's where the connection happens. We open our homes and our hearts to them, and they do the same for us.

It's worth mentioning here that money and income remain one of the great taboos that we're not supposed to talk about, and, for the most part, lawyers are among the higher income earners in our society. Even in those years of our careers when we're struggling to repay law school loans, living with housemates, and using our credit cards to make ends meet, we're still doing way better than most of the country. The vast majority of our clients over the years have not been high earners. So is it weird when we bring them to our homes and they see that we have more "stuff" or nicer "stuff" than they do? Nope.

We've already connected with our clients before we bring them home. We've already met them at their homes, spent time with them, shared meals. We know them, and they know us. And though we are two girls who didn't grow up with any of the "stuff" we have now, we are very proud of what we have built for ourselves and our families, and we want to share what we have and who we are with our clients.

When we first met John and Jane Smith,[1] their son had been stabbed to death at the bar of a national restaurant chain. They were

---

[1] Out of respect to our clients' privacy, we've fictionalized their names.

devastated and not ready to connect with anyone new. One of the really special times we spent with them, and the day of the biggest breakthrough in connecting with them, was an afternoon and evening with them at the Rowley's house. We both had new babies. Our husbands were there. The Smiths were there. And a handful of our other friends were there. We spent time together, talked, ate, watched the sunset, got to really know each other as people. In listening to John and Jane talk to us about our babies, we learned how the loss of their own son changed their lives, without having to ask the question. At dinner, after spending the afternoon bonding, John was moved to share some words with all of us.

Essentially, he shared that he felt his family was truly in good hands with us. We all connected with John and Jane that day, and that connection affected the trial. Although we were involved in the case preparation, we both chose not to participate in the trial because it would have required significant travel, and we wanted to be with our babies at that time. Nick Rowley and Keith and Angela Bruno went on to get a $40 million verdict for the Smiths.

What If the Client Is Corporate or Criminal?

What do you do if your client is a corporation, or if your client is a criminal? How do you invite a corporation to your home?

- **A note for lady lawyers who have corporate clients:** There is always a human behind the company. Find the human, get the story of the company, and connect.
- **A note for lady lawyers who have criminal clients:** We understand that you can't go to your client's house or invite her to your house. But you can make the most of the time you do have with your client. Fast-track your connection: get to know your client, be

inquisitive, find out who she is, and relate and bond where you can. Above all else, use your judgment to keep yourself safe.

Step 2: Build Your Team of Experts Early

Experts are often necessary in civil litigation, and they're often used in family law cases, including divorce cases and custody cases, as well as in criminal cases and business litigation. Put your expert team together *as soon as possible*.

On the plaintiff's side, if you've filed your case and you don't have experts retained, you've waited too long. On the defense side, you should be retaining experts as soon as you get a demand package with some medical records. We often get cases referred to us well into litigation that do not have retained experts. With very few exceptions, we could have made those cases far more valuable if the trial team had retained experts early. Some lawyers even go to mediation without experts. That is futile. You really can't have a meaningful discussion about case value if you don't have your case sufficiently prepared; and if you don't have experts, you aren't sufficiently prepared.

Experts aren't hired guns. On the damages side, for example, they are real doctors with real insights. If you get all of the medical records to your expert and meet with him early on, he'll give you a lot of valuable insight into your case that will shift your perspective on case value and how you will present your general damages case in discovery, in deposition, and to a jury. The same is true for liability experts. Take their insights, and you may elevate the way in which you present your case in discovery, deposition, and to a jury.

Gather your experts, but be smart about how many you hire. There is an old-school view that says the more experts the better, but we've found this isn't always true. Extra experts may not improve your case, but they will add significant costs that can impact your ability to make clear decisions when it comes to trial and settlement. Don't perpetuate the status quo.

First, trust yourself. Read your jury instructions and make your trial plan. What do you have to prove? What evidence do you need to prove it? In California civil cases, for example, one witness is enough to prove a fact.[2]

Second, know what your jury needs. What do we know from jurors? They ignore competing expert testimony unless one of the experts is not credible. How does this impact jurors? Some wonder why you have an expert telling them what's obvious, which can make them question their interpretation of the evidence. Some feel insulted, as though the lawyers don't trust them to figure out the evidence. Neither of these scenarios is helpful to your clients.

Third, once you've formed your team of experts, meet with them. The time to find out your experts' opinions is early in your case preparation. If you are waiting until just before your expert testifies to find out his or her opinions, it's too late. Send your experts everything they need to form an opinion. Meet with them. Find out what opinions they will offer and why. This will always give you valuable insight into your case because, in addition to being an expert, this is another human with another point of view, just like your jurors.

The best experts are the ones who can *teach* their area of expertise to lay people. How to get full bang for your buck? Let your expert teach *you*. The idea that "you don't need to know the medicine" is outdated and amateur. These days there are so many resources available to you, but the best resources are the ones you're *already paying*. Are you a prosecutor? Take your detective out to lunch. Have a brain injury case? Get

---

[2] CACI 107—Witnesses: "If you believe it is true, the testimony of a single witness is enough to prove a fact."

a stack of questions together and purchase an hour from your expert that will pay off dividends for the rest of your career.

Some practical tips for civil cases:

- In an injury case, use your client's unbiased treating physicians as experts. When you first meet with your client, talk about all of the doctors she has seen. These are your best experts. They are unbiased. And they often knew your client before this injury.
- In an injury case, you don't always need a biomechanical expert to prove causation. Often, doctors can establish causation based on their experience.
- In an injury case, you don't always need an accident reconstruction expert, unless there is a true question about how the crash happened.
- In an injury case, you don't always need an economist. Many lawyers believe they need an economist whenever they have future economic damages because all damages must be awarded in present value. However, in lieu of presenting expert testimony on the present value of future economic damages, and in lieu of requiring the jury to undertake the time-consuming and error-prone task of determining present value, the parties can stipulate that the court will make the present value determination after judgment is entered. We routinely do this in our cases.
- In all jury cases, there are often witnesses other than experts who can prove facts, including friends, family members, coworkers, and third-party witnesses.

Move Fast and First— Witnesses

Our actions drive our cases. We are always focused on trial and focused on moving a case toward trial. That means we dig into a case immediately. We look at the case from every angle—look for the good, the bad, the ugly—and embrace it all. We're honest with ourselves, honest with our clients, and honest with our jury. Because life isn't perfect, and neither is any person or any case.

In practice, this is how it looks:

- Go to the scene as soon as you get the case, even if it's a criminal case, to see what your client saw and felt. Sit down. Breathe the air. Connect with the space. Don't put yourself in danger, obviously, but making those human connections, to people and even to places, gives you valuable insight into what your case is really about. This is how you become the authority on your case.
- Meet with witnesses as soon as you get the case. In person is best, but do it by phone if you have to. Just sit with them. What happened? What can they tell you? What can you learn from them? Be curious. This is not a job for investigators. This is a job for you—the lawyer trying the case.
- Get sworn affidavits from witnesses early. Ask the witness, "Can I type notes while you're talking?" And type up the witnesses' statement as you sit with them, or listen over the phone. Then send them an email with what you've drafted in Word format, and ask them to read the statement, make sure it's accurate, make sure you didn't leave anything out, and make sure you didn't misstate anything they said. Ask them to make any changes in the Word document so that the statement is accurate and then print, date, and sign the statement. Doing this creates a paper trail so that when your opponent deposes your witness, the witness's

recollection can be refreshed, if necessary, with the statement that you typed for them and that they had a chance to immediately review and approve.
- Schedule the depositions of important witnesses early on, including treating physicians, witnesses who have given you statements, and anyone else who helps build your case.

Going all-in on your cases right away establishes momentum, moves you toward your ultimate target of trial, and puts you in control of the litigation.

Don't Get Dirty along the Way

You set the tone for your cases. You cannot be affected by opposing counsel's behavior unless you allow yourself to be. Your actions direct the course of the litigation.

We don't accept an invitation to get into the muck with opposing counsel. We take the high road. We are reasonable. We do not reward bad behavior. We avoid being the subject of discovery disputes because we are happy to hand over all of the information we have about our clients. More on that later.

We don't get caught up in fights about the little stuff because our focus is always on the following:

1. Moving the case forward to trial
2. Making sure that all parties have all of the information they need to see that we will be successful at trial

Admittedly, this takes work and focus. But after hundreds of cases, we've seen common truths emerge:

- The lawyer who is angry is either feeling threatened by you, or is panicked about something in his or her case and, in either scenario, is losing.
- The lawyer who is freaking out in a deposition, at a hearing, in a letter, in a phone call, is either feeling threatened by you, or is panicked about something in his or her case and, in either scenario, is losing.
- The lawyer who is rude is threatened by you and is losing.

These are truths. Keep this in mind. Stay focused. And know that you are winning.

Documents? Don't Fight about Them

As a general rule, we don't waste time fighting about documents in discovery. If the documents are discoverable, we turn them over, and we don't block production of subpoenaed records, even if the subpoenas are overbroad and the production could technically be blocked.

For example, in civil litigation, we don't move to quash subpoenas that include W-2 and payroll records if we have a lost earnings claim, even though those records are protected by federal law. We don't move to quash ob-gyn records where they are requested in non-ob-gyn injury cases. We don't move to quash cardiology records in a non-cardiology case or pulmonology records in a non-pulmonology case or orthopedic records in a non-orthopedic case, for example.

First, the scorched-earth approach to discovery always backfires on the party that subpoenaed all of the unrelated records during trial. Second, courts' calendars are incredibly impacted, and we ask for court intervention only when it is absolutely necessary. Finally, we move *in limine* to exclude irrelevant or protected information before trial after demonstrating to the court that we've held nothing back and have not interfered with document production but that particular documents are not admissible, and it's time for the court to exercise its role as the evidentiary gatekeeper.

Note: always discuss subpoenas and medical care received with your clients before deciding upon this course of action.

Organize for Trial

Trial organization is critically important. During trial, every document needs to be accessible at a moment's notice. We have our complete trial file in court, and we have an identical electronic file that's searchable.

Courtroom Organization

We had a judge say to us that we were the most organized trial lawyers that had ever been in that department. Here's how we do it.
- First, invest in school library carts with wheels.
- Second, create a Redwell folder with a spine label for each witness, titled "Last Name, First Name." Include the witness's statements, depositions, reports, and so on in the Redwell.
- Third, alphabetize the Redwells on the library cart.
- Fourth, add copies of your joint trial notebook, motion *in limine* notebook, exhibit notebooks, and witness scheduling notebook.
- Fifth, add a Redwell for documents filed by either party during trial.
- Finally, add a plastic storage bin for trial supplies, including pens, pencils, pads of paper, a stapler, a hole puncher, flash drives, computer adapters, a small desktop printer, printer paper, markers, and sticky notes.

Electronic Organization

All of our files are scanned and stored in Dropbox. An electronic copy of every document we have on our trial cart is in Dropbox and is organized under subfolders that make them easily accessible.

Things You Can Do Today

All of this organization should be happening as soon as evidence exists in a case. If you're the entry- or midlevel attorney working on a case, you should be drafting a trial exhibit list and a trial witness list as you work the case. Draft your trial jury instructions immediately so you know what you have to prove or disprove in your case. Draft your special verdict form immediately so you know what the jury will have to find. These are ways for you to use a Trial Perspective approach. If you're not doing these things now, and you're working on cases, you're working them blind. Trial exhibit lists, trial witness lists, jury instructions, special verdict forms—these are not documents that you should throw together right before trial, and they are not documents that your support staff should draft. It's the trial lawyer's job to marshal the evidence. Start doing these things today, and you'll see your case performance increase dramatically. That's discovery by woman.

Chapter Takeaways

- Connect with your client by seeing them as a human being.
- Build your team of experts as early as possible.
- Move fast and first—go out and get the information you need.
- Don't get dirty—be honest, sincere, and aboveboard.
- Don't fight about documents—give your opponents what they request and expect the same in return.
- Organize for trial from the beginning.

14

Jury Selection by Woman

Do you find yourself trying to incorporate what the most successful trial lawyers do into your own practice? And not getting the same results they get? Or feeling like you're putting on an act, being someone else? Feeling like what you're doing doesn't fit?

Us too.

It's because the role models we're looking to are men, and men are inherently different from women. When women try to act like men, it doesn't work. It's not authentic.

For us, the biggest breakthroughs and successes came when we let go of trying to try cases the way men try cases and when we committed to trying cases based on our own intuition and being authentically ourselves.

There is so much more power, and a well of success available to you too, if you act like a woman. Because you are one. Be yourself. It begins in jury selection.

Jury Selection: Learn to Use Your Strengths

Jury selection is where we first get to meet, connect, and form a relationship with our jurors. It is the only time in trial that we get to fully interact and have a back-and-forth, open conversation with the humans who will be deciding our client's case. It is our one chance to learn as much as we can about these decision-makers, get to know them as human beings, and show them who we are.

Jury selection is about one thing: connecting with the people in front of us. If we can connect with them, we've succeeded. As women, we are made to build connections with other people. It's how we are wired, and we are so very good at it. Embrace this.

In this chapter, we'll show you how to capitalize on women's greatest strengths in jury selection and teach you how to apply those strengths to pick the best jury for your case, whether you are preparing for your first trial or whether you're a more seasoned attorney ready to enhance your practice.

Voir Dire: A Liberal and Probing Examination

A liberal and probing examination—sounds daunting, right? It's not, actually. And women are naturally really good at liberal and probing examinations. Need proof? Ask your husband, your best friend, or your kids.

For those of you reading this who are new to trial work, just getting into trial work, or coming back after a hiatus, we want to give you a quick overview of the nuts and bolts of voir dire. Voir dire is the process of selecting a jury, conducted in most states by both the judge and lawyers for each party. In some venues, in some federal courts, for example, there is no voir dire. In those places we suggest you carry crystals. For the rest of us, we conduct voir dire with the goal of selecting a group of people who can decide a case fairly and impartially for all parties involved.

All humans have biases and prejudices. The goal is to find jurors who can set those biases and prejudices, whatever they are, aside and decide a case based on the evidence presented and the jury instructions given, while giving consideration to the views and opinions of the other members of the jury during deliberations. To achieve this goal, it's critically important to have a meaningful conversation with your potential jurors to find out if each one of them can give both sides a fair shake in resolving the dispute.

Effective jury selection is both a science and an art. Simply asking people whether they can be fair and impartial, which is the way some judges and lawyers do it, isn't anywhere near what is necessary to select a jury. We must do more. If we don't, we end up, from the outset, with a jury that will be unfair to one side or the other and, thus, an injustice that defeats the whole purpose of a jury trial.

When you connect with potential jurors you don't have to be afraid of them. When we are functioning from a place of fear, which is what we're doing if we're not connecting, our instinct is to reject a juror who says something negative about our side of the case. If jurors say they don't agree with something about your side of the case, but you've connected with them and they've expressed a sincere willingness to be open-minded, you don't have to get rid of those jurors. You have no reason to fear that they will hurt your case because of the connection between you. We've seen it time and again. Those people stay true to their word, stay open-minded, and end up fighting for our side in the deliberation room. So, how do we get there?

Effective jury selection takes time. Our first job as lawyers is to have a conversation with the court before jury selection begins to make sure we are given the time for voir dire that our case needs.

In California, for example, the law gives us the ability to conduct a liberal and probing voir dire and forbids arbitrary or unreasonable time limitations on jury selection. California Civil Code of Procedure 222.5 gives us important rights that we can use to pick the best possible jury:

1. A Liberal and Probing Examination

    During any examination conducted by counsel for the parties, the trial judge shall permit liberal and probing examination calculated to discover bias or prejudice with regard to the circumstances of the particular case before the court.

2. No Arbitrary Time Limits

    The trial judge shall not impose specific unreasonable or arbitrary time limits or establish an inflexible time limit policy for voir dire.

Even though these rights are codified, that doesn't mean it's a given in every courtroom. After all, judges still have the inherent right and obligation to control the proceedings and keep things moving along. We file a motion in every trial specifically requesting the rights we are entitled to under the law. We let the judge know how long we estimate a meaningful voir dire will take in our case and what the specific issues are that warrant more time than a judge may be accustomed to allowing. Jury selection takes longer in some cases than others. Judges know this.[1]

This approach lets the judge know the following:

1. We know the law.
2. We've done this before.
3. We don't intend to waste the court's time or the potential juror's time.

---

[1] You can find a sample of this motion in appendix C at the end of this book.

Then, as we do our jury selection, we prove it to them. We show the judge with our examination that we aren't wasting time, that we are looking to pick a jury that is fair to both sides, and that we are following the rules.

Why a Liberal and Probing Examination Takes Time

Voir dire is often the first time a lawyer speaks to the panel of potential jurors (unless your jurisdiction allows mini opening statements, which we'll discuss later). At that point, you are a lawyer, not a human being. The jury pool looks at you and sees all of the stereotypes they know from TV, from lawyer jokes, from their own life experiences, and from what their friends and family say. As you well know, most of the time, those stereotypes are not positive.

So, we don't start out with a dynamic where the jury pool wants to open up to you and tell you their closely held biases. You and the jury pool are strangers. And for the most part, you are not a stranger these people want to get to know.

And there's more. These people didn't want to come to court today. They got a letter in the mail saying where and when they had to show up, threatening them with criminal prosecution if they didn't show. No one considered their schedule, whether their family would miss a meal if they couldn't work, or who would watch their children.

For the dutiful folks who show up, they are rewarded by being reduced to a number. They don't even have names anymore. They wear a paper sticker on their shirts. All morning, they are held hostage in a room in the courthouse, forced to watch outdated videos about how great the judicial system is, and told when they can leave the room and for how long. Eventually, an announcement is made, but it's not what they're hoping for. A list of names will be read. It will be the only time they are addressed by their names during this process. The announcement threatens: if your name is called, you are going to a courtroom, and you're one step closer to being "stuck" with jury duty.

When these folks get up to the department where you are trying your case, they are told where to sit, they are told when they can speak, they are told when they can use the restroom, and they are told when they can eat. And maybe the one other person they spoke with and connected with today either didn't get called up to the department or isn't allowed to sit next to them. And then the lawyer stands up, says, "Good morning," and starts trying to engage them in conversation. This is tough stuff.

If you look at this process from the juror's point of view, you can see why most lawyers don't really get anywhere with voir dire. How, in this scenario, would a prospective juror ever feel comfortable revealing personal thoughts, beliefs, or biases?

These people, who will decide your case, are sitting in a room they've never been in, with people they've never met, and they are being asked to speak publicly. Any idea how difficult it is for some people to speak in public? The National Social Anxiety Center says the fear of public speaking is the most common phobia. The Center cites a National Institute of Mental Health study showing that the fear of public speaking affects 73 percent of the population. Did you process that? Seventy-three percent of the population! That means, roughly three quarters of your potential jurors may have a phobia of public speaking. Not only are they being asked to speak in public, but these potential jurors are being asked to describe what closely held beliefs they have that may prevent them from being fair and impartial jurors.

So, how do you get past that? Jury selection is about connection. Let's take a look at how to connect in a few simple steps.

How to Connect

If we want jurors to be open and honest with us, we must be open and accessible to them. We can't stand up, ask probing questions, and expect they will share their deep, personal thoughts and convictions with us. They have to want to share. As women, we are particularly well suited to creating an environment where people feel safe to talk and share.

So, how do we connect with complete strangers? It's something we do every day. We have a real conversation and connect.

Connection with other humans happens when we are good listeners, open, honest, vulnerable, and kind. When we let down our guard and become real, authentic, and approachable to the people in front of us, they, in turn, open up. And that is an amazing experience.

Conversation is something we all do, and we're all good at it. We're talking about *real* conversation. This isn't chitchat. It's not surface-level stuff. When you really *care* about what someone is saying, when you're really *interested* in what someone is saying, it shows. Your eyes engage; your mind engages. You are listening to what the person in front of you is saying. You're not thinking about what you're going to ask next. You're not worried about how much time you have left. You are there, and you are sincerely invested in the conversation and in the person you're speaking with. When we really *do* this, the person we're speaking to and listening to feels it. And the people listening to the conversation feel it too.

Have whoever is sitting at counsel table take notes. Specifically, make sure that they write down direct quotes, word for word, when it comes to cause challenges, so that you are armed when you make your arguments later. Your job is to focus on the connection, the conversation.

The key is to start with one person—one member of your pool of potential jurors. Engaging and connecting with that one person allows the other people to see that you have created a space where it's safe to talk and an energy that makes people want to *get in on the conversation*. That's the conversation, and that's the connection.

Then, one by one, you engage other potential jurors in the conversation. It looks like this: "How do you feel about what your fellow juror just said? Do you feel the same, or do you feel a little differently?" And really *listen*. What is he saying? You're now engaging with a new person. Give this person the same energy, respect, and interest you gave the first. You are connecting the rest of the group to the conversation they just watched. And you are leading them to form a group. A group doesn't mean that everyone has the same opinion. A group means that these people have formed a unit, a bond, and they will work together to come to a just resolution.

When you really invest yourself in these conversations, there will be no question in your mind that you are "doing it right." You're engaged, and you're open to whatever course the conversation takes.

Sometimes, opening yourself up this way and allowing yourself to be vulnerable to what the jurors may say can be really, really painful. Here's an experience Courtney had.

Courtney:

A few years ago, Theresa and I tried a case together in Van Nuys. We represented a sixteen-year-old who was hit by an AT&T van while he was riding his bike in a crosswalk. I got up to start voir dire, and as the conversation started unfolding, one of the men on the panel of prospective jurors started getting agitated. He interrupted other potential jurors while they were talking. His behavior escalated. I knew that he wanted to be heard; so I started talking to him directly. He immediately attacked me. He said he felt like he was watching a play. He called me a liar. He said that every smile, every word I said, was putting on an act.

"Thank you. You say, thank you. It's a lie." He was raising his voice.

Jurors get hostile, and it's a really, really good thing. Reframe how you see "hostile jurors," and you will be unstoppable. It's honesty, and really, that's what we are looking for in voir dire. We want to create a space that allows potential jurors to say how they really feel so that both sides can get a fair and neutral jury.

Jurors can say things that trigger us to feel emotions. Our job is to be honest about what we're feeling.

The truth was, in the moment, I got a little scared. I don't do well when people raise their voices. I tend to do the rabbit thing and freeze when people raise their voices. I had a father who used to pick us up and drink and blast loud music when I was really small and scared; so, loud noises still scare me. When the man finished his tirade, I didn't know what to say next. I had just had a kid a few months before, and my body was still pretty out of control and I felt myself tearing up. So, I stopped. I took a breath. I got honest. "I'm sorry," I said. "I have a lot of hormones going on. I need to step away from you right now." I took a few steps to the other side of the jury box, looked at the group, and asked, "I think I need to change the subject now. Would that be all right with everyone?"

We won on the liability phase of that trial and went on to receive an eight-figure verdict for our very deserving client.

By being honest in the moment, and allowing myself to not know the "right" thing to say next, I gave the jury a chance to see who I really am, without walls. The group, in response, accepted me.

Being a woman in the courtroom has a lot of advantages. I used to worry about whether or not I would be judged for being a woman, that I would somehow have less authority than if I were a man. But this experience and many, many others like it have taught me that the opposite is true. Had I been a man, I don't know that the group would have rallied to protect me the way they did. When the case finished, the jurors told me that they admired my courage in contuining on when that man said those ugly things to me, and that I stood strong and stayed professional but that I was honest. They said it made them feel like they could trust me. When we expose our human side, when we allow ourselves to be seen, we build a bond.

Theresa:

I remember that moment so well. I can still feel the feelings of what it was like to be in that moment, sitting at counsel table and watching and listening to this man abuse my dear friend. Courtney's back was to me, but I didn't need to see her face. I knew how she felt because I knew how I would feel if I was up there. Both of our babies were in the hall, and we were both counting down the time until our next break so we could nurse them. I couldn't believe that this man was attacking her, and no one was doing anything about it.

But then I looked at the jurors. Every single one of them was very uncomfortable. The ones who were sitting closest to this man were creating physical distance between themselves and him, leaning away from him in their chairs. I could see the big picture from my seat, and I was able to see that this man had given us such a gift. He had kicked the baby doe in the face, and the rest of the tribe was appalled and was going to jump in and save her as soon as possible.

And that's exactly what they did. Later, another juror spoke up and said that what that man did was wrong. And, again, from my seat, I could see all of the others agreeing.

Above all, I was proud of my friend. She was brave, and at the same time, she stayed true to herself and true to her commitment to be herself in front of the jury. The moment came and it went, and she handled it with grace.

Being open and engaging with the people who are in front of you is how you connect. Be open; be interested in what you're hearing; and, most importantly, be present.

Get the Conversation Going

Step One: Get Present

Getting present can be as simple as touching an inanimate object—the desk, the hem of your jacket, maybe a photo or even a medicine bag—and saying to yourself, "I am here." Take a breath. In and out.

Why touch something? It's grounding. It brings your mind into the physical space. In other words, it brings your mind to the same place your body is. It stops the mind from worrying about what just happened or what will happen next.

If you want to elevate your mindfulness practice, touch an object that means something to you: a lucky coin in your pocket, a drawing from your child tucked into a file folder, anything that reminds you that you are a human being with emotions, thoughts, opinions, people whom you love, and people who love you—just like the panel of potential jurors you're about to connect with.

Then physically get yourself in front of the jury. Sometimes, when we are nervous, we start speaking while we are walking somewhere. Don't. Allow for silence. Invite it. That is how you take control of the room. Silence can be scary, but it's very, very powerful. Silence before you begin builds anticipation. Silence in between questions and sentences gives everyone a chance to think and, more importantly, to feel.

Step Two: Will You All Please Talk to Me?

Ask for what you want:

> I am hoping that you will all please promise to talk to me. In fact, I am hoping you will somehow magically become the most talkative group of people who have ever been in a courtroom. This is our one and only chance to get to know one another and, importantly, at the end of this process, to make an important decision. Is this the right case for you, as the person you each are, to serve as jurors? Can you be the fair and impartial decision-makers that everybody in this courtroom needs? So, would that be all right? Will you do that? Will you talk to me?
>
> Mr. Jones? . . . Thank you . . . Ms. Hernandez, will you do your best to be talkative? . . . Thank you . . . Mr. Jackson? . . . Thank you . . . Mrs. Parks?

Or

> "Juror No. 1? Juror No. 8?"

Or even

> "Ma'am? Sir?"

Do this while making eye contact. If you have the names of the jurors in front of you and are comfortable using them, great. If you need to use numbers, that's fine too. We aren't big on memorizing names. It's a great parlor trick, and if you have a photographic memory, then by all means have at it; but we find, especially if you are at the beginning of your career, that it tends to be a distraction that can interfere with our main goal: connecting with the jury. Being respectful, acknowledging the human, in our experience, trumps the anxiety of trying to be a superhero:

> Thank you. Now, if for some reason it's not working and if there is a lull in the conversation, or that uncomfortable silence, could we have a cue? To get the conversation going again, could I say something like, "Would someone please talk to me?" Would that be all right?

Tell them what you need them to do, and they will do it. Remember, for most of these potential jurors, it's the first time they've done this. They don't know what you want unless you tell them.

As women, sometimes we don't ask for what we want. We sometimes expect people to know what we want. There's no space for that behavior here. Know what you want, communicate that to your potential jurors with sincerity, and they will be happy to give it to you.

Step Three: Brutal Honesty

"Brutal honesty." Pause. Wait. Then say it again. "Brutal honesty." And the third time, they will hear the words, "What do those words, *brutal honesty*, mean to you? Will someone please talk to me?"

Now it's time to keep your lips closed and look around and make eye contact. We promise that there will be a few people ready to talk if you commit to not saying a word and just let it happen. When they talk, in response, all we say to them is, "Thank you." We don't even have to speak the words. We can say thank you with our eyes or a smile and then look for the next juror who is ready to talk. Let the answers come from wherever and however they come. Just keep your mouth shut. You'll get all sorts of responses:

"It means not caring what the other person thinks."

"Saying what you really think no matter what."

"It means not being politically correct."

"Not being worried about hurting your feelings."

In a San Diego trial, one woman shouted from the back of the courtroom, "You look fat in that skirt!"
We all laughed.
"Thank you. That's what we are asking you for. Brutal honesty, without worrying about hurting our feelings."

Step Four: Time to Talk about Topics and Issues We Need to Cover

Before you start the substance of your conversation, you should pause. Check in with yourself. What's on your list of issues to talk about? The order in which you planned to talk about them doesn't matter. This is the time to check in with yourself and feel what you should talk about first. Talk about what feels right in the moment. Stay connected, continue to be a good listener, and use the fewest amount of words possible.

Two Categories of Topics

There are two categories of topics we need to cover.

First Category: Big-Picture Topics

This category pertains to the kind of case you're handling and includes issues that could affect a juror's ability to be fair and impartial. These aren't fact-specific questions for the jurors. We're not preconditioning the panel by asking, "If these were the facts, would you think that was negligent?" We're talking about big-picture issues. For example, in a civil case, we ask how jurors feel about the burden of proof being less than in a criminal case, and how they feel about awarding money for pain and suffering. For both sides to get a fair trial, we need to know that we have jurors who don't have beliefs about these types of big-picture issues that would prevent them from following the law.

Second Category: Case-Specific Topics

The second category covers case-specific issues you need to address with the potential jury. Here again, we're not asking jurors how they would decide a case given particular facts. We're making sure we get a fair and impartial group of jurors on our panel.

We start compiling this list from the day we get a case. We keep a running list in our electronic file for each case. Every time we read discovery responses, review medical records, talk with our client or other witnesses, talk with our experts, defend a deposition, or take a deposition, we add to the list as things come up.

How do you know what to put on your list? When you first find out what your case is about, which parts scare you? Which parts make the case more difficult to win? Which parts could be affected by someone's opinion or beliefs? In a car crash case that involves an elderly driver, for example, do any of your potential jurors believe that all elderly drivers aren't as safe as younger drivers? Or that all teen drivers make bad choices?

Some topics that always show up on our lists: the burden of proof, money for pain and suffering in a civil case, representing a corporation rather than an individual, and experience with assault or other crimes in a criminal case. We discuss things we think our juries may have biases about so that we can make sure both sides have a fair jury. Remember, as women our unique perspective means we see additional issues that may have gone overlooked by an all-male team. This gives us a significant advantage when it comes time to picking the right jury for our case.

Working with the Topic List

Once our list is made, it is our resource during voir dire, not our script. We may skip around depending on the conversation with the jurors and how much time we have.

A great resource for civil voir dire questions and topics is David Ball's book, *David Ball on Damages*.[2] We have also found it to be a great starting point even when we are trying criminal cases. Last, we find some of our most important issues when we do focus groups, which we discuss in chapter 12.

Once we know which topics we are going to talk about, the approach is simple. We just ask the question:

"In a civil case, our burden is not beyond a reasonable doubt; it's more likely than not. How do you feel about that?"

---

[2] David Ball, *David Ball on Damages*, 3rd ed. (Portland, OR: Trial Guides, 2012).

"Money for pain and suffering. Does that stir up any feelings for anyone?"

Or

"Some people might say I'm OK with big numbers when it comes to medical bills, but not when it comes to pain and suffering. Anyone feel that way?"

This is not to give you an exhaustive list of questions but rather to give you a flavor of using few words to elicit an informative response.

We promise that every person is able to communicate, in very few words, and get a discussion going about the topics that are important in each type of case.

As long as we stay open and accepting of what we hear, the jurors will share how they think and what they feel without filters, without restrictions, and with brutal honesty. This is because we have asked them for it, and they have promised to be talkative and brutally honest about whatever you need to cover in your case.

We especially love the brutal honesty method when the court has limited our time for jury selection. When we are limited for time, we go to the topics that are most dangerous for our case or that we feel are going to have the biggest impact on whether or not a juror can fairly decide our case. For example, in a case where our plaintiff was drinking when he was hit on his bike, we ask the jury how they feel about alcohol, first question. It is the most inflammatory part of our case. There are a lot of people who have strong opinions about alcohol. They may have a hard time awarding money to someone who was drunk and riding a bike when he got hurt. That's something we need to know. We have other topics on our list—the use of bike helmets or whether anyone has been hurt in a car accident—but if we are limited for time, we start with the scariest bits first and get right to the meat. Brutal honesty cuts out the small talk.

In our experience, jurors actually love that approach. It's rare that we are given a chance to speak our minds. It's even more rare for someone to ask us what we are feeling and to care about our response, with no limitations. Judges love it too. We had a really great judge in a farming town in northern California that said he was going to use it in every one of his cases. We have heard rumors that one of our favorite judges in LA is doing the same thing. It cuts the crap. And that is what we need to do in order to connect.

Avoiding Common Pitfalls

When a Juror Says What You Don't Want to Hear

When these strangers open up to us and share their beliefs with us, we have to accept them. That's how you keep the connection. Jury selection is never a time to cross-examine a juror or argue against a juror's beliefs or positions on issues. We must be accepting and respectful of whatever our prospective jurors say—no matter what.

Being open means listening and hearing things we may not want to hear—even things that may seem to hurt us in the moment. Some lawyers teach that we don't want to hear a prospective juror say something adverse to the case because it has the potential of poisoning the minds of the rest of the jurors. We don't believe that, not at all. We want to know how people feel about our type of case and whether they have biases or prejudices before, rather than after, they are sworn in as jurors. We have found that an open and honest discussion that invites, accepts, and respects adverse beliefs will ferret out jurors who cannot possibly be fair and impartial.

Equally as powerful, taking this approach and getting the jurors' opinions and beliefs out into the open gives us an opportunity to ask those who might have preconceived adverse opinions and beliefs to keep an open mind and maybe see our side as the one that is just. Quite often, when we do this, jurors who we think are against us, turn around and become willing to be part of the team we need in order to win the case.

Don't Speak or Act Out of Fear

One of the fatal errors lawyers make in voir dire is acting out of fear. One of the most common ways they do it is by attacking the other lawyer.

Courtney:

When I was trying an employment case in downtown Los Angeles, I talked to the jurors about damages, and I said I would be asking for "millions and millions of dollars." I don't think the judge was letting us talk about actual numbers, but I wanted to make sure I was up-front with the jurors about what I would be asking for in the case and listen to how they felt about it.

The defense lawyer was a very well-respected, prominent, and highly successful older woman. She went through the usual schtick and then asked about "Mrs. Rowley and her millions and millions of dollars." She said it with a sneer. Then she said it again. And again. It was like she was in on some joke with the jurors and I was the punch line. I started feeling really defensive, thinking I had screwed up, said or done something wrong. I started worrying that my connection with this jury was disappearing—that they didn't like me because of what she was saying.

When the lawyer finished, and I had to get up again, I was a little meek. But I had to do it, so I asked the next group the same questions. I made a little fun of myself, but I kept going and I did my job. I didn't hide the fact that I was embarrassed.

As the day went on and on, she kept it up, sneering and angrily making fun of me, and I kept on going, politely, maybe sheepishly at times, but without acknowledging her.

For the rest of the case, our team made the decision to keep putting me physically near her. When we would walk to the bench, I would stand near her. When we came to and from chambers, I would walk in front of or behind her. We exploited her anger and polarized our case, in part, by capitalizing on her bad behavior.[3] We got a great result for one of the neatest and most brilliant men I've had the privilege of representing, and creating that contrast played a role.

It is our responsibility to constantly step back and evaluate our own behavior. Can I look at this from the outside? What does it look like? Is it classy? Are my actions aligned with my higher self? You can tell. You can feel when you are out of alignment. It feels like anxiety, discomfort, pain, depression, embarrassment. It feels unbalanced.

As women, we are all too good at second-guessing ourselves. However, there is a clear distinction between feeling the inevitable nervousness of being in trial and reacting out of fear and insecurity. You know you're acting out of fear when your actions are not aligned with your highest self—with who you are and who you want to be as a human being. You feel your energy draining. You feel yourself getting ugly. When you feel that way, stop. Fix it. And then move on.

We aren't talking about the general fear and anxiety that comes with trying a case. No matter how many times we go to trial, there are moments that we feel scared and moments that we feel anxious, because we

---

[3] See the excellent book by Rick Friedman, *Polarizing the Case: Exposing and Defeating the Malingering Myth* (Portland, OR: Trial Guides, 2007).

care. Overcoming that fear might take a lifetime, and like a lot of things, it comes and goes, sometimes trial to trial, other times every five minutes. Any time we take on a challenge, take a risk, there will be fear—that means we are alive. But the key to managing the fear and rising above it isn't pretending it isn't there. We cannot shut it out. When we do, we become inauthentic and cold. We have to turn into the fear, into ourselves, by embracing our emotions and using them to fuel our task at hand. One way to do this is by maintaining an awareness of ourselves and our behavior in the courtroom. When we are aware of what our behavior looks like from the outside, the jitters of being up in front of a crowd, worrying about whether anyone will talk to us, being afraid that we won't represent our client well, all lessen, and we find clarity, a bit of a calm in the storm.

Consider Using Written Jury Questionnaires

We love using jury questionnaires on complicated cases and cases where we have potentially polarizing and sensitive issues. However, they can be very useful in otherwise run-of-the-mill cases too. Most of all, jury questionnaires save time and give us a lot of information that we can use to prepare for jury selection. They also save time by giving us all of the biographical and background information both parties want on jurors without taking the time for the judge to have each juror verbally respond to a standard list of questions.

The other benefit of jury questionnaires is that we can ask the hard, polarizing, and sensitive questions without jurors being under the pressure of having to respond in public. Here again, we can get right to the point.

Also, if there is a time crunch on voir dire, we have more direction, based on the jury questionnaire responses, on where we need to go with the jurors. In a recent case, because we had questionnaires, we knew that we had only a few chances to get a jury before we would hit a section of jurors that weren't good for our case. That information informed our decisions and how we exercised our peremptory challenges.

Most of the time, we draft our own jury questionnaires. On the birth injury case I talk about in chapter 15, "Opening Statement by Woman," we used questionnaires that Wendy Saxon, the best jury consultant we know, drafted for us. With over a thousand jury trials under her belt, she's an incredible resource for lawyers, but an even more significant resource for women. Also, she's a wild motorcycle-riding lady, a connoisseur of good food in even the most dire circumstances, and a hell of a good time.

In developing questionnaires, we use the topics we compiled in our list for voir dire, but we tweak them to make them more specific. When you are writing questions, think about what answers you are looking for. "Yes" and "No" don't give you very much information. What we want to know is how people feel about a topic and how strongly they hold those opinions. We all have opinions. That's part of what makes us unique. What we want to know is whether someone's opinions are so strong that they prevent that person from listening to both sides and making a fair decision. One of our favorite ways to ask the right questions is to use scales.

For example:

On a scale of 1 to 10, 1 being the least strong and 10 being the most strong, please answer the following questions and rate the following statements:

I believe large verdicts for pain and suffering are justified.

1 2 3 4 5 6 7 8 9 10

I believe anyone arrested for a crime is probably guilty.

1 2 3 4 5 6 7 8 9 10

Scaled questions are a quick and easy way to see what people believe and, more importantly, whether they have strong opinions about something. This helps us identify questions that we want to follow up on in voir dire.

"Mr. Spalding, I see on question 5, you circled a 1. Would you say a little more about that?"

We attach some questionnaires we have used at the back of this book, and we encourage you to join listservs and other professional groups to share and swap questionnaires with other lawyers.

Regardless of whether you draft the questionnaire yourself or use the help of a jury consultant, it's important to use the questionnaires as extra information, not as a replacement for actually connecting with the jurors. We have had the experience of having a massive stack of lengthy questionnaires returned with very little time to go through them before jury selection. It's always more important to focus on connecting instead of trying to shuffle through papers and revisit flat questions.[4]

Picking the Jury and Making Challenges

We believe that jury selection is a process of *inclusion*, not *exclusion*. We look at it like building a group, creating a team that will represent the community, working together to make an important decision. We find that this approach helps us in two important ways.

First, it builds better juries. When we eliminate everyone we think we *don't* like, we are stuck with whatever is left over—a leftovers jury—which is about as appealing as the leftovers one finds in the fridge after a long week of work and play.

---

[4] See appendix D for a sample juror questionnaire.

On the other hand, when we build a fair and impartial group by initiating the conversation that will eventually carry over into the jury room after closing arguments and by building connections among ourselves and among the jurors, there is a sense of unification, or camaraderie. That fosters better communication and, in our experience, better results.

The second reason we seek inclusion is selfish: when you walk into a room of strangers and you're already on the offensive, with critical eyes and a judging heart, the process is scary, daunting, and not very fun. As trial lawyers, as leaders, we carry the energy of the courtroom and set the tone for the trial. If we walk in angry and disappointed, we have found, we tend to walk out the same way.

Challenging Jurors

Let's talk about how to challenge jurors.

The voir dire process happens in groups. In other words, each side gets to talk to a group of potential jurors at once. Some judges start with eighteen, for example. In that case, one side gets to examine the first eighteen potential jurors. Then the other side follows. Ask your judge how he or she conducts voir dire. This varies from courtroom to courtroom. Know how many people are included in your initial voir dire and where those people are sitting in the courtroom. After each side has conducted voir dire of the initial group, the judge will ask for challenges. Jurors can be challenged for cause when they have shown the following:

1. Implied bias—as when the existence of the facts as ascertained, in judgment of law disqualifies the juror

Or

2. Actual bias—the existence of a state of mind on the part of the juror in reference to the case, or to any of the parties, which will

prevent the juror from acting with entire impartiality, and without prejudice to the substantial rights of any party.[5]

This is the law in California. The law in your jurisdiction may be different, but this is the general idea.

That said, part of our job in picking the jury is making the right challenges. In most states, there are two types of challenges:

- challenges for cause
- peremptory challenges

After the initial voir dire, the judge asks the lawyers whether there are any challenges for cause.

There is no limit to the number of cause challenges that a party can make. A challenge for cause is made when a lawyer or a party asks the court to excuse jurors because they lack the ability or have demonstrated a likelihood of bias or prejudice that will prevent them from being fair and impartial to one or more parties in a case. An example of a cause challenge would be a juror who has experience with being the victim of assault and has expressed a likelihood of believing the victim over the defendant and convicting the defendant before ever hearing any evidence. An example of a juror in a civil case who should be excused for cause is a business owner who has been a defendant in other cases and who has expressed a dislike for personal injury lawsuits and an opinion against compensating injury victims for pain and suffering regardless of the evidence. When potential jurors say they will not follow the law or they will decide the case a certain way regardless of the evidence, that is the basis for a challenge for cause.

Challenges for cause are generally made outside of the presence of the jury, and lawyers have to argue to the judge the factual basis for why a particular juror should be excised for cause. It's often helpful to have a

---

[5] California Code of Civil Procedure § 225(b).

court reporter recording the voir dire so you have a record of what the potential juror said.

If the judge does not grant a challenge for cause as to a particular juror, you can protect your record by using one of your peremptory challenges to excuse that juror. Judges allow peremptory challenges after challenges for cause are made and ruled on.

Peremptory challenges are different from challenges for cause. While challenges for cause are unlimited, each side has a specific number of peremptory challenges to use, depending on the jurisdiction and the number of parties involved. You can use a peremptory challenge to excuse a potential juror from the case for any reason other than race, gender or sexuality. So in other words, if your gut just tells you, "I really don't like juror number 5, Mr. Spalding. There is something about him, and I would just rather have somebody else as a juror, and I don't want him on this case," you can exercise a peremptory challenge. If, however, you are excusing him because in your mind you wanted someone of a different ethnicity, that would be wrong, and that would not be a valid basis for a peremptory challenge.

Depending on whether you're in federal or state court, and depending on the state and the number of sides to a case, a party may have up to eight peremptory challenges. It is important to know the number of peremptory challenges each side has before beginning jury selection. If you're unsure, ask. In fact, ask just to be sure. We try cases all over the country—there are different rules in different courts for different cases. Ask the judge how many peremptory challenges each side gets and in what order those challenges are executed (that is, who goes first). In some jurisdictions we practice in, it is mandatory to use all of our peremptory challenges.

The typical magic words used to exercise a peremptory challenge are along these lines: "Your Honor, I'd like to thank and excuse juror number 5, Mr. Stone."

This is by no means an exhaustive how-to for voir dire, nor is it a step-by-step guide. In fact, that's the best part about what we do—we are always learning more. These are arrows to add to your quiver, tools and ideas to either get you started or add to your experiential base. These are the methods we've used and refined over the years through jury trials, focus groups, and a lot of teaching and learning with and from some of the best trial lawyers in the country.

Always Request a Mini-Opening

Mini-openings are *brief, nonargumentative* statements of the case that each side gives before jury selection. These are three- to five-minute summaries of the issues in the case to give the potential jurors a flavor for what the case is about. In more and more jurisdictions across the country, case law is changing to include mini-openings. In California, for example, California Code of Civil Procedure 222.5 now states that mini-openings *must* be given:

> Upon the request of a party, the trial judge shall allow a brief opening statement by counsel for each party prior to the commencement of the oral questioning phase of the voir dire process.

We ask for a mini-opening in every case for two reasons: First, it brings honesty and clarity to jury selection. Second, it improves the juror's experience and makes voir dire go faster.

With a mini-opening, the very first thing the jurors get to hear is—YOU. Instead of some sterilized statement of the case that gives the impression that there are "two sides to every story" or that there is a legitimate "disagreement," you get a chance to actually state your case and let them know what you are asking for. This facilitates a much more honest, focused voir dire that takes less time. Because the jury knows what the beef is, when jury selection starts, we can get right to the heart of it. Is this the right case for them where they, as the humans that they are, can be neutral, fair, and impartial, and give both sides a fair fight? It eliminates a lot of ambiguity and confusion.

In our experience, a mini-opening combined with brutal honesty in voir dire helps jurors efficiently decide whether or not they are a fit for the case. We do a lot less dancing around what we are *trying* to say and get right to it. It's great for both sides and for the trial process. Some jurisdictions allow mini-opening statements, in the discretion of the court. In California, it is now mandatory, if requested, after many years of being discretionary.

If we are in a jurisdiction with no mini-opening, or in a courtroom where the judge denies it, we still write one. We have found that mini-openings are the best way to organize our themes and the most important points of our cases. If it turns out we can't use it, then we keep to the same plan: focus on connection during voir dire, and tell our story in opening.

What to Do When We Don't Get Voir Dire

In some jurisdictions, lawyer-directed voir dire is not permitted. This is a shame, but it is what it is until the laws are changed. And we still have an obligation to do our best for our clients, even when the law limits us. Be proactive. Write out the questions you would ask and submit them to the judge.

Find Out What You Can about Prospective Jurors

You can learn a lot about jurors by doing a simple internet search. This information isn't a substitute for voir dire in any way, and information on the internet shouldn't be the basis of a challenge. And while simply reading the information and looking at the pictures publicly available is not prohibited and is informative, make sure not to interact in any way with a prospective juror by requesting to become Facebook friends or following a person on Instagram or the like.

We have found that a simple search across social media can yield considerable information about potential jurors, as well as witnesses in our cases that can add to the focus of our conversations.

On Listening

Jury selection is about connection. We make the connection through communication. Communication is about listening.

A great activity to practice communication—and by communication, we mean listening—is the "tell me more/say more" exercise. The next time you are having a conversation with a family member or with a teacher at a parent-teacher conference, or are having a meeting with a coworker over lunch, let the other person finish what he or she is saying and then respond with, "Say more." And mean it. Then hush your mouth and *listen*. When they finish, resist the urge to *respond*. In fact, don't. Take it in. The advanced version? Do this during a conversation where there is a disagreement or conflict. When we listen without responding, we hold space for the other person's emotions. You can always come back later and respond. In fact, you might find that taking a break to reflect makes your response better, more empathetic, and less clouded with emotion.

Not going to court? Your mini-opening still matters. In a way, it's a statement of the case, but it's more a statement of *your* case. What is your case about? Can you edit your case down to a few sentences and still convey your side of the story? It's a difficult skill. Often, when we teach trial skills in different parts of the country, we find that many lawyers can't. Take a shot at your mini-opening as soon as you get your case, and then keep refining it as your case develops. Being able to give a brief and compelling summary of your case will help you when you are interacting with the judge, other lawyers, in focus groups, in legal writing, and in finding focus and direction as you work your case.

Jury selection is about connecting, which we, as women, are uniquely suited to do. It is about inclusion, not exclusion—we walk into the room with an open heart, ready to build the group that works together to make the best decision for the case. We come armed with a list of topics that we believe can affect whether or not the jurors can make fair decisions and, sometimes, armed with questionnaires. We begin by asking for brutal honesty, and we are prepared to deliver the same throughout the trial. We ask for and are prepared to give mini-openings, to provide better context for a more productive voir dire. Jury selection is the first time we get to meet the human beings who are going to listen to both sides of a complicated case and work together to make a difficult decision. We come to them appreciative, open-minded, openhearted, and ready to listen.

That is jury selection by woman.

Voir Dire outside the Courtroom

If you're not picking a jury tomorrow, here are some things you can do to improve your Trial Perspective approach:

1. Arrange an inexpensive, one-hour, lunch-time focus group and practice your voir dire.
2. Practice these voir dire strategies in your next deposition and see how much more helpful a witness is, even an expert, when you take a true and authentic interest in trying to relate to and understand where he's coming from as a human being and why he has the opinions he does.

Chapter Takeaways

- Women are uniquely suited to conduct jury selection because we know how to connect.
- Connect with the jury by listening to them.
- Start conversations and keep them going.
- Don't be afraid to talk about the tough stuff.
- You can do this even if the judge won't allow voir dire.

15

Opening Statement by Woman

Remember how we talked about that research showing that nearly three quarters of the public has a phobia of public speaking? Believe it or not, there are a lot of trial lawyers who aren't comfortable speaking in public either. If you sweat through your shirt when you have to stand up to give your opening statement, if your hands shake, if your breathing is shallow, if your mind runs wild with thoughts of self-doubt and everything that could go wrong, if you suddenly can't remember your opening, if you won't stand in front of the jury and instead are hiding behind the podium and have a death grip on the podium sides, even if you're barely suppressing the urge to run out the back door, *you are not alone*. We have all been there. It's normal. It's your body's natural reaction to adrenaline. You're about to do something big. In this chapter, we'll show you how to prepare and deliver your opening so that less adrenaline pumps through your system. And we'll give you some practical tips to calm your body down and calm your mind down in those high-stress moments.

Opening is where we first present our case to the jury. We have already touched on our themes in mini-opening and voir dire, but this is where we get to tell the whole story. What we say to a jury in opening and, very importantly, how we say and deliver it, can determine the fate of our case.

Many of us have had the daunting experience of getting up to give our opening and feeling like we had to convince the jurors then and there. And for those who haven't tried cases, the same fear is there. Will they like me? Will they choose my side? So, we argue, we repeat ourselves, and in the process of it all, we lose credibility. Sometimes, in trying to show our case in the best light, we overreach, making promises we can't or don't keep during trial, again, losing credibility. Some of us think we have to have a perfect script memorized, so we end up looking mechanical and frozen, while we agonize over our lines and end up forgetting important pieces of our story, which makes us lose our confidence.

Opening statement is the first time that we have full control over what is going on in the courtroom. The spotlight is on us and, if we choose, we can make the courtroom so quiet and filled with suspense that the jury could hear a pin drop. They are interested and engaged. We can be very matter of fact and not show any emotion, which is the right thing to do in some cases with some juries. Or we can put on a show, have fun, and entertain. Every case is different and so is every jury. There is no right way to do an opening statement, but there are wrong ways. Much of what we can do depends on who our judge is. In the end, no matter what course we choose to take, the most important thing is that we have credibility, show the jury and the court that we are an authority on the case, and present a story of the case to the jury that is true and supported by the admissible evidence.

Before getting into specific techniques and dos and don'ts, Courtney shares a story.

Courtney:

An "Opening by Woman" story that still stands out in my mind makes me sad, but also makes me shake my head and half smile, and is one of the motivations for this book and the Trial By Woman movement.

The weather outside is cool and crisp, and the courtroom isn't much different. There is dead silence. These people don't know me because I did not do voir dire. I am representing the child, and my co-counsel is representing the parents. It is a medical malpractice case where a child was injured at birth. We split the trial up and designated separate counsel for each party, and the judge only let one lawyer do voir dire. I stand up, walk over, and am now standing in front of the jury. There is dead silence. All eyes are on me. Slowing down all the things rushing through my mind, I am really hoping my shoes were the right choice. Then I think to myself, "I wonder what everybody is thinking looking at me." I have had so many lawyers, in particular male lawyers, tell me over the years what I should be wearing, and it is in this moment that insecurity strikes. Maybe it is because this is a big case—one that really matters. I know from my time at the Los Angeles super-firm that hired me during law school that I should be standing in dark blue power pumps. But, then again, they would never let me do an opening statement on a multi-eight-figure birth injury case. Certainly, they would have expected me to wear a skirt. But hey, I'm not a downtown LA attorney-at-law. I'm a California trial lawyer, but I am also a trial lawyer licensed in Iowa and Wyoming, and I try cases all over the country. I am not LA Law—I am a woman who is less confined by the superficial. At least that is what I have told myself.

Besides, I had a baby this year and none of my pumps fit anyway. (No one tells me these things.) So, I am wearing loafers (leather, of course) because they feel comfortable. I tell myself it's OK because I have a jury of people who care about comfort more than fancy appearances. I'm standing up in front of a jury of farmers, nurses, warehouse workers, forklift operators. They are salt-of-the-earth people. I will be in front of them with the spotlight on me for two hours, and it is my responsibility to explain and tell the story of a very complicated birth injury case. Thinking about whether my shoes are OK is my insecurity and fear coming through. I am trying this case in a little farming community, where winning a medical malpractice case is said to be an impossibility. The least of my worries should be shoes, right?

This is where I shut myself up and tell myself again that "I am prepared, ready, and I am the best person to do this job." Deep breath in. Deep breath out. I look at the people in front of me, slowly. I make eye contact with the jurors, one by one. I find someone, speak my first words to that person, and we connect.

As I look into the juror's eyes, I think, "Sir, I have something you need to hear, something you'll want to hear because it is important, something that happened in your community, something we need your help with." This slows me down and helps me feel what is going on. The tone and rhythm of the beginning of an opening statement is so important.

I tell the story about a mother with a baby in her belly, the hopes and dreams, and everything that was to be with the birth of her little girl. How negligence changed it all.

The nurses and doctor in charge ignored signs that the baby wasn't doing OK. He wasn't the doctor the mother had been seeing; he was someone she hadn't met before. His nickname, which he gave himself, was "the king of forceps." I show the jury what he did with those forceps. I show the jury what happened to the mother's body when he yanked, inside of her, on her baby's head. I break down the science, explain why this never should have happened. I talk about the parents and how much they love their little girl. Her father, an engineer, designed and built a bike so he can take her riding by the beach. I introduce her, in her wheelchair, to the jury, and I introduce every member of her family.

When I sit down, my heart is pounding. I did it. I was in the moment, I was connected with the jurors, and I told this little girl's story. I squeeze her hand on my way back to counsel table. I'm feeling really proud about myself. The next two defendants (very good and well-known and respected medical malpractice defense lawyers) give their separate opening statements, but they don't work. I can feel it; they can feel it. I had already hit every one of their points. They're dead in the water. I killed them with a compelling human story before they ever stood up.

When the judge goes off the record for the day, I grab my bag and get up to head for the car. I'm starving and exhausted. A pretty blond woman, about fifty years old, gets up from the back of the gallery. She's a little taller than me, dressed really well. She has a big smile on her face. She is walking toward me, making eye contact. She introduces herself, just her name, and shakes my hand. I'm higher than a kite. I think that this is a local woman trial lawyer who came to watch this high-profile case, and I know I did a good job. She leans in to say something quietly, and I follow the lead.

"You know your ta-tas were hanging out the whole time? Everyone could see them—your ta-tas. You probably should think about getting some clothes that fit. It's pretty unprofessional to use your tits to distract the jury. Just so you know, that's all anyone was looking at. From one woman to another, I thought you would want to know."

She laughs and so does her friend standing next to her.

I freeze. *"Don't cry, don't cry, don't cry,"* I tell myself. The truth is that I had just had a baby, and yes, I have rather large, engorged, milk-filled, ready-to-burst breasts that now are starting to drip down my obscenely hormone-smelly armpits and which stain my clothes. I am absolutely mortified. I have no idea what to do. My whole team is men. My face is hot, and my chest is locking up.

I think, "*I've blown it, completely destroyed this case, this little girl, this family. I've disappointed everyone. I'm an idiot and I knew I didn't belong here. I am totally wrong, about everything. I've got to get out of here. I knew this shirt was too big, and I knew I should have worn the sweater.*"

I stand there, dumbstruck. "*Say something. Say something*," I tell myself. I say nothing. Finally, I laugh politely and say, "Thank you."

I go back to the room, and one of the men on our team, Pat Logan, who I've known for years, is sitting at the little table. I tell him what the woman said.

Then, quietly, "Pat. You need to tell me the truth."

Poor guy. He tells me I did a great job, no boobs that he noticed. He turns bright red and starts slamming a Diet Coke. I don't believe him at all.

I get in the car with my husband. I tell him what happened. I'm trying not to cry. He tells me I'm wrong, that it's untrue. I don't believe him either. As we pull out, the woman is walking by the car, so I point her out.

Nick rolls down the window. He starts yelling into the parking lot, "You the one that went up to my wife? She's breastfeeding. She just had a baby. And she did a great job. And you're wrong."

"Well," she says, "when I had my kids, I didn't go to work and I wouldn't have gone out *like that*."

I cry all the way home. And while I make lunch. And while we all sit and eat it, quietly.

The next day, the defendants all offer their policies. My opening takes the case from zero to full policy limits by all health-care defendants and gets this child the multiple eight figures she deserves. The Good Samaritan lady, the one with the fashion advice, it turns out she is the wife of one of the defense lawyers.

I did a great job. The jurors told me. The judge told me. The defense lawyers told me. My husband told me. But the truth is, even after such a great success, I still doubted myself. And it wasn't just the boobs. (Which were *not* hanging out. I did a few hundred takes in the shirt later that night to convince myself.) But what was it in me that still doubted myself? That still doubts myself?

I had been through years of trying to fit some sort of mold, trying to overachieve and have my work be seen. All the old stories and experiences and doubts were right with me, along with a lot of conditioning. The defense lawyers were older, experienced men. They knew what they were doing. The defendants (hospitals and doctors) were well established in their community. And me? I was a just a mom and felt like I was less than what I was before as a trial lawyer. So, I fought with my husband because I needed him to fight my stories out of myself, for me. I needed that push—that confidence. I couldn't do it on my own. We forget that sometimes. That we need help.

A Woman's Place Is Opening the Case

Women are uniquely and often best suited to giving opening statements. It's an area where women can really shine.

The majority of our cases are referred to us by men. Therefore, we try a lot of cases with men. When we try cases with men, we almost always give the opening statement. We have found, in talking to juries on case after case, that between us and male lawyers we've worked with, even including Courtney's husband, the great Nick Rowley, jurors are more receptive to us, as women, versus men, in the early phases of the trial, and this is especially true in opening statement. Our energy is less aggressive, less demanding. We are able to show the story of the case without overreaching or arguing, and in doing so, we build credibility with the jury and continue to develop the connection and relationship that began in voir dire.

Women tend to connect with others quickly and in a nonconfrontational way. This means the jury is more likely to listen with an open heart and an open mind. Chief Carla Provost, the first woman chief of the United States Border Patrol, told *Politico Magazine* in November 2017 that she found that, many times, she had an advantage over her male colleagues. She explained that in a high-stress, high-stakes situation, her being a woman tended to have a calming and facilitating effect. She also talks about the advantage she had being a female law enforcement officer and encountering people who expected to see a man, particularly in the U.S. Border Patrol, where women comprise only about five percent of all agents. Sometimes being a woman disarms your audience in a good way.

From our nonbiased, totally neutral mentor, friend, and husband Nick Rowley:

> Brutal honesty, women have more credibility than men in a courtroom. The opening statement is the most important part of the case after voir dire. It is a time to present the case to the jury in the most credible way. I have asked Courtney and Theresa to do openings on cases we are trying together because they have huge credibility in front of the jury. Our friend Brittan Cortney did an opening on one of my cases when she first started working with us. People trust what women have to say more than they do men if the women speaking say it in a professional tone and back up what they have to say with facts and evidence. Toe

to toe with equal skills and experience and equal facts and evidence, a woman will beat a man every time.

Practicing with Courtney is awesome. It was great before we were a couple, when we were best friends, and now it's hit a new level. She does have a better name now, and that certainly is a boost. But, seriously, having my wife and best friend up doing an opening statement or any other part of the trial, well it's just the best thing ever. And juries just love her, more than me actually, and they love me more because of her. I have never seen anybody who has more credibility in a courtroom than Courtney, and I would not say that if it weren't true.

Beginning and Maintaining Connection

Connections, just like relationships, require work to be maintained. You took time to build connections with your jury pool in voir dire. Don't abandon them now! Those connections should grow during opening statement. You have to start with the right mindset. Explain what the evidence will show and deliver that information in a way that is understandable, relatable, succinct, and engaging. How? By telling a story.

Always start out slow. By doing so, you can better connect and capture your audience. When you take the time to make this happen, you can soon be off and running because the jury is with you. It's important to check in with the jurors as you move forward or speed up your pace. Even though they cannot reply to your opening, you want to be sure that the opening is a story and a conversation, that you are talking *with* the jurors and not just at them.

The Bird on a Wire Perspective

The *bird on a wire* technique is about taking a scene in the story of your case and presenting it in a way that the judge, adjustor, or jury—whomever your audience is—can have an experience and feeling of actually being in the moment that you're talking about. We tell part of the story of our case from the perspective of a bird on a telephone wire or power line. What would that bird see, up above it all? The bird would see who did what, in what order, and how. Just the facts. Not arguing. Not pushing the boundaries of "what the evidence will show." When we tell part of our story that way, the jury is shown that moment as though they were there.

You want to bring your audience to the scene. Think of it like going to a movie. If your friend sees a movie and tells you about it, you listen and create pictures in your mind to go with what you're being told. For example, if your friend says there was a murderer walking through this big house looking for children, your mind will pull up an image of what a big house looks like to you, based on your life experience, and what the murderer in the movie probably looked like, and your mind will make up information, like where the children were and what they were doing. If you actually saw the movie yourself and had the experience of watching the murderer walk through the big house and look for children, the picture could be very different. For example, maybe this movie scene took place in an abandoned English manor that used to be an orphanage and the murderer was actually a ghost that was wandering the halls of the empty orphanage. That's probably a different picture than what you had in your mind. And it would create a different experience for you.

The goal is to present the evidence as efficiently and effectively as possible so that we honor the court's time and the jurors' time. One way to do that is to bring the jury right to the heart of a scene. Put them there and let them watch the movie instead of being told about it.

The advanced or elevated version of this bird-on-the-wire technique is to create a scene in the courtroom. You don't just tell the story; you turn the courtroom into a scene from the story and put our audience in the position of being there, observing for themselves what happened on a particular day.

For a liability scene in a civil case, you could turn the courtroom into the scene of a crash (or if it's a criminal case, the scene of an alleged crime). You can use this technique for a damages scene as well.

Theresa:

I was giving an opening statement in a brain injury case. As with all brain injury cases, the way to understand the damages is to understand what parts of the brain control different behaviors and what happens when those parts of the brain are injured. For that case, I turned the courtroom into a brain and described what each part of the brain did. The frontal lobes, which control our executive functions and decision-making and put the brake pedal on our emotions, were in the front of the court where the judge sits. The temporal lobes, part of where we store our memories and find words, were on each side of the courtroom, including in the jury box. The parietal lobe, which controls how we navigate our bodies in space, was where the lawyers sat and where they would stand up and move around and handle evidence and question witnesses. And the occipital lobe, which takes in visual images and starts to make sense of what we're seeing, was in the back of the courtroom, where the doors were (with small windows so people could see into the courtroom). Assigning a physical space to these parts of the brain and explaining what the brain parts do made it easier for the jury to understand a very complicated topic and made them part of a scene from our story.

The bird-on-a-wire technique is one that you can start using today in your cases. You can use it in your demand letters to draw the reader into the experience. You can use it in depositions to set a liability or damages scene. You can use it with your experts or even a treating physician in deposition.

Unexpected Sequencing

Another technique we use is unexpected sequencing. We can build anticipation by changing the sequencing of our story. Some of the best movies start with a scene that grabs our attention. Then they take us back to the beginning to show us how we got there. Not all stories have to be told chronologically. In *Trial by Human*, Nick Rowley calls this technique *Pulp Fiction* sequencing.[1] By removing some of the predictability, we give the jurors more incentive to engage in the story.

Consider the ideas of *primacy* and *recency*. People are going to remember what they heard first (primacy) and what they heard most recently (recency). Whether it's an opening, a presentation, or instructions, people tend to remember the first thing they hear and the last thing they hear better than what is said in between. That means you have a window of opportunity when you stand up to give your opening. You have their attention. Don't waste it on something meaningless, like small talk, or introductions, or the date ("It was August 4, 2017…").

Begin at the heart of your story with the rules that were broken, the conduct that caused the damage, the theme of your case. Give the jury the most important piece of the case that you want them to remember. Then say, "Now let me tell you what happened in this case . . ." and tell your story.

---

[1] Nicholas Rowley and Steven Halteman, *Trial by Human* (Portland: Trial Guides, 2013).

If you want to learn more about sequencing, *Rules of the Road* by Rick Friedman is invaluable.[2] No matter what area of law you practice, it will help you frame your case and focus on what's most important.

The Undersell

There are some views that the lawyer shouldn't be an advocate during opening. We don't agree. From the moment you walk into the courtroom, it is your job to advocate for your client and tell your story. That means that you are moving the ball down the field from the first time you speak. Keep finding ways to get your themes in front of the jury. But do it while still maintaining your credibility and following the rules.

If you want credibility, don't overreach. In fact, *undersell* your case in the opening. Many times, we feel we need to try to cram in all of our very best facts in the opening out of fear of losing. The result is we build up the shiniest, rosiest case we possibly can, and then, for the rest of the trial, we struggle like hell to prove it. You have to be able to back up everything you say in opening. Trial is a battle of credibility. So if you are the one setting your own bar, why not lower it a bit so you can exceed it?

Have the confidence in your cases to cut out what you don't need. Before trial even starts, some of the best decisions we've made are the ones where we cut out pieces of our case. Claims, aspects of damages, entire back surgeries, all economics, you name it. Don't carry dead weight into the courtroom. The more you can streamline your case and streamline your story, the better the likelihood that (a) it will be understood and (b) you will keep your credibility.

Once you've cut out the pieces of your case that you don't need, take some of your good stuff out of opening to leave for trial. Leave

---

[2] Rick Friedman and Patrick Malone, *Rules of the Road: A Plaintiff Lawyer's Guide to Proving Liability*, 2nd ed. (Portland: Trial Guides, 2010).

the jurors some surprises! Stories with surprises are more interesting and allow the jurors to have a more interactive (read: engaging) experience. A good start is to go through your opening and cross out all the adverbs. Then take a step back, and take a hard look at what you can and cannot prove (with 100 percent confidence) and edit accordingly. In storytelling, it's important to know your punch line. When we overemphasize emotions, we set ourselves up for a lot more work. When we undersell in the opening, there are still punch lines for the jury throughout the trial.

In some cases, for example, we don't go through all of the individual damages in opening. We leave that for the doctors and the lay witnesses to do on the stand. Instead, we give a brief overview of the damages, tell the jurors how much we are asking for, and then sit down. This gives us the opportunity to add color and richness with witnesses and stories throughout the trial.

For example, on a wrongful death case of a Chinese immigrant, along with our pal, Cortney Shegherian, we represented the adult children of the man who was killed. Our clients were very uncomfortable talking about themselves; in their culture it was not something they were used to doing. One of the children had a story about her father teaching her to cook. It was one of her most precious moments with her father. In fact, when we met her and her family, she cooked us a giant meal of all of her father's favorite foods and recipes. In opening, we talked about the different elements of damages, but we left that story for the client to tell. In her very few words, the love and the honor and the admiration of her father poured out of her and lit up the courtroom. It was beautiful, and surprising. Because of that, the jury got to have that experience for themselves, in the moment.

Another reason it helps to undersell your case in opening is that trial, like life, does not always go as planned. Actually, the truth is trial never goes as planned. That's why we are junkies. It is an organic unfolding, and a lot of times what we think will come out in testimony doesn't and vice versa. Giving yourself that space in opening pays off.

Any extra goodness that comes out becomes gravy, instead of the life or death of the case.

When you allow jurors to uncover facts on their own, you elevate their experience. Human beings are more likely to trust their own experience. Also, you give the defense a little less of a chance to prepare for what's coming. As our good friend Amy Solomon says, "Keep your powder dry." By setting the bar a little lower for yourself, you may find that you have a little less pressure throughout the trial and more ammo for when you need it. Bottom line: if you can make your life easier, we say go for it.

Be the Most Reasonable

Be the most reasonable person in the room. The most reasonable *woman* in the room. If there is something you can give on, GIVE. Whenever you have the opportunity to admit the shortcomings in your own case, to acknowledge where your side falls short, do it. To find the shortcomings, go through your case and look for the parts you don't like, the ones you want to hide. Those are the pieces we are talking about.

At the end of the opening, you want the jury to say to themselves, "Hey, this is a big deal. I'm here for a reason. This lawyer is honest, thorough, methodical, and entertaining; she knows her case. This lawyer is an authority on this case. But she is also fair. She is not unreasonable. She is being straight with me." You want to find that balance in your presentation of the story—that credibility. You can do it by being honest about the case: owning what is yours.

For example, in civil work we sometimes establish balance by using the theme of "shared responsibility." In a case where the plaintiff we were representing was a child who rode his bike into the street and was hit by a bus, we knew the crux of the liability case was going to be about whether or not our client "darted out." We knew that the evidence would show that yes, he did, but no, that does not mean it was his fault. Instead of hiding from this fact, we handed it right over to the jury in opening:

> This is a case about shared responsibility. He should not have been riding his bike on the sidewalk, and he admits that. But the driver of that bus, she should have looked right before driving through that crosswalk. Yet the defense here, they are claiming no responsibility. Zero.
>
> If you can own what your client did was wrong, you set yourself apart and above the other side that is unwilling to do the same. You build credibility. It's always better to give a little than to lose it all.

And it makes you reasonable. When the other side does what most lawyers do—goes all or nothing—you become the reasonable one, and you earn trust.

Be in the Moment

Being in the present moment is powerful. There is no gift we can give that is more precious than our presence and our attention. Our physical presence, if our minds are somewhere else, means very little. When we are here, now, we are honest, clear, and better able to convey our thoughts and emotions to other human beings.

What does that look like? Giving eye contact. Taking the time to communicate directly with the individual jurors. Joshua Karton is a fantastic resource for being present. One of his exercises is practicing holding a mock juror's hand while you make a point, and then reaching out and holding the next mock juror's hand before you start making your next point. What he is teaching is connection—true, live connection. One of the things we do when we are uncomfortable and anxious—not present—is shotgun-spray our eye contact. We glass over and pepper the jury with our eyes and words. We do so to protect ourselves from our own fear of failure, of rejection. We end up closing ourselves off and blocking the emotional exchange that is required to connect and convey our story.

If you want to get more comfortable talking with people, then practice. Make the world your laboratory. Talk to strangers. Give eye contact. Make connection. Find comfort in the silences. You can do this out in the world, and you can run focus groups. When you get comfortable connecting out in the world, it becomes second nature, and it is seamless in the courtroom. What's more, we have found that getting comfortable communicating doesn't just improve our experience in the courtroom, it improves our lives. Cultivating communication skills is a lifelong practice that enriches your relationships with others and with yourself.

One of the hurdles to communication is insecurity. ==Confidence is not some gene that is out of our control; it is like a muscle that we can work, grow, and strengthen.== So, we practice. The simplest way to do this is to get out into the world and communicate with strangers. The next time you are in line at the grocery store, ordering coffee, out for a hike, or waiting at the doctor's office, connect with another person. Say hello, ask her a question, maybe even get a little racy and ask about something other than the weather. Look into her eyes, breathe slowly and deeply; consciously relax your body. Imagine what the world would be like if we all reached out a little more, genuinely, generously.

Want to get crazy? Like the stoic Seneca, consciously put yourself in an uncomfortable situation. In doing so, you raise your own tolerance for discomfort. Ask someone if you can have a dollar. Not borrow. Or, as suggested by Tim Ferriss, walk into a coffee shop and lie down on the floor for one minute. You might not have to go to those extremes, but if you do, standing up in front of twelve people will be a piece of cake.

We Can, and Must, Out-Prepare Our Opponents

We both had trial coaches in law school who were dedicated to training students to be the best trial lawyers. Their dedication wasn't to win awards for the school. It was to build great trial lawyers for the world. Our coaches demanded hard work, grit, confidence, dedication, and accountability. The single most valuable lesson each of us learned from our respective trial coaches is that preparation is the key to success.

This is not about charm, charisma, storytelling, or the elusive brilliance that some of these great winning trial lawyers have. This is about ugly, messy, down-in-the-trenches preparation—reading every piece of paper in the file, deciding which evidence should be excluded, preparing witness lists and evidence lists, preparing a statement of the case, seeing themes emerge as you read the file, seeing the story of the case come together in your head as you read and prepare, understanding what each witness will say beyond what is in his deposition, anticipating every move your opponent will make. By knowing your case through and through, you become the authority on the case. When you are the one who knows everything about a case, you start taking ownership. Then you become the one the jury wants to follow.

This is true in a lot of contexts. When you have a business project or a school curriculum or a surgery, preparation translates to authority. It breeds confidence. And confidence is irresistible.

- Read the discovery—all of it, including your own answers.
- Do your homework on the experts. Look them up on the internet and ask other lawyers for their resources and experiences with those experts.

- When you get the exhibit binder for the other side—GO THROUGH IT. It's a treasure trove of everything you can expect and, almost always, a whole bunch you didn't.
- Know the depositions—don't just read them.
- Put the time in with your clients by going to their homes, having them to yours, and sharing meals.

Every ounce of your work will shine through in your opening and give you more credibility.

Early on, when we started doing brain injury cases, neither of us knew a lot about how the brain actually worked. We had a case with a little girl who had suffered a brain injury when she was hit while riding her bike in a crosswalk. Along with getting violent with her mother and shutting herself in her room, she was having problems with hygiene. So, we sat down with the expert neurologist in the case, and he educated us about brain injury and how injury to certain lobes of the brain causes certain symptoms. Our client's injury to her frontal lobe meant she had less control over her behavior and emotions, was sensitive to sound and light, and had an impaired sense of smell, so she didn't notice her own. Eureka! It all made sense!

- Be curious.
- Ask questions.
- Seek out experts.
- Get answers.
- Prepare to the fullest extent.

Theresa's Opening Preparation Routine

Go to War with Your Doubts

Trial is war, no doubt. But the war isn't always or only against our opponent. If we're really honest, the war is against our own fears and doubts. Do you ever notice how doubt hits when you suddenly realize *that you are trying this case or you are giving the opening statement or you are arguing the motions* in limine *or you are examining a really important witness or you are making the closing argument*? As much as you want to do it, suddenly, your mind is about to explode with overwhelming thoughts of self-doubt. *I shouldn't be the one making the opening statement. I'm not experienced enough. I don't try enough cases. I'm not good enough. I'm not a good enough trial lawyer. I'm not really a trial lawyer at all.*

You have to win this war against your own doubts before you step into the courtroom. The way you win the war is through love. We all have these thoughts and feelings sometimes. That's normal. But the thoughts you're having aren't true, not even a little. If you are in a position to be trying any part of a case, then you are enough.

The best way I've found to keep these thoughts from creeping in is a daily meditation practice. Even a few minutes a day can teach you to better control your mind, your feelings, and your actions. You can become an *observer* of your thoughts rather than an *experiencer* of them. You learn to separate the thoughts that don't honor and promote you from the ones that do. And the power in that is astounding.

Before I started meditating, I thought it would be hard or a little too hippie-dippie for me. After years of practicing yoga, I still can't keep my mind from wandering in class—how could I sit still and think about nothing? A person must have to be really enlightened and not busy to be able to do that, I thought. That's not me. I have two kids; I have a husband; I run a household; I run a business; I have to buy groceries. I'd be missing out on valuable planning time by *not thinking!*

Wow, was I wrong. Meditation takes all of the random thoughts in my mind and clears them out. After I meditate, as the thoughts drift back in, they make more sense and are more organized and less frantic. I feel refreshed and better able to make a coherent *plan* for the day ahead. I feel calmer. There's not a mad rush to get my kids dressed and ready for the day. I have a plan. I know when that's going to happen. And I know that it will happen. That's probably the biggest thing. There's no unreasonable fear that my kids are going to be in their pj's all day with dirty teeth and with breakfast smeared on their faces. Because I know and trust that I'll accomplish all that I need to in this day.

And all of that happens from just five to ten minutes of meditating. I make it easy and use the Calm app. Others use Headspace; Stop, Breathe & Think; or Omvana. You can choose a guided meditation if you're just getting started; or, you can choose a timed meditation that you do on your own with nature sounds in the background. It is time well spent.

Video Is Your Best Coach

If you want the truth about how you look, how your voice sounds, whether you talk with your hands too much, and generally how you present yourself—video yourself! This has been the most effective tool I have ever used, and it started back in my television reporting days. The news was recorded every night; so, after we put on a show, I would come back to the station from my live report in the field and watch my segment. I would analyze how I looked, how I sounded, whether my clothes or makeup or hair was distracting (that is, if I noticed it, it was distracting), how fast or slow I spoke, how loud or quiet my voice was, whether my pitch was high or low, whether I looked stiff or relaxed, and whether I told a compelling story. Then, when I had a segment that I thought I did a really good job on, I would take the video to every other reporter whom I admired and thought was better than me and ask them for their feedback. That's how I learned and how I got better.

I follow the same practice as a lawyer. I set up my iPhone and start recording a video of myself as I work through my opening from start to finish. I don't say, "Whoops, I messed up. Let me start over." I don't stop the video when I say something I don't like and then start again. I go through the opening from start to finish. And then I watch it. I notice where my voice isn't full or where I make a weird hand gesture. Then I do it again and fix those things. I keep doing it until I eliminate the distracting habits and make sure that I'm using my voice, my body, and my movement to tell the best story I can tell. I'm not so much practicing *what* I'm going to say as much as *how* I'm going to say it. Our voices, our bodies, the way we use the space in the courtroom, are incredibly important to the story we're telling. As lawyers, if we're just writing a script to follow in court, we're missing one of the most powerful components of the storytelling—ourselves as the storytellers.

Let the Jury Light the Fire

Less is more, always. Openings can be thorough and meticulous. But they never should be repetitive. Keeping a story entertaining means keeping it fresh. When we repeat ourselves and keep mowing the same field, we suck the life out of the story and take our listeners out of the moment.

If you represent the plaintiff, you want the jury at the end of the opening to be ready to burn all the defendants at the proverbial stake. But we want to hold off on lighting the fire. We want to have the defendants all tied up and ready, matches waiting. But we still have to prove our case first.

The goal of the opening is to provide a full road map for the jurors. You become the authority on the case by addressing all aspects, good and bad, and by doing so fairly. Then you sequence your trial to match up with your opening. Use the first witness to back up your opening, point by point. Sometimes that's an adverse witness. You have laid out your promises to the jury of what you will prove, and you are going to honor every single promise. If you're unsure about any one of your promises, leave it out of the opening.

At the end of the opening, you should have laid out the kindling with the logs on top; all your opponent's arguments are neatly arranged and ready for the bonfire. But you don't light the match. Instead, you hand it to the jury. That way, as you connect your trial evidence to your opening, you let the jury light each one of the defense's arguments up and burn them to the ground.

Read David Ball

The bible on opening statements is David Ball's *David Ball on Damages*.[3] He and his partner Artemis Malekpour have made it their life's work to help trial lawyers do the very best job for their clients by providing the tools and guidance they need to try cases. But even if you aren't trying cases, *Damages* is a valuable resource. It is a handbook on the anatomy of a lawsuit.

It's also helpful if you work in criminal cases. It's the best and most thorough outline of presenting a case to a jury. Whether you are a young attorney or simply looking to improve your practice, you need it.

---

[3] David Ball, "Opening Statement," in *David Ball on Damages*, 3rd ed. (Portland: Trial Guides, 2010).

Opening Is a Road Map, Not Evidence

Lastly, many judges will explain to the jury that your opening is a road map. All judges will make sure, consistent with the law, to tell the jury that nothing we as attorneys say is evidence. We believe in bringing that into context right away and embracing the words the jury is going to hear over and over again by telling them at the beginning of opening:

> Nothing we say is evidence, just like nothing the judge says is evidence, and nothing the jurors say to each other when they deliberate is evidence. But the human voice and advocacy for what we believe in is one of the most important things about our justice system. We are the voice for our clients. We are standing before the jury because, without our voice, there would be no justice. Without the voice of the jury, there would be no justice, but it's not evidence.

So, it is with that in mind that we respectfully acknowledge what the judge says, embrace it, and then ask our jury to please listen to every word we have to say.

> Please pay close attention and see if what we lawyers say matches up to the true story of what happened here.

Each Case, and Lawyer, Is Different

There are many resources and conflicting schools of thought on how to open. What is important is that we have fun, we learn and consider them all, and we find what fits. We must always remember that every case is different. The way we need to open on one case may differ from how we open on the next. Good storytelling and sequencing are what let us do this and are the most important skills to learn to get good at this part of trial.

Opening statement is your chance to establish credibility with the jury, and you do that by being brutally honest about your case and all its flaws, by underselling your case, and by trusting your jurors.

You don't have to be the most talented, the shiniest, the smartest to win. You can out-prepare the other side by knowing your case better than anyone in the courtroom. Video yourself. Fight the war of self-doubt by finding something to center yourself, be it meditation, hiking, or lying down in a coffee shop. Practice these communication and storytelling techniques in your day-to-day life and you will have more confidence when it's time to get in front of a jury.

Remember, we don't tell the jury what to think, we give them the evidence of the case so that they can draw their own conclusions. Opening is where you lay out the kindling, and we trust that the jury will light the fire. That is opening statement by woman.

Opening outside the Courtroom

What if you're not giving an opening statement tomorrow? What can you start doing tomorrow to give yourself more of a Trial Perspective approach? Try the bird-on-a-wire technique in your next demand letter or deposition. In a demand letter, for example, choose a moment in the case and communicate it to the adjustor from the bird-on-a-wire perspective. The reader is immediately taken out of defensive mode and inserted into the experience of the story, and that is powerful. In a PMK (Person Most Knowledgeable) or 30(b)(6) deposition, have the witness tell you from a bird-on-a-wire perspective what *should* have happened if the safety rules had been followed. You'll have a beautiful picture to contrast with what actually happened in an injury case, for example.

Chapter Takeaways

- Opening is about building credibility, and you're the best one to do it.
- A woman's place is opening the case.
- Use the bird-on-a-wire perspective.
- Be in the moment.

16

Direct and Cross-Examination by Woman

Direct and cross-examination are two parts of trial where you can shine and bring your feminine energy into the courtroom. Don't let your fears, your worries, or the idea that only experienced lawyers can do this hold you back. You got this.

Direct Examination

Direct examination is a part of the trial that most of us need to spice up. You are calling witnesses who are under your control and/or favorable to the stand, and some lawyers even rehearse their questions with the witness or client in advance. We do not do that. But even without rehearsing questions, direct exam can feel somewhat rehearsed and, frankly, can feel a little stiff and boring sometimes. Jurors almost always perk up on cross-examination because there is a little tension and a chance that something exciting might happen. You can feel that energy in the courtroom. The trick is bringing some of that energy to direct.

So, let's talk about some ways to make direct a little more exciting.

Cross-Examination in Direct

We use a technique on direct examination where we cross our own witness. We call it the "Hold On a Minute, Let's Keep This Real" approach.

It's easy to put on a pretty show on direct. You ask the good questions and get the good answers from a compliant and agreeable witness. However, when you do that, when you paint a pretty picture and you leave out the ugly parts that you know are going to come out later, it looks like you're hiding something. How do you keep things from getting too pretty? Jump in and keep it real. Here's what it looks like:

Q: How's your life different now?

A: I can't walk anymore.

Q: Hold on, are you saying you can't walk anymore at all?

A: Well, no, I can walk.

Q: How is it different? Tell us what you meant.

A: It's not the same as before. I can only walk from my car to the grocery store entrance, and I have to sit down. I skip most of the grocery aisles now and just get what I need that's closest to the entrance so I can get back to my car as quick as possible.

When you inject some cross into your direct, you're answering the questions the jury has. If you're tuned in and present in the moment, and you're really listening to the answers your witness is giving you, follow-up questions will naturally arise. It's our job as leaders in the courtroom to ask the follow-up questions and get the answers. An unanswered question hanging out there is a distraction. Think about that from your own perspective. When you have a question to ask, and you can't ask it, you keep thinking about the question and what the possible answers could be, and you're no longer focused on what's happening in front of you. You're no longer focused on what's being said to you. As lawyers who lead in the courtroom, if we ask the follow-up questions as they arise, we're honoring and respecting the jury.

Using the cross-in-direct technique also keeps things from getting too pretty and forces you to own all of your case—not just the good parts. Owning the good and bad parts of your case continues to build your credibility in the courtroom with the jury and the judge. It's sexy. It takes some of the sass out of the defense when they cross-examine your witness. When you take the "gotcha" moment from your opponent, you take the power of the "gotcha" moment.

Show-and-Tell

Another technique we use to make direct come more alive is Show-and-Tell. We use the witness's testimony to create an image that brings a moment of our story into the courtroom. In auto crash cases, if liability is an issue, we set up the physical scene of the crash in the courtroom. In injury cases, we have the medical witness take us inside the body to understand the parts of the body that were injured, the significance of those parts, and even how those injuries were corrected with surgery.

Direct Examination outside the Courtroom

What if you're not in trial and doing a direct examination tomorrow? What can you start doing now to give yourself a better Trial Perspective approach? Try using the "Hold On a Minute, Let's Keep Things Real" technique in a deposition. When a witness says something that's too perfect, too pretty, or doesn't acknowledge less-than-ideal facts that we know are already out there in the litigation, guide the witness down the path of keeping things real. Or try the show-and-tell technique in deposition. Ask a medical witness, for example, to demonstrate or use a model to create a visual of what happened. That's direct examination by woman.

Cross-Examination

Everyone, it seems, has a firm opinion on how to conduct a cross-examination.

- Don't get in the cage with an expert.
- Get in the cage with the expert.
- You'll always lose an argument about medicine with an expert.
- You can win an argument about medicine with an expert.
- You don't need to know the medicine.
- You need to know the medicine.
- Just get in and get out.
- Take all afternoon.
- Don't get angry.
- Tear them up.
- You win or lose your case in cross.
- Cross doesn't matter.

Heard any of these tips before? Us too. All of them.

Cross, for us, has been the part of trial that we were least confident about for the longest time. We have found very little instruction on cross over the years, and what is taught tends to be geared toward either how to imitate the styles of others (generally older men) or how not to get hurt (too badly) doing it. Above all, the problem we found was all the conflicting information about how to conduct a cross-examination. Frankly, when we tried to figure out the rules to follow for cross, we couldn't get a straight answer. The story we were sold was: it's really hard to do a good cross. (Read: This isn't something you'll do well for a really long time; so, you might as well give up before you even start or just let an *experienced* lawyer handle that part of your case for you.)

If you think about it, can that really be true? Is it really true that there is a single element of a trial that is so difficult to perform that only certain people are even capable of doing a decent job at it? Unlikely.

What is it about cross-examination that strikes fear into the hearts of trial lawyers and makes our underarms get moist? What people fear about cross is that it's the only part of trial for which there is no script. While we don't recommend it, it's very common practice for lawyers to script out voir dire, opening, all of their direct examinations, closing argument, and even rebuttal. But cross is dynamic. It's you, interacting with a witness, and you can't control what that person will say. The witness could say something that hurts your case. So, the fear of cross is the fear of losing control of your trial. If you take control of the cross-examination, you have nothing to fear. We'll show you exactly how to do that, and, along the way, we'll show you how the law is actually designed to make cross-examination easy. So, dab your underarms and let's get going.

Successful Cross Is about Control

The secret to a successful cross-examination is control. We can control a witness by making very short statements and asking the witness to agree. And the law was actually written to make cross easy for us. Cross is the only time in trial that we're allowed to ask leading questions, which are questions that suggest the answer.

Q: Mr. Smith, your corporation does not have any policy requiring a driving record check before giving an employee a corporate truck; correct?

That's not a question we can ask on direct.

We know from Mr. Smith's deposition and discovery responses that he will agree with that statement because he already said it under oath. That's another way the law helps make cross-examination easy for us: discovery. Cross isn't seeming as scary or hard after all, is it?

When we look at cross as a series of statements that we already know the witness will agree with, it shifts from being an intimidating exercise in trying to outwit the witness, to being a simple, clean, much-less-scary exercise in ticking off points you have to make to prove your case.

And while you could simply write out the five or ten points you need to make with a witness on cross, we like to kick it up a notch by not just ticking off points, but *storytelling*.

How do you make this work for you? Write out the simple story you want to tell with this witness. We tell our story from big picture to small picture, meaning, we start with the macro, big concept (*It's important to be complete when writing a police report*) and end with the most important point we want to make with this witness (*The fact that

Mr. Jones was seen drinking two martinis in less than forty minutes, an hour before this crash, is not in your report, is it Officer?).

Here's an example of a simple story:

> A hospital is somewhere people go to get help. You work in a hospital. You work in the ER. Most people who come into the ER are coming because it's an emergency. Hence the name. So you are used to working in high-pressure environments. You have to think on your feet. Your job is to assess the patient as quickly as possible. You need to determine whether they need lifesaving medical attention. And to do this, you have protocols. One of those protocols is the Glasgow Coma Scale. That's where you assess how conscious someone is. The Glasgow Coma Scale is one tool to help you figure out whether someone has a brain injury. And you didn't use the Glasgow Coma Scale to assess Ms. Johnson.

You can then break it down into as few statements as you can. The simpler the better. Then, if you're practicing civil law, you go back and match each statement with a statement made in deposition, page and line number, or something you have in a medical record or other exhibit, so that you have the resources you need to impeach the witness if he tells a lie or disagrees. In criminal, you can do this with exhibits if you have them.

Here's the story broken into individual statements:

Q: A hospital is somewhere people go to get help, correct?

Q: You work in a hospital?

Q: You work in the ER?

Q: Most people who come into the ER are coming because it's an emergency?

Q: So you are used to working in high-pressure environments?

And so on.

The point is, with every statement, you are building toward a major point with your witness. If a statement doesn't advance the story directly toward your point, eliminate it. With this tight building, you will reach a point in your cross where the witness and the jurors see exactly where you're going, and no one can do anything to stop it. Together, we're all barreling toward the fact that the police officer didn't include in his report Mr. Jones's statement that he had been drinking earlier that night, or the fact that the doctor didn't evaluate Ms. Johnson using the Glasgow Coma Scale. Since you've worked from big picture to small, narrowing your focus with each statement, you've already established that there was a protocol, that the protocol was important, and that it wasn't followed here. The point that you don't have to make is "and that was a bad, bad thing."

Preparation Is a Key Element of Control

We write our trial cross-examinations in advance, short statement by short statement. Beside each short statement, we write the deposition page and line or discovery where the statement was previously made. Use whatever medium you prefer. If we are really organized, it's typed out; otherwise it's on our legal pad.

We are ready with the deposition transcript or discovery response or other exhibit to impeach the witness if he suddenly decides not to agree with the statement.

If the witness changes his testimony, you impeach him. Impeaching a witness means that you use the witness's sworn deposition or sworn discovery or other exhibit to expose the witness's inconsistent story or lie.

Courtney:

> I was cross-examining a nurse in a medical malpractice case where a young mother died because the doctor failed to give her the epinephrine she needed to reverse a severe adverse reaction to contrast dye. During the cross, the nurse blurted out a new and significant fact that was very helpful to the defense's theory of (non) liability. Fortunately, I had done my homework and was able to show that not only did she not mention this fact in her deposition two years prior, but she also stated the opposite in the notes she authored the day this took place. I'm a super-nervous crosser, so I keep page and line references under each topic I plan to cover (Susan Poehls you are my hero). When something like this happens, I know exactly where to go. Sometimes, if I'm neurotic enough, I even add page and line numbers to the "background section." For example, "What's your name? (13:1-6)"—that's usually a good indication that I've gone overboard.

Impeachment only works if there's a real inconsistency or lie or change of testimony. Don't argue over semantics. You always want an impeachment to be on point. How do you know if it's on point? Because it is different or opposite from what the person said in deposition, in the medical records, in the police report, in a statement, in the affidavit, and so on. Second, get in and get out. You need to have the evidence in hand. And you need to know what to say next. Here's what we say:

Q: Sir, you gave a deposition in this case on [whatever] date?

Q: And you gave that deposition under oath?

Q: You had a chance to check that deposition after to make sure it was a full and fair representation of what you said?

Q: And you signed that deposition on [whatever] date?

Q: Your honor, may I approach the witness?

Q: That's your signature right there, Sir?

Q: Your Honor, I'd like to read from this witness's deposition page X, line X through page Y, line Y.

Then you read the testimony and move on to your next question. Although you may be tempted to jump up on the table and shout out something like, "See? See you liar-face?" or "So were you lying then or are you LYING NOW?!?" like you've seen in the movies. Don't do it. The jury heard it. They always do. Let *them* get pissed at the liar-face. You, the cool cat that you are, keep going with your next point. Also, we never want to give the witness a chance to *explain*. Next leading question/statement. Proceed.

Know When to Stop

When we finish, we sit down. In almost all settings, but especially on cross, it's important to know when to stop. As we learned from Aristotle, stories should have a beginning, a middle, and an end. Ideally, your cross-examination should be structured so that when you reach your main point, your punch line, you are finished, and you sit down. Leave the jury with that point.

Remember, it only takes one witness to prove a fact in most jurisdictions. But if you are making the point, for example, that there was a systemic failure, that is, that everyone knew about a rule and chose not to follow it, you would be justified in calling multiple witnesses to say they knew the rule and ignored it. But it is 100 percent unnecessary to go through your entire list of questions again with each witness. ==Just establish who they are, make your point that they knew the rule and didn't follow it, and call your next witnes==s.

Let's use our Glasgow Coma Scale example from above. With your first witness, you would go through the cross as we've written it above. When you call your next witness, it would look similar to this:

Q: Sir, you were working in the City ER on [whatever] date?

Q: And you evaluated Ms. Johnson?

Q: You were aware she had an injury to her head?

Q: You were aware that at the City ER, one of the protocols was to use the Glasgow Coma Scale to determine whether a patient has a brain injury?

Q: And you didn't use the Glasgow Coma Scale to assess Ms. Johnson; correct?

Going through the same details, over and over with every single witness is cumulative and will bore the jury. If you spend one-and-a-half hours methodically questioning one witness and the next witness says the same thing, based on the same inaccurate assumptions that you have already exposed, trust that the jury gets it and you can cross-examine the second witness in five minutes. Have faith in your jurors.

They are intelligent human beings that are paying attention. They heard you, and they get it.

We find that in this technological age of instant gratification and short attention spans, ours included, juries appreciate when we move it along. Respect their time by being mindful of when you can shorten your examinations or even eliminate witnesses instead of risking repeating yourself.

Lead by Example

Cross-examination is adversarial by nature, but it doesn't have to be antagonistic. Speaking in broad generalizations here, most women are nonconfrontational. This means when we are in a high-stress situation, a couple of things could happen that will not advance our cross.

- One, we can get angry.
- Two, we can get emotionally reactive.
- Three, our voices can jump into our throats and become shrill.
- Four, we can lose our voices and get really meek.

This is where having a centering practice like meditation or Kundalini yoga—two of our favorites—can help. These practices, which we will talk about later in the book, train you to develop a place of calm centeredness that you can immediately go to and draw on when your body or mind kicks you into crisis mode. This is exactly the type of reserve you need to draw on when you're in cross.

Instead of giving up control, catch yourself. Center yourself. Get back to your baseline and remember that you have a goal and purpose with this witness.

We know it's hard. When we stand up to cross-examine our opposition's brilliant, board-certified expert in all things and he just dumped all over our case, we don't feel calm or centered. We want to react and attack or walk out the back door of the courtroom. It's easy to lose focus in those moments.

But here's the deal: we knew this was coming—months in advance. We knew exactly what those opinions were, and we prepared our cross as best we could anyway. We know our opponents are going to make good points with their witnesses. That's what trial is all about. And it's going to suck. Every. Time. However, it's our job to get centered, get up, and do what it is that we're there to do. Pick up all that hard work we've put in, take a look at that paper (our confidence), take a breath, and proceed with grace and decorum.

Rick Friedman, in his book *Becoming a Trial Lawyer,* said, "If the system were fair, we'd hardly be needed.... For us to complain about unfairness is like firefighters complaining there is too much smoke for them to put out the fire."[1]

Using Their Witnesses to Prove Your Case

Now that you've got the basics, let's kick it up a little bit. The number one way we use cross is to prove elements of our own case using our opponent's witnesses. In a civil case representing a plaintiff, for example, we call the defense witnesses first in our case, with very few exceptions. In California, you can cross-examine an adverse witness in your case-in-chief under Evidence Code section 776. That means you can use leading questions.

For example, in a case against a corporation or company, we call the safety manager first to establish that the company had certain safety rules in place. All employees were trained in these safety rules and expected to follow them, following the safety rules would have prevented

---

[1] Rick Friedman, Becoming a *Trial Lawyer: A Guide for the Lifelong Advocate*, 2nd ed. (Portland, OR: Trial Guides, 2015), 214.

our client from being injured, and, in this case, there was a failure in the system and the safety rules were not followed.

In a car crash case, we call the defendant driver first. We establish the story of how the crash happened and establish that our client did nothing to cause the crash and that the crash was the defendant's fault.

We don't spend a lot of time with background or setup with these witnesses. We establish who they are and what they're going to testify about, and then we get right into the substance of the cross.

The result is, right out of the gate, you've continued to build your credibility with the jury by proving what you said you'd prove in opening, *using your opponent's witnesses.* Sure you could, and you probably will, cover some of the same territory with your own witnesses down the line, but having the evidence come from your opponent's mouth makes the point much stronger.

A Little Fishing

Sometimes, it's good to break the rules. Here's an example of that. You've heard the oldest rule in the book: *Never ask a question you don't know the answer to.* We agree, but we'd add: *IF there is a potential answer that can hurt your case.*

This is the oldest rule of cross for a reason: cross-examination is not the time to conduct discovery. But, even though we want to construct our cross using leading questions and we want to have the witness's prior answers cross-referenced to the depositions, discovery, exhibits, and so on, if you're plugged into your intuition and you're not on autopilot, there are times where you might do a little "nonrecourse fishing."

For example, we've been in trials and examined opposing experts whose testimony had clearly been methodically prepared and likely rehearsed. If our gut tells us that this seems apparent to the jury too, we may dip a toe in the water:

Q: When did you and the lawyer who's paying you to be here today rehearse your testimony?

A: Over dinner.

Q: Who was there?

A: Another expert.

The defense lawyer starts objecting, further emphasizing the point. The more questions we ask about it, the more the witness starts to look strikingly like the cat who ate the canary. Of course, sometimes a witness has an epiphany over the lunch hour. We just like to know who was helping them pluck out the feathers first.

We want to avoid being too rigid, too stuck on rules and on dos and don'ts. You are a creative and interesting person. If, as you are listening to the direct, you hear something that you have a question about, chances are, someone on the jury feels the same way. The more prepared we are, the more we are able to be in the moment. If you have your statements prepared with their corresponding evidence, then you can sit back, listen to what that witness is saying on direct with fresh ears, and ask questions in the jurors' minds that aren't getting answered.

When you hear something fishy, don't let it just slip by because you don't know the answer. Evaluate it. Ask yourself, How far can the witness go, and could he hurt my case here, or is this something that doesn't make sense that I want to explore? Test the waters, statement by statement, nice and slow, and pull back and resume course if it doesn't pan out.

Discrediting the Witness Isn't the Goal

There is a misconception that cross-examination is all about discrediting the witness. That's all fine in a late-night TV crime show that has a bunch of writers who have scripted a dramatic outcome. In real life, the jury gives most of the witnesses who come to the stand the benefit of the doubt. Remember, jurors don't have any backstory. They don't know that a witness was a royal jerk in deposition. Jurors come in clean and evaluate what's being put in front of them. We will do better if we respect that witness as a human being as well. Most witnesses, especially experts, have a lot of credibility. When we attack the witness, we lose credibility.

If and when we encounter hostile witnesses, we have found that the calmer, more respectful we are, the nastier and dodgier they seem to get. We don't have to fight fire with fire and burn the courtroom down. Similarly, it's important to keep ourselves in check if we gain some ground or earn some points with a witty question or a particularly helpful admission. We can cross with grace and without humiliating or mocking the witness.

Different Crosses for Different Witnesses

In addition to making the points you know you can and must make to prove your case or disprove your opponent's claim, keep in mind that there's also a story going on in the background. There's a reason people do what they do, and that's the story that can become a theme in your case. Here are some examples of motivating factors that may apply in your case that you can incorporate into your cross.

The "Motivated by Money" Cross

Some experts have a lengthy history of being paid *for* their opinions rather than being paid to *offer* their opinions. With those witnesses, you can usually find ample evidence from prior cases, such as the following:

- how much the experts make
- what percentage of the experts' time is spent working in their industry versus working to give opinions to lawyers
- what percentage of the experts' income comes from working in their industry versus working for lawyers
- how many cases the experts have worked on
- How many times the experts have worked for the lawyer or firm that's paying them to be there in court
- how much money the experts have made from the lawyer or firm that's paying them to be there in court

One of the defenses in a civil case is that the plaintiff is bringing the case because she is motivated by money. But, in most cases, the defense experts are motivated by money. Expose that truth.[2]

Many experts are titans that lawyers call upon to destroy cases. For some of these lawyers and experts, things have gotten out of hand. Instead of having objective views, we find people who are motivated by the hand that feeds them. A lot of the time, the focus is on whether the expert does more plaintiff or defense work or more work for the prosecution or the criminal defense bar, but if we look at it from a

---

[2] Patrick Malone talks about how to do a fantastic cross-examination of a paid expert in chapter 11, "Shooting It Out with the Hired-Gun Witness" in his book, *The Fearless Cross-Examiner: Win the Witness, Win the Case* (Portland, OR: Trial Guides, 2016).

bird's-eye view, what we are dealing with are witnesses, paid experts, whose opinions are for sale.

This is a story that's set up in discovery and depositions before trial. Join your local trial lawyer groups and Listservs and get information on the experts and get prior deposition and trial transcripts. You'll find that the best lawyers out there—the successful lawyers, the experienced lawyers, the lawyers you want to learn from—want to share. They want to help you do well at your job. Because they know that there's enough room for us all to succeed and that the better we do as individuals, the better we do as a whole.

The "Expose the Faulty Foundation" Cross

An opinion has to be built upon a strong foundation in order for the opinion to be credible. A witness can be credible, a witness can be qualified, a witness can be a good person and a hero in the community, but if the foundation of the witness's opinion is faulty, the opinion is worthless. When we have that situation, our job is to systematically reveal the shaky ground upon which the expert's opinion is built. We don't need to destroy the witness or contradict the opinion. All we need to do is show that the foundation is unstable.

For example, you have a medical expert testifying that the defendant physician or nurse or other medical provider did not do anything that violated the standard of care.

Q: Dr. Johnson, your opinion is that the standard of care was not breached, correct?

Q: And that opinion is based on your review of the medical records?

Q: Reviewing the medical records, you didn't find any violation of the standard of care?

Q: Then you looked at the depositions of the medical doctors, correct?

Q: And you saw that they had no independent recollection of treating the patient?

Q: And their testimony was based solely on their review of the medical records?

Q: So the medical records are the only history of the case that you relied on?

Q: And it was the medical defendants here that wrote that history, true?

That can be the extent of your cross. And you show through other witnesses and your own experts how the medical records are inaccurate

The "Sympathetic Witness" Cross

Sometimes there are witnesses who are sympathetic or who don't hurt your case. If you think as a lawyer that you have to cross-examine every witness—you're wrong. This goes back to courtroom awareness and monitoring your own behavior.

Ask yourself:

- Did that witness hurt my case?
- Is there something I need to fix?

If the answer is no, then the next question is,

- Can this witness advance my case?

If the answer is yes, then the next question is,

- Is this witness the best person to advance my case, or can I get what I need from someone else who is going to be better?

For example, a mother gets on the stand and testifies on behalf of her adult son. Is it really necessary for you to stand up and point out that she's in a really tough position and that she's a biased witness because she loves her son? Or could you ask no questions and save that for closing argument?

Jurors appreciate it when we choose not to stand up and ask questions when it's not really necessary. It also shows that we are confident in our case.

Sometimes our opponent will call a witness that is either a complete waste of time or hurts her case. Why would we need to ask any questions? In most jurisdictions, we have jury instructions that say that the testimony of one witness is enough to prove a fact.

If something has been nailed down and established, our opponent is going to lose credibility by calling witnesses presenting evidence to contradict that which has already been established in the case.

Cross outside the Courtroom

Understanding cross-examination isn't helpful for trial only. These techniques and tools are invaluable as you are working up your case. Using a Trial Perspective approach as you take depositions, draft discovery, and especially respond to discovery, anticipating the cross from the other side, you build a better, more valuable, more winnable case. Also, understanding the goal of cross in trial is an invaluable aid when helping your clients and witnesses respond to discovery or prepare for deposition and when constructing and evaluating your case.

Deposition, for example, is when you want to discover what a witness will or will not agree to. For deposition, write out the points you want to make with this witness at trial. What are the best things this witness could say for your case? What might this witness say that would prove elements of your case? Preparing for the deposition of an adverse witness means, in essence, writing out your cross-examination wish list. The same is true when you are deposing third-party witnesses, including medical providers.

Cross-examination scares people most often because they fear losing control of the witness. They don't know what the witness will say. That means someone failed to prepare for a deposition using a Trial Perspective approach. Another bonus: when you prepare for a deposition using a Trial Perspective approach, there's less work to do to prepare for trial. Your cross is basically already written for you.

Chapter Takeaways

- Use techniques from cross-examination in your direct exam.
- Remember the secret to a successful cross-examination is control and preparation.
- Use your opponent's witnesses to prove your case.
- Don't discredit a witness unnecessarily on cross-examination.

… 17

Closing by Woman

Closing is when we get to argue, passionately, about something we care about. There is nothing more exciting than knowing what you believe, having conviction, and getting the chance to share that passion.

As women, we haven't always been rewarded for speaking up and arguing for our point of view. Throughout history, we were often punished. We don't need to get into the Salem witch trials, but even in America, women have been conditioned to speak softly and be agreeable. There were many times in the history of our country when women didn't have a voice. Over the course of history, from ancient Greece to medieval England to late nineteenth-century America, women who have spoken up have been scorned for being insubordinate, punished for being mad, marginalized, and even institutionalized for being "hysterical." Even today, as Jay Newton-Small writes in *TIME* magazine, "words like shrill, caterwauling, shrieking, yowling, and screeching are all associated with women—not men."[1] Studies show that when women voice their opinions, their voices land in the ether, unheard, while men, voicing the same opinions, receive praise and promotions for their assertiveness and leadership.

However, a court of law is the great equalizer. The courtroom is where the playing field gets leveled. We are not only heard in the courtroom, but we are heard from an advantageous position of great respect.

This is something that we, all of us, men and women, need to embrace. It is a privilege and a responsibility that gives us the opportunity to change how women are heard and treated *outside the courtroom.*

Know the Remedy You Want

Humans are sentient beings. We can feel when something is inauthentic, and we can feel it in our cells. A picture may be worth a thousand words, but a feeling is worth a whole lot more. Jurors are looking to you, the leader in the courtroom, and sizing you up. If your channels aren't clear, if you aren't certain about what you are asking them to do, how can you expect them to do it? How can you ask them to do something that you yourself won't do?

Understand why you are here. In the civil world, we are here for a remedy. The only remedy under our civil justice system is money. We are here about the money, whether we are the plaintiff or the defense. We don't subscribe to barbaric eye-for-an-eye justice anymore. We don't grab the defendant and tear up his leg or break his back or kill his wife. Our system is about civil justice, money justice, and that makes us civilized. That's what makes our society great. We are part of that system that we believe in.

---

[1] Jay Newton-Small, "How Hillary Clinton Is Trying to Avoid Being 'Shrill'," *TIME* (February, 3 2016) available at http://time.com/4206660/hillary-clinton-sexism-shrill-yelling.

In criminal law, we are here because the Constitution guarantees everyone the right to a fair trial and presumes us all innocent until proven guilty. The prosecution has the highest standard, beyond a reasonable doubt, because we, as a society, since the beginning of our nation, have put the highest value on liberty, which means freedom.

Let the Jury Instructions Be Your Guide

If there is one thing you do at the beginning of every case, it should be to print out the jury instructions for your case and highlight them and stick them on your wall. We see so many lawyers who address the instructions—the *law of the case*, the only guidance these lay people jurors are given by the judge, the most important rules of the whole thing—for the first time in closing. That's crazy. Don't do that.

Think about it from the jurors' perspective. When they all sit down at the end of the case to figure out what decision to make, what do they have? They have two sides of a story and a set of rules. We have done hundreds of focus groups. Every single time, the first thing the jurors did when we left the room was pick up the instructions and look at them.

The jurors want to do the right thing, and the only guidance they have are the jury instructions. Make it easier on them! From the very beginning of your case, from depositions to voir dire to opening to closing, use the words and the language of the jury instructions in your case. When we are trying a wrongful death case, where one of the damages is "loss of companionship," we use the word *companionship* in discovery, depositions, voir dire, opening, direct examinations, crosses, and then closing. By the end of the case, it's our goal that the jurors see *companionship* and know exactly what evidence they heard that addresses that element of damages.

Jury Instructions in and out of the Courtroom

The jury instructions give you the language you should be using in your case from initial pleadings through closing argument. Know the language and integrate the language into your witness preparation, witness depositions, expert depositions, and trial. Use the language when you write and respond to discovery, and as you argue motions to the judge.

Believe Your Client Deserves What You're Asking For

The biggest hurdle we see in civil cases for women and men is asking for money.

The first step to talking about money is "getting right" with it. And this goes for whatever you are asking for at the end of the trial. If you are a civil plaintiffs' or defense lawyer, you need to know exactly what you want at the end of the trial and why. If you are doing criminal law, then you need to know why you are asking for that acquittal, and it has to be something that you feel and believe.

A lot of us have a hard time asking for money. We have a hard time even *talking* about money. There's a few reasons for this: we have been socialized to think that asking for money is taboo, we are afraid that the jurors won't like us (reject us), we are afraid we won't get what we asked for, and often, we have a lot more riding on our cases than we would like to admit. Our reputation, our ego, our self-worth, our overhead. You name it. So it's a tangle of emotions and fears and circumstances that ball up and end up creating a barrier between us and the jury. When we take responsibility for our own thoughts and emotions, we unravel the ball of yarn.

Courtney:

I have tried cases where I was asking for a defense acquittal that I didn't believe in myself. I have also asked for an amount of money that I wasn't comfortable with. I know the feeling. I know the iron wall that slams down between me and the jury when I do it—which is part of why I can identify it in others when I see it out in the world—and I know it's most or all of why I lost those cases, big time.

This really hit home for me recently when I saw it from the other side. In a wrongful death case, when it came time for the defense lawyer to get up and ask the jury for a verdict, things went a little sideways. First, he held up the special verdict form and said, "In a minute, I'm going to tell you what my number is." Then, he talked for a while and repeated the same thing.

Then he said, "When I tell you my number, I'm going to write it down. And when I write it down, you're going to see it. And that's what I'm going to do in a minute."

Pause. No joke. When he finally wrote it down, it took longer than it should have and it was illegible. He couldn't own what he was asking for, and it got worse and worse. It was clear that he didn't believe in the number he was about to give the jurors. We can't ask people to do something unless we are willing to do it ourselves. Own whatever it is you are asking for, or reevaluate what you are doing there in the first place.

Theresa:

I had a client who I didn't like as a person. I believed the client was injured, and I believed the case had merit, but I had a bad gut feeling about the client from day one. I ignored the feeling. I represented the client, and it was the longest, most excruciating experience of my career. The client became verbally abusive and was difficult at every pass. The case hung around for a long, long time. I couldn't get that case to trial no matter what I did. I think it was the universe teaching me a lesson: listen to your intuition. Fast-forward to the time when we finally had a firm trial date. I knew that my dislike of the client would affect my energy in the courtroom and the energy I was subconsciously communicating to the jury. So, I brought in a friend and trial partner, with full disclosure of the circumstances, to act as a buffer. Doing that gave me the space to disconnect emotionally from all of the prior nastiness and come to trial clean.

My partner picked the jury; I gave the opening statement. We put on a handful of witnesses, and before we were halfway through the trial, we got a very large settlement offer that was a huge victory for the client and the case. The nature of our relationships with our clients shines through at trial. If you put in the work, it shows. If you don't believe what you're doing, if you don't believe your client deserves what you're asking for, or if there's discord between you and your client that you haven't buffered or addressed, it will be apparent to your jury.

Ask, Specifically, for What You Want

The next step in asking for the money or for your acquittal is to *ask for it*. We start this process at the beginning of the trial, in voir dire. We file motions with the court to have a mini-opening, a short statement about the case before voir dire, where we let the potential jurors know that we are going to be asking for a lot of money. We want to be upfront with them from the very beginning so that they know this case is about money and that is what we are asking for.

So how do we get to the number? We talk about value. Most jurisdictions we have tried cases in have jury instructions that say that the value of damages must be reasonable. We embrace that word. Being reasonable means we are not going to be cheap. The reasonable value of a loss under the law is 100 percent of the true value of that which was taken from a human being. The value of these things are expensive.

So why, as a culture, do people say you should give very little in a civil injury lawsuit? Because we are asking for money to compensate for intangibles. Some people may find it offensive to put a dollar value on such things. But that's the remedy the law gives us. It's the only remedy.

We ask our jurors to appraise the loss. If we had an original piece of fine art, or an original sculpture, or a rare gem, something a person could never get back, never replace, and our job was to do an appraisal of that very valuable item, we would have no problem doing it. The same is true in a civil jury trial. We're asking the jurors to appraise the harm to a unique, irreplaceable human being with a special, incomparable life she created. We value the civil rights—life, liberty, and the pursuit of happiness—that is, the loss of enjoyment of life due to another person's negligence. We look for metaphors and analogies that help contextualize a particular client's loss in the scope of this big world.

At the end of the case, we tell the jurors that our job is done. We are now handing our client and her future and her life over to them, to take great care and do what is right and just. We hand them the case, and we believe that they will work together to do the right thing.

Increasing the Value: Noneconomic Assets

In our justice system, civil injury cases are about money. That's the remedy prescribed by law for the harm.

You are not limited by the economic damages in your case. When we talk about economics—sometimes it's a little, sometimes it's a lot. Sometimes it's zero. Maybe we are representing a retired person. Or a stay-at-home mother.

Most of our cases are general damages cases. We focus on building our general damages and tend to put an emphasis on the mental suffering over the physical suffering damages. Why? Because the real damages are the experience, the life changed, and how the change in the body changed the life.

It's the happiness of camping with your son, having Sunday dinners with your family, watching movies on the couch with your beau. It's about being able to provide for your family as opposed to being a disabled person who is no longer able to provide for the family. The most valuable damages are the loss of the noneconomic freedoms and gifts. We work hard in our lives to avoid losing those things because they are precious.

This takes us back to that Trial Perspective approach we keep talking about. We start working our cases with the perspective of building our general damages story from the beginning. What does that look like? It means making a connection with our clients. We go to their homes, we bring food, we sit down, and we talk. We connect. We learn about our clients as human beings. Many times, when we visit our clients or meet them at their kids' basketball games or meet them for breakfast at their favorite café, we don't talk about the case. We just talk.

It's through that connection that we learn the finer details, the values, and the quieter, richer nuances of who that human being is and what is special and dynamic about him as a person. As lawyers, we act as the conduit between our client and the jury. The more depth of understanding you have about your client, the better you are at connecting your client with the jurors, and the more powerful you are going to feel every step of your trial. We guarantee it. You become the expert on the case by living it through your client's eyes.

General Closing Content

If you are just getting started or you want to enrich and expand your closing arguments, there are a lot of great resources that speak to the content of closing and give examples of outlines and arguments to be made in closing. For example, *David Ball on Damages* teaches us to remind jurors of the laws in our jurisdiction regarding how many jurors have to agree.[2] In California, it's nine out of twelve. In Iowa, it's unanimous until a certain amount of time passes. It's different in different jurisdictions, and whatever the rule wherever you are, it's critical that you are the one to explain it to the jury. We say this every time, sometimes at the very beginning of closing, in every case. Rick Friedman and Pat Malone's *Rules of the Road*, Rick Friedman's *Polarizing the Case*, and Keith Mitnik's *Don't Eat the Bruises* are all great resources for closing argument.[3]

---

[2] David Ball, *David Ball on Damages*, 3rd ed. (Portland: Trial Guides, 2012).

[3] Rick Friedman and Patrick Malone, *Rules of the Road: A Plaintiff's Guide to Proving Liability*, 2nd ed. (Portland: Trial Guides, 2010); Rick Friedman, *Polarizing the Case: Exposing and Defeating the Malingering Myth* (Portland: Trial Guides, 2007); Keith Mitnik, *Don't Eat the Bruises: How to Foil Their Plans to Spoil Your Case* (Portland: Trial Guides, 2015).

The Power of Visuals

We love visuals. More importantly, so does everyone else on the planet. Look at Instagram. It has been proven over and over that all humans have some component of visual learning and that we all benefit, albeit in different ways, from visual learning. Visual aids do three things: they help the audience learn and remember what you are trying to present, they make what you're doing more interesting (more interest = more attention), and they act as cues to help you remember what you are doing and keep you on track.

We have used all types of visuals, from the insanely expensive and complicated version of paying a tech company to design and project visuals onto top-of-the-line, high-tech plasma screens, to writing on the back of some paper with a Sharpie. We are not above charades. What we have learned, over and over, is that visuals can enhance your case, and not just in closing.

We use photographs, diagrams, and other visuals in our demand packets. We integrate them into our depositions, and we use them throughout trial, during all parts of the trial. We have flip charts—big stacks of blank paper bound together, preferably the ones that are sticky on the back—and big sharpies everywhere we go. We write down points we make in opening, we write down words from jury instructions during directs, we show diagrams of anatomy and injuries during our expert testimony, and we use analogies and illustrations during closing to help make our points creatively and in an interesting, more digestible way.

In injury cases, we like to show a visual where we take the different general damages from the jury instructions (loss of enjoyment of life, pain and suffering, disfigurement, humiliation), put them in boxes, and stack them up one by one (click by click if you're using PowerPoint) as we talk about each, to show how the damages our client suffered pile up to create a loss that is worth a whole lot of money. We also like to write out exactly how much money we are asking for during our opening, if we are in a jurisdiction where this is allowed. We do this either with a black marker or we put it into a computer-animated presentation.

Non Economic Damages:	
27.8 YRS Love	$_____
27.8 YRS Companionship	$_____
27.8 YRS Comfort	$_____
27.8 YRS Care	$_____
27.8 YRS Assistance	$_____
27.8 YRS Protection	$_____
27.8 YRS Affection	$_____
27.8 YRS Society	$_____
27.8 YRS Moral support	$_____
27.8 YRS Guidance	$_____
Total	$_____

When you write things on a board, STOP TALKING while you write. Give yourself the space to write legibly, and give everyone else the space to take it in.

Courtney:

I was in an employment case where our client, a writer for a prominent newspaper, was discriminated against and fired. The defense argued that they did not fire him for discriminatory reasons but rather because his work product was poor. They produced five articles into evidence to show the jury that his writing was bad and then argued that they had to fire him. I was trying the case three months pregnant and was sick as a dog. I made the long trip from the giant courtroom we were in, in downtown Los Angeles, to the bathroom many, many times each day of the two-month trial. I had moved my family into an apartment near the courthouse because I couldn't do the drive back to our home in Ojai. The night before closing, I couldn't stand the cooking smells from the other apartments, so I went wandering through the nearby Target. It was late October, and there was candy everywhere. I bought bags and bags of Hershey kisses, took them home, poured them out on the living room floor, and started counting them.

In rebuttal the next day, I picked up my giant tote bag full of 2,000-plus kisses and dumped them out all over our counsel table. Then I sorted through them in front of the jury and picked out five. The jury got to see what the defense did: they took a lifetime of work, picked through thousands of articles over twenty years, and could only point out five articles to make their fraudulent case, and it stunk.

==Finding ways to make your case come to life, with objects, with pictures, with phrases, even with music and sounds, makes your case more convincing, dynamic, effective, and fun.==

In another case, we represented a Chinese immigrant family who lost their father. There were four plaintiffs, and they had about three words between them. They were very quiet, shy, humble people. They spoke through a translator and did not have a lot of stories or photographs to help connect them to the jurors. But I was fascinated with them; these were people who fled China to get to Vietnam to end up making their way to America to have a better life. That story was compelling and became the foundation for understanding the man who got them here, their father, and what it meant to them to lose his direction and guidance in their lives. So, we told the story visually, with our graphic designer Pat Logan, in the opening. Pat showed a spinning globe, and then, as the globe slowed its spinning, we panned into the little village in China where our plaintiff was born. We showed a truck taking him over the terrain far out to the coast, then the boat floating across to safety, then finally the airplane to the United States. For each of the kids, we showed when their airplane flew across the ocean to California.

Closing by Woman 255

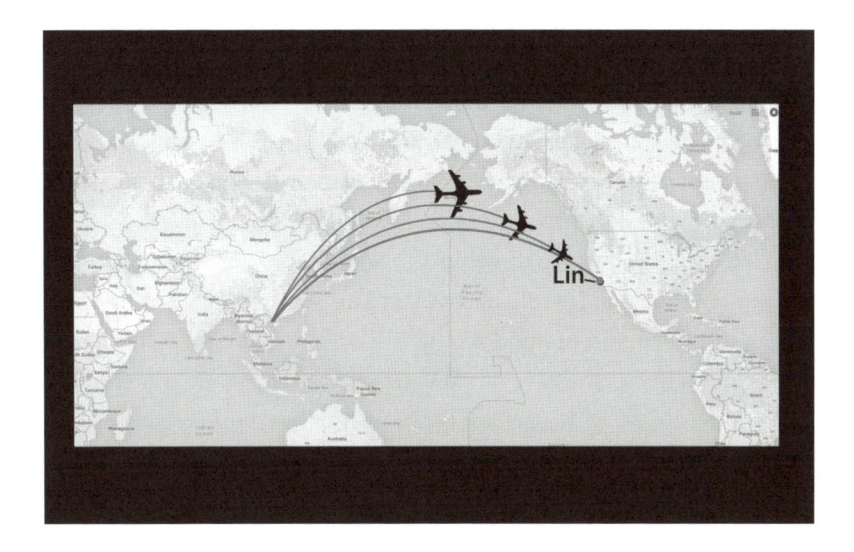

It's one of my favorites we've done. It's terribly interesting (who drives across China in a pickup?) and gives the viewer a sense of the character of a person who would go to such impossible lengths to make a better life for his family.

Here are some tips you can start using today:

1. **Use Diagrams.** Before your expert depositions, get yourself a diagram. It can be of the part of the body that was injured, of the scene where the injury or crime took place, of the concept the expert has been hired to explain. You can have one made by a professional legal medical company, or you can print one off the internet. Give it to your expert and ask her about it. Ask her to explain, using visuals, what she is referring to. Better yet, ask the expert in advance to help you find visuals that she would like to use. When we do brain injury cases, we always use clean, easy-to-see diagrams of the major lobes of the brain so that our neurologist can give an overview on how the brain works before going into how our client was injured.

2. **Less is more.** When making visuals, cut out as many words as possible. When you put something up with words, people are going to read them. While they are doing this, they are not listening to YOU. So you have two choices: cut out words so there is less time digesting and more time listening, OR, be quiet for a second and give them a chance to take in the information you have put in front of them.
3. **Get creative.** For years, we used a visual of an ostrich putting its head in the sand. It's ridiculous. And funny. Theresa loves it. It drives Courtney nuts, but she loves it too. In every case, we find some unique and creative way to show the jurors what we are trying to say. Sometimes, to find ideas, we type our concepts into google and just see what images come up. You'll be surprised at what you find, and what it sparks in you. You are a creative, interesting, artistic being.

Revisiting Old Ideas: Loss of Consortium

Courtney:

We have tried two cases in the last two months that had either a loss of consortium or "secondary" (adult daughters) wrongful death component. Traditionally, the view on these cases, especially the loss of consortium cases, is that they bring down the value of the main case. The idea is that if someone connected looks money-hungry and opportunistic, no one wins. The last two months have changed my mind completely. In both cases, we were blown away during jury selection. The secondary cases tended to help trigger emotions in the jurors, which helped to identify hostile jurors while simultaneously bolstering the main case. Over and over, potential jurors would say, "Well, I can see how the mom has the case, but not those adult daughters." Or, "I understand how the lady who was hurt could be here, but her husband is just an opportunist and I wouldn't give him anything." Our cause challenges, in both cases, were easier, cleaner, and faster than normal. It's a working theory, but it goes to show that these hard-and-fast rules we think we know are always up for reevaluation.

Here's our working hypothesis: anyone who can't be fair to the secondary claim is never going to be fair to the main claim, but without that secondary claim, you might never know that. (Until it's too late.) Our suggestion: have a separate lawyer represent the secondary claim, and make sure you do that thing that boxers do—ice the face, Vaseline on the eyebrows—before you send the lawyer into jury selection (it's going to hurt). Also, we have found that when we follow our trial by woman, Trial Perspective case development, these secondary cases can actually become valuable and important cases that allow more insight and connection to the human stories of the case overall.

The important point here is that our collective consciousness is always changing, so the way we try cases (and which cases we choose) has to shift often, as well. Science has proven that when we learn, we activate dormant and sometimes undiscovered neuropathways that reveal more energy and more creativity. This leads to increased success and satisfaction with our lives and work. Regardless of the area of law you practice, it can really pay off to look at why you do the things you do and revisit your rules from time to time.

Ask yourself:

- Do you have any hard-and-fast rules? *What* are they? *Why* are they?
- When was the last time you looked at why you do what you do?
- Do you get curious often, or do you tend to repeat old patterns?
- Where can you incorporate new or different approaches to the way you work? To the way you think?
- What about incorporating new approaches to other parts of your life outside of trial? Your relationships? Your beliefs?

Embrace the Truth of Your Case

In jury selection, we focused on listening. In closing, we do the same thing, but in a different way. We heard what the jurors think, we learned about their beliefs, and we watched the trial unfold. Closing is about addressing the defense's points and the jurors' questions as well as making our own points. When you get to closing, ask yourself, "Where did trial go differently from what I expected? Was I able to meet all the promises I made in my opening?" If so, say that. If not, name it and own it. When we own the truth of what happened during trial, we remain the leader in the courtroom. Leaders don't hide from the truth; they acknowledge and embrace it.

Courtney:

In a car crash case, during opening statement, I told the jury that the plaintiff's car was sent crashing into a "concrete barrier." That was my understanding from the depositions, but

> the way the testimony came out during trial, it turned out to be a flower pot. I knew opposing counsel was going to go wild on me during their closing, so I owned it, up front, before they could. I told the jury I made a mistake, that the evidence at trial showed it was a flower pot, and I apologized. I asked them not to hold it against my client. Then I held up the photo of the front of the car, which was smashed in, and said that, regardless, there was no question that they had a second hit, and moved on.

We have tried cases where it became clear, over the course of trial, that we had weak evidence on one of our injuries, and we acknowledged that during closing. Obviously, you want the evidence to match your opening. But we have found that whenever you have to concede an argument or a fact, you can turn that into an opportunity to gain credibility with the jury.

In closing, list out your opponent's defenses and put each one into context. Address them head-on, with evidence and confidence.

For example, in a car crash case, our client had a fall *after* the car crash. Naturally, one of the defenses in the case was that the *fall* caused her current symptoms, not the car crash. So, in closing, we put up a slide that said, "Defense Number 2: The Fall at the Church," followed by the slide "All of Her Symptoms Existed before the Fall," and then went on to list all of the evidence that her current symptoms were all documented, in multiple places, *before* the fall at the church. We showed different evidence from trial including neuropsychological testing, ER records, doctors' notes, and testimony from various lay witnesses. We went defense by defense, showing the evidence to back up each point. We ended the section with this:

> So, when you get back to the jury room, if someone says it was the fall at the church, you say all of her symptoms existed before the fall.

Be credible and reasonable in an effort to polarize the case and push the other side into an unreasonable position. See Rick Friedman's *Rules of the Road* and *Polarizing the Case* for more on this, but here's the short version: if there are points on which you have to concede or can concede without hurting your case, do it.[4] This builds credibility and gives you the advantage of being the most reasonable person in the room. For example, in a lot of our cases, we embrace shared responsibility. If we see that our client is at fault, even a tiny bit, we embrace it from the outset. We tell the jurors that they may find this is a shared responsibility case and that we accept our responsibility. Then, when the other side refuses to take any responsibility whatsoever, they look unreasonable and untrustworthy. Even if you are in a pure comparative fault state, it is worth giving a little to get a lot. Where can you give? Where can you be the reasonable one?

Pragmatic Tools

1. Write out your opponent's points and put each one into context.
2. Go through your trial: What went wrong for you? Own it.
3. Before you even get to court, write out the defense points in your case as soon as you start working on the case and keep adding to the list as the case progresses. This gives you competitive advantage and a clear view of what it is you need to address with your evidence, the law, and your arguments.

---

[4] *See* Rick Friedman and Patrick Malone, *Rules of the Road*; and Rick Friedman, *Polarizing the Case*.

Courtney:

I come from a very loud dinner table. Growing up, my parents were teachers. They were both working days, sometimes two jobs, and going to school at night to complete their master's degrees. We ate a lot of canned bean burritos. But dinner was never boring. A lot of the time, when they weren't touring the United States with their square-dancing group, my grandparents would join us. My grandfather was about six feet three, the runt of his brothers, and almost deaf in at least one ear. He would stretch his long legs under the table and lean back in his chair and start the conversation. There was only one prerequisite for being heard at the table. It didn't matter how old you were, what you believed, or whether you even knew what anyone was talking about, the only way to be heard in my family was to be loud. My mother is a passionate person, and she always had something she wanted to talk about, laugh about, share, or discuss. And we all jumped in. Arms would start swinging, bread would be burning, and we would be shouting, laughing, disagreeing, and agreeing until we all ran out of energy and piled into baths and bed. I remember feeling important, included, and I remember wanting to learn more so that I would have more to add the next night. I also remember, as I got a bit older, when I started to understand the value of convincing others to agree with me, and that it meant a lot more than simply shouting out my own opinions and beliefs. Winning arguments, I learned, had a lot less to do with understanding my opinion and a whole heck of a lot to do with understanding theirs.

Closing isn't just about arguing. Closing is about connecting all of the dots and tying all of the pieces of evidence together. The way we approach trial, closing in particular, is this: we have an obligation to *teach*, not to *convince*. When you're teaching, you're standing in the full truth and conveying the complete, whole story. When you're trying to convince, you're obfuscating in some respects. Teaching allows for other perspectives and answers questions with a spirit of curiosity and guidance, not superiority. Try it the next time you're in a spirited conversation with someone. Try to teach instead of convince and see how that shifts your energy and the energy of the other person.

On Being Clean

Courtney:

We just finished a medical malpractice case in Northwest Iowa in what is considered to be the most conservative part of the state. It's a Dutch town. They have an annual tulip festival. All the window displays have clogs and tulips, and it's beautiful, with well-manicured grass and pristine white fences. We represented a family whose young mother was killed when the doctor failed to give her epinephrine after an adverse reaction to contrast dye during a routine CT.[5] Awful. Probably one of the most stressful cases we've done. We came into it with a lot of very broad rulings about what we could and could not say (value of life, community), where to stand (podium or table), what we could show the jury (defense has to agree, so no demonstratives, no timelines). As it goes when you start

---

[5] This case is also discussed in chapter 16, "Direct and Cross-Examination by Woman."

doing well, the defense made quite a few motions for mistrial, and the parameters within which we could work kept getting smaller and smaller.

At closing, the judge took out most of our slides and ruled we could not say *justice*, *money justice*, or *civil*, or make any reference to the Constitution. (He did, however, remind my husband that if he wanted to participate he would have to put his "big boy pants" on. I was sitting next to my husband in front of the group of ten young women, age nineteen to twenty-one, who came to support one of our plaintiffs, so I spun around and looked at all of them and said, "Welcome back to 1954, girls. Check your pants, please.")

I guess it was a little worse when the defense continued to repeatedly refer to cooking dinner, taking care of the kids, running the house, and doing the bookkeeping as "ladies work." Again, I turned around and unquietly reminded them that I would pay for any of their law school tuitions, any day, here's my phone number. I digress.

Long story short, we didn't just try a clean case; we tried a case where anything we had been doing in the last however many years of trial work wasn't going to fly. So, we tried something new: not "trying" anything at all. We referred to what was owed in this case as reasonable damages. We called it compensation. When I crossed the nurse and she blurted out some planted prejudicial nonsense that she had been fed, I simply reminded her that she had not said anything like that in any record nor in her deposition. I didn't need to ask, "Is that something you prepared for last night at that dinner with the lawyer?" (No reference to expert interactions with counsel ruling.) We didn't put up any cheeky visuals about ostriches or famous people who are worth a lot or priceless paintings or any of the other go-to bullshit in our arsenal. We proved our case. And in closing, we dissected Every. Single. Piece. Of. Evidence. At times, painstakingly. Then we connected it all to what this family lost. And why reasonable value for what was taken, their mother, was not cheap. Reasonable compensation for something so valuable to this family could only be a lot.

The jury came back unanimous. We got the first plaintiff's verdict in that county for medical malpractice, and one of the largest verdicts in the history of the state.

We have a lot of nonlawyers and lawyers who don't try cases (either anymore or ever) writing books and putting on seminars and telling us that we have to use the "right words" or that we shouldn't say *this* but call it *that*, and so on.

We are orators. What we do is creative. But sometimes we have to go to Occam's razor: What is the simplest solution? When we take out the manipulation, the tricks, the pizzazz, the sideshow, and we focus on proving our case and matching the evidence to the jury instructions, pretty amazing things happen. I think we are all yearning for authenticity, veracity, and fairness. Plain talk, using the words from the jury instructions, obeying the court, and putting on your evidence like a boss—these things work. Also, it's not so bad to finish a case knowing you have a clean record to put up when the other side asks for a new trial.

Practical Tips for Closing

Practice, practice, practice. Get in front of a mirror. Even better: record yourself. We use our iPhones. Practice asking for money and giving your reasons with people in line at the grocery store, with your family at the dinner table, with the guy who makes your coffee in the morning.

Outside the courtroom, long before closing: Spend time with your client. Identify the lay witnesses who can add flavor and value to your case, who can talk about before and after, who can give insight into who your client is and what matters to them the most. Understanding that this is how you come to the big numbers in closing is what will make your work on the front end all the more specific and valuable. From the beginning, during discovery, go to the client's *house*, meet them, bring food.

1. **Jury instructions.** Know them, use them, plug evidence into them, and then argue them. Show exactly how your case matches with the instructions and then what to do about it with the verdict form or jury charge. This is something criminal lawyers are really good at, because they know cases come down to instructions. In civil cases, we have seen lawyers who don't look at the instructions until trial. This all goes back to Trial Perspective case development. On day one, when you get a case, get out the instructions and take a good hard look at them. That way, when it comes to gathering your evidence, putting on your cases, and finally arguing, you remain the authority and teacher of how the jury does their job and, ultimately, what decision they should make.
2. **Cut it down, cut it out.** Arguments are artistry and an important part of what we do, but don't be afraid to speak plainly and be straightforward. How can you cut out your personal opinions and replace them with more facts, more truth? Can you replace a long, belabored explanation with an analogy?
3. **Speak from your heart.** Find what connects to the deepest parts of you and speak and write from there. Close your eyes and imagine traveling to the depths of you, to where your light and love and spirit play, and then start writing and speaking about your case from that place. What is the absolute truth of what happened here? Can you feel it? Where? What does it feel like?

Closing in and out of the Courtroom

If you're not in a position to close yet, maybe you're writing a demand letter or about to present your case to a mediator or even about to give a case summary at a weekly meeting. How can you simplify? How can you take away the crap in order to amplify what really matters? What can you cut, and how can you say it more plainly, more directly?

Lastly, passion is infectious. Find the pieces of your case that fire you up, that connect you to your deeper self, and then speak from that place. You might call it righteous indignation, and that has a place in many cases, but not all cases. What is the emotional tone of your case, and where, emotionally, does the jury need to go? Maybe that's anger, maybe it's joy, or maybe this case gives you a sense of yearning because it triggers emotions in you about the family you wish lived closer. Argument is just words without passion. It's the passion that moves the needle and inspires action.

Chapter Takeaways

- Know what remedy you want, believe your client deserves it, and ask for it clearly and directly.
- Refer to actual evidence that the jury was given throughout trial.
- Get creative! This is the time to use everything you have to get your point across.
- Answer the defenses and arm your jurors: remember that people are going to argue for your client, show them how.

18

Negotiation and Settlement by Woman

What if you want to try a case, and your client wants to settle? What if your client refuses to go to trial under any circumstances? What if you don't know whether it would be a better outcome for your client to settle or try the case? What if you don't have enough money to try the case? What if you are low on cash and really need a case to settle so you can make payroll, pay the bills, and so on? What if you're afraid to try the case? We've all felt all of these concerns at one time or another. The answers to these questions aren't always easy, but we can give you a method that helps you work through it.

We are trial lawyers. We want to try cases. We prepare and plan and expect to try cases. But there are also times when we settle cases. When we settle cases, it's because it is in the client's best interest to settle the case.

In this chapter we'll discuss the following:

1. How your fiduciary duty to your client impacts whether or not a case goes to trial
2. Tools to evaluate whether to settle a case versus try a case
3. How to discuss with your client the options of settlement and trial
4. A trial by woman approach to negotiations

Fiduciary Duty

All lawyers have a fiduciary duty to every client. That means we have to put our clients' interests above our own interests at all times:

> The most fundamental quality of the attorney–client relationship is the *absolute and complete fidelity* owed by the attorney to his or her client.[1]

As a practical matter, that means we can't pick a case and decide we're going to try it no matter what. In fact, in many jurisdictions, including California and Iowa, where we primarily practice, the client has 100 percent authority to decide whether or not to settle his or her case.

The decision on any matter that will *affect the client's substantive rights* is within the client's sole authority.[2] When such matters arise, the lawyer has a duty to advise the client and suggest particular courses of action, but the ultimate decision is the *client's* to make.[3] The client has

---

[1] *Flatt v. Sup.Ct. (Daniel)*, 9 Cal.4th 275, 289 (1994); *Yorn v. Sup.Ct. (Hesemeyer)* 90 Cal.App.3d 669, 675 (1979); Cal. State Bar Form.Opn. 1984-83; ABA Model Rule 1.7, Comment (1).

[2] *Blanton v. Womancare, Inc.* 38 Cal.3d 396, 404-405 (1985); *Maddox v. City of Costa Mesa* 193 Cal.App.4th 1098, 1105 (2011).

[3] ABA Model Rule 1.2(a). *See also*, Rest.3d Law Governing Lawyers § 22.

the unilateral right to settle or refuse to settle.[4] And a lawyer must abide by the client's decision.[5]

The bottom line here is that, in many jurisdictions, even if we're dying to try a case, we can only do so if it's in our client's best interest and if our client agrees. While it's the client's decision whether to settle or try a case, naturally, clients need our guidance in making the decision. And that begins with our ability to evaluate the case.

Practical Tools: Settle or Try

Theresa:

> We were set for trial the day Courtney got back from her friend's wedding out of town. It was a slip and fall case set in Orange County. We were brought in about six weeks before trial, which was perfect timing because we were both itching to try a case. A week before trial, we had our trial documents done, our opening written, and our witnesses lined up.
>
> There were a few things about the case that were troubling me. Courtney was ready to charge full speed ahead. One of the great things about working together on cases is that we get two different perspectives on the case—and often those perspectives switch and change depending on the case and what else is going on in our lives. Another thing: the advantage of coming into a case late is that we get to look at it with fresh eyes. When lawyers have been living and breathing a case for two, three, or even more years, they are in the foxhole, mired

---

[4] *In re Guzman*, 5 Cal. State Bar Ct.Rptr. 308, 314 (Rev.Dept. 2014).
[5] *See also*, Iowa Rules of Professional Conduct, Rule 32:1.2.

in the details and emotional ups and downs of working a case for a long time. When we come later to the case, we get a different perspective—almost a bird's-eye view. We get to see the case *as a jury would*. Once we were brought into the case, we finished up discovery and did a focus group. At this point, we had a pretty good understanding of the strengths and weaknesses of the case.

Courtney and I divide up work. We believe doing so is essential to doing right by our clients and remaining sane in the process: no one can do it all. So, as trial approached, we began our process of evaluating a case for settlement. We do this before every trial because it is our job to know where we stand so that we can advise our client properly throughout trial.

Evaluating a Case for Settlement

Below, we'll walk you through our process of evaluating a case for settlement.

Step 1: Excel Spreadsheet

We have an Excel spreadsheet for each of our cases that allows us to quickly run the numbers and see a client's net recovery whenever a settlement offer is made. The spreadsheet accounts for attorney's fees, costs, liens, and so on. So we can give clients a very close estimate as to how much they will net in a civil case whenever our opponents make an offer.

Looking at that spreadsheet also helps us, as lawyers, evaluate a settlement offer. How far are we into a case? How much have we spent litigating the case? If we continue to litigate the case, how much more can we expect to spend? How does that affect the client's net recovery? If we go to trial, how much more than the settlement offer will the jury have to award to offset the additional costs?

Just looking at the numbers can give us a good sense of where we are and where we're going. If we're within $15,000 of our assessed case value, for example, it doesn't make sense to spend $40,000 to try the case. These are the types of things we're thinking about when we're running numbers.

In our case, the costs were pretty high. The client had a few different serious injuries that required separate experts. As we looked at the numbers, it wasn't black-and-white. This was a close call. There was a decent amount of money on the table before we came into the case. Having just finished discovery, including treating physicians and experts, we knew there was a small chance of losing at trial and a slightly larger chance of comparative being assigned to our client, which could potentially reduce her overall recovery.

On to the next step.

Step 2: Assessing the Value Based on the Facts

Do you like your client? Will the jury like your client? In a civil case, what are your real chances of winning on liability? Will there be comparative fault assigned to your client?

What is the range of damages a jury may award? Does your client have other medical conditions that detract from your case? Does your client have other medical conditions that made her more susceptible to injury in your case?

Looking at our case, we knew there were a lot of other medical issues that could detract from our case. We had decided to waive economic damages, so it was going to be a general damages case. We knew it was going to be very difficult in trial to parse out how much our client's damages were going to be for her disputed injuries and how much was for unrelated injuries. We knew at that point that we had an obligation, as the new lawyers on the case, to reach out to opposing counsel and make a final effort to settle the case. So, that's what we did. We reached out, said we wanted to make a final effort to see if the case could be settled before trial, and when we did that, the amount being offered increased. After a few rounds of negotiating back and forth, the offer was in a range that convinced us to recommend that the client consider accepting the offer. The client's net at that moment was quite likely more than she would net at trial under the most likely (pretty good) scenario.

It's important to note that the *reason* that offer went up was that we were *prepared for trial*. This is huge. If we had reached out, and they had stayed where they were before, we were *100 percent ready for trial*. This goes back to what we are talking about when we say that you have to work your case from a Trial Perspective approach. Your duty to the client means you have to be ready to try the case just as much as you understand when it's time to settle. I was finalizing my mini-opening, and Courtney was having a terrific time at her friend's wedding and practicing her opening, up until we got the defense's email settling the case.

Step 3: Discuss Settlement versus Trial with Your Client

So how do we talk about settlement with our clients? How do we make sure that the clients understand what may (and may not) happen in trial so that they are prepared to make informed decisions about their case? We do it with brutal honesty, and we do it early and often.

It's important to be up-front and *clear* with your clients about the risks of their cases, both early on and as issues arise during discovery. That way, when it comes time to make a decision, there are no surprises. We talk about case-specific risks with our clients, as well as the approximate cost to litigate the case throughout trial, and the best possible outcome at trial. And we talk about the appellate timeline and potential for new trial. Remember, a verdict does not always mean payment. Our job is to do the best job we can *for our client*. Sometimes that means asking ourselves, "Is this what's best for me or for the human being I'm representing?"

When we work our cases from a Trial Perspective approach, weighing the risks of the case *in trial* from the beginning, we are better able to navigate settlement and give our clients the right information so they can make the best decision *for them*.

Negotiations by Woman

Everything in our lives is built on relationships—getting jobs, making friends, getting married, having children. Our relationships with opposing counsel are important too. A better relationship means professional courtesies are given. A better relationship means less unnecessary adversarial time-wasting and more productivity. A better relationship means our reputation improves among our adversaries, making it easier in the future to build good relationships with new opposing counsel. And, in our experience, a better relationship often means a better settlement for our client if we are not trying the case.

We have had countless cases where, because of the relationship we built with opposing counsel, we got policy limit offers or substantial movement on a case where there otherwise would not have been any. In the criminal world, better relationships can foster quicker discovery and more options for our clients.

This effect is amplified, in our experience, when opposing counsel is a woman. Women are inherently relationship-builders. We build connections between ourselves and others, and we help build connections between other people—our kids and their friends, our husbands and our friends' husbands, and so on. Don't lose or bury this valuable skill as a lawyer.

How to do it? Focus on building a relationship between yourself and opposing counsel; your client and opposing counsel; and your client and the insurance company decision-makers. What does that look like? It doesn't mean forcing an actual relationship.

It means making your client a real human being to opposing counsel and the decision-makers, rather than just a case name or file number. We've done this by inviting opposing counsel and the insurance company decision-makers to come to our clients' homes and visit with them, talk to them about how their injuries have impacted their lives. We've taken candid iPhone videos of our clients and sent them to opposing counsel and the insurance company decision-makers. When you speak to opposing counsel, refer to your client by name rather than as "my client." And refer to the opposing counsel's client by name. Refer to your clients by describing their relationship with opposing counsel's client. For example, if you represent the wife in a divorce case, and opposing counsel represents the husband, you would discuss the parties by referring to your client as "Mr. Smith's wife." All of this humanizes and respects everyone involved. And you are building connections among the parties, the lawyers, and the decision-makers involved in the case.

Chapter Takeaways

- Your fiduciary duty to your client impacts whether or not a case goes to trial.
- You have the tools you need to evaluate whether to settle a case versus try a case.
- You need to discuss with your client the options of settlement and trial.

PART FIVE

The Highest and Best Use of Your Time

The Highest and Best Use of Your Time

Time. Sometimes it feels like a peaceful winding river, lazily curving around the rocks and trees; other times if feels like storm waves crashing on our heads, relentless and suffocating. When we're kids, summers seem to last forever, and during the end of December, Christmas feels like it will never get here. When we're grown, time flies. Our kids seem to grow up overnight, and we seem to always be barreling toward something. Scientifically speaking, however, time doesn't exist. Certainly not the way in which we have organized it with schedules and clocks and deadlines. Philosophically (and in the mirror), we agree with Aristotle's version of time as a measurement of change. It's easy to forget that we are entirely in control of our own experience of time, and that it is our responsibility to ourselves and our loved ones to find the highest and best use of the short time we are given. Let's work on feeling gratitude in each moment of our precious and short lives.

In this next set of chapters, we will talk about the following:

- finding and pursuing the highest and best use of our time
- how making space for our spirit with tools like meditation, walking, and self-care can improve our experience
- why food matters, and how to treat our bodies and minds better with the food we eat and the water we drink
- just for new moms: how to balance being a lawyer and being a new mom

19

The Importance of Physical, Mental, and Spiritual Health

Historically, men held positions of leadership and power outside of the home. Now, women also hold positions of leadership and power outside of the home. Historically, it was men who died earlier and who were more likely to have illnesses and conditions caused or aggravated by the stress and pressures of their jobs, being sole providers for their families, and not taking care of themselves. Now, we stand on the cusp of a time when women feel those same pressures and have those same responsibilities, along with the responsibilities of caring for the home, family, and, often, extended family. What will happen to us if we don't take the time now to cultivate time and space to care for ourselves?

As women, we are responsible not only for our work and careers, but also the caretaking of our families, as the leaders of our homes.

Whether or not we have children or spouses, we end up being the matriarchal leaders of our families. We know that there are many happy, satisfied, and whole women who either choose not to, or cannot, have children, and we celebrate them as well. Many of us will find ourselves caring for our parents, our siblings, our relatives, and even our friends. We are looked up to and depended upon for the leadership and care of others. In order to do provide that care, we have to take care of ourselves.

Women have been socialized to put others first. We tend to give all we have to the ones around us and neglect ourselves in the process. Culturally, some women have learned to embrace their fatigue and self-sacrifice as badges of honor. We need to flip the script. Who we are and what we do as lawyers takes great strength and fortitude. Part of embracing our power means honoring our bodies, minds, and spirits by learning how to take time to nurture ourselves.

Women are different from men. We have different emotional, physical, and spiritual needs than men. This section talks about our personal explorations, discoveries, and experiences in the realm of physical, mental, and spiritual health and practical suggestions for self-care. When we are healthy, in body and mind, we are unstoppable. Statistically, our profession has a poor track record for addressing and promoting self-care and is well-known for self-medicating with drugs and alcohol. Not anymore. It's time to honor our unique abilities by nurturing ourselves and making space in our lives and careers for well-being. When we feel good, we do better.

In framing all of this self-care and care of others, we ask ourselves and one another regularly, "What's the highest and best use of our time?" What we mean is we have a fixed amount of time in a day, in a week, in a year, and in a lifetime. On an even more tangible level, we have a fixed amount of time in any given experience. When we're being intimate with a partner, that experience lasts for a fixed amount of time. When we're pregnant, that experience lasts for a fixed amount of time. When we're in our wedding ceremony, when we're at our wedding reception, when we're in labor, when our children are infants, when our children are toddlers, when our children are school age, when they are teenagers, when we are on a vacation, when we're in retirement—all of these experiences are transient. So, are we devoting the time we have in each moment with intention, and are we using the time we have in these moments to make the best use of the time we have? That's what we mean when we're talking about the highest and best use of time. Our time matters tremendously. We always want to be aware of how we are spending the precious time we have.

Health and Lifespan

Well, we know we have a fixed lifespan. We all have a fixed amount of time to live on this planet. We decided that we want to be healthy and well and disease-free during the time we have here. We want our life to consist of a much longer span of health than span of disease or disability. One of the physicians whose work we follow is Sara Gottfried, MD. She's an integrative medicine physician and scientist who has the data to show that only about 10 percent of any disease we get is caused by our genes. The rest are caused by lifestyle. And she says we can activate or deactivate the genes we have that may predispose us to illnesses and diseases. That means just because certain people have the genes for diabetes doesn't mean they are going to get diabetes. Even if everyone in their extended family has it. You can do things today to deactivate those genes, increase your health span and decrease your disease span.[1] Amazing stuff, right? We heard about Dr. Gottfried's work about a year ago and immediately started implementing as many of her recommendations into our lifestyle as we could. While we had both practiced yoga for years, around the same time as we discovered Dr. Gottfried's work, we began Kundalini yoga practices, meditation practices, and

---

[1] See Sara Gottfried, MD, *Younger: A Breakthrough Program to Reset Your Genes, Reverse Aging, and Turn Back the Clock 10 Years* (New York: HarperOne, 2017).

infrared sauna practices. We are also both avid walkers and hikers and believe 100 percent that, above all, it's critical to listen to our bodies. They know what we need. Here's what has worked for us to make our lives and our practices richer. Let's start with food.

Food First

Food is fuel for your body. The quality of the fuel directly impacts your body's performance. We don't diet. We don't restrict. We don't deprive. We listen to our bodies and eat what makes our bodies feel good.

Developing mindfulness practices like Kundalini yoga and meditation have made it much easier to connect with how we feel after eating certain foods. Dr. Gottfried talks in many interviews about how all calories are not created equal. She has a great analogy where she explains how equal calories in broccoli and diet soda do very different things to your body. Basically, the soda shrinks your brain and makes you fat, and the broccoli sweeps all of the junk from your insides and is an antioxidant.

In general, we have mostly plant-based diets and eat real foods, that is, whole foods, as much as possible. We rarely eat processed foods, and if we want cookies, we bake them from scratch so we know what we're putting in our bodies. We eat a couple and put the rest in the freezer for another time.

There's so much information out there on what foods are "good" and what foods are "bad," and it seems that now some experts are saying that even some "good" foods are actually "bad" for you. It's confusing. And we're not experts in medicine, nutrition, or any of those related subjects. So, instead of trying to sort it all out and figure out who is most credible and qualified and who to believe, we have become more intuitive about our food. Does this make me feel good? Do I have sustained energy after I eat this? Or does it make me crash? Do I feel tired after I eat this food? Does it make me jittery? Do I crave more of this food after I eat it even though I know I'm not still hungry? Do I feel satisfied after I eat this food? Or am I still hungry or craving something? Does my stomach hurt after I eat this food? Does my skin break out the next day or look uneven or splotchy?

The more in touch we become with our bodies and our minds, the easier it is to answer these questions. If you listen, your body tells you what you need.

We have both made small, permanent changes over time rather than launching into a complete food and menu overhaul for ourselves and our families. Yes, we eat chocolate, but when we do, it's a few squares of an organic chocolate bar. (If we're going to eat chocolate, we eat the good stuff!) Yes, we drink wine on occasion. Yes, we give our kids birthday cakes.

But, mostly, we eat real food that's grown in the ground, and when we eat those other things, we throw extra broccoli, blueberries, leafy greens, thyroid tea, and lemon water into the mix that day to balance it out.

We eat organic food because what we were reading about pesticides in our bodies scared us. We grow some of our own herbs and fruits and vegetables in our own backyards for fun, and, honestly, you can taste the difference. If you need any encouragement to go organic, check out the study out of Australia showing that after seven days on a plant-based organic diet, people had a 90 percent reduction in the amount of toxic pesticides in their bodies. The study was performed by Dr. Liza Oates and her team at RMIT University in Australia, and the report was published in Environmental Research.[2]

OK, that's all we have to say about food. It's a complex subject. As with all things, do your research, take your own health and health conditions into account, listen to your body, and do what will lift you to your highest and best.

---

[2] Liza Oates et al., "Reduction in Urinary Organophosphate Pesticide Metabolites in Adults after a Week-Long Organic Diet," *Environmental Research* 132 (July 2014): 105–111, https://doi.org/10.1016/j.envres.2014.03.021.

Move Your Body

This is a big one. Moving your body is so good for you, that we'd probably pick exercise over any other self-care technique if pressed to choose. There's no shortage of information out there on how good it is for you to move your body. Exercising creates endorphins, which are magical peptides produced in the pituitary gland that make you happy and even block pain receptors. Numerous studies show that exercise can alleviate anxiety and depression.[3] Right now, according to the Centers for Disease Control and Prevention, women are twice as likely to use antidepressants as men.

And on top of all that, exercise can help you live longer.[4]

Pretty neat stuff.

We are avid walkers. We hike in the mountains where we live. If we're traveling, we put on our sneakers and start walking as soon as we get where we're going. Yogi Bhajan, who introduced Kundalini yoga to the United States, recommended walking four to six miles per day. Think about how it was done in earlier times, all of that walking, and how, despite a less than ideal diet and no exercise per se, the incidence of disease was lower in many respects.

We move our bodies every day. Some days we walk, some days we hike, some days we run, some days we do yoga, some days we do Ballet Beautiful with Mary Helen Bowers, some days we do the Class with Taryn Toomey, and some days we do BBG with Kayla Itsines.[5] Some days we chase our kids around the yard. But we always move.

---

[3] Elizabeth Anderson and Geetha Shivakumar, "Effects of Exercise and Physical Activity on Anxiety," *Frontiers in Psychiatry* 4 (April 23, 2013), https://doi.org/10.3389/fpsyt.2013.00027.

[4] Office of the Assistant Secretary for Planning and Evaluation, *Physical Activity Fundamental to Preventing Disease* (Washington, DC: US Department of Health and Human Services, 2002).

[5] Ballet Beautiful: https://www.balletbeautiful.com, The Class: https://taryntoomey.com, BBG: https://www.kaylaitsines.com.

Nourish Your Spirit

Our industry is known to be one that puts people at an increased risk of drug and alcohol abuse.

Back in 2012, the American Bar Association published a bulletin about substance abuse. The rate of problem drinking for attorneys was 18 percent, compared to 10 percent in the general population, according to a study in the *International Journal of Law and Psychiatry*. Substance abuse problems in our industry start early and get worse if they're not treated. According to the research, 15 percent of first-year law students, 25 percent of third-year law students, and 18 percent of two- to twenty-year attorneys reported problem drinking, and the figure increased to 25 percent for lawyers who practiced more than twenty years. But that data was from 1990.

In 2015, the ABA Commission on Lawyer Assistance Programs and the Hazelden Betty Ford Center gathered new data, based on responses from nearly thirteen thousand lawyers in sixteen states. What they found was troubling:

- One-fifth had problematic drinking, nearly twice what would be expected from a highly educated workforce based on comparable data from other industries.
- More than one-quarter had suffered from depression.
- One-fifth had suffered from anxiety.
- More than one in ten had suicidal thoughts while practicing law.
- 0.7 percent had attempted suicide at least once.
- If the suicide attempt rate was extrapolated over the 1.3 million lawyers in the country, that would mean 9,100 have attempted suicide.
- Lawyers are reluctant to get help for substance abuse and mental health issues.

The stress is high. The stakes are high. Your colleagues are slugging back four to five cups of coffee to get going, skipping breakfast, not eating well when they do eat, slamming through the day at 150 miles per hour and then coming home, crashing on the couch, and drinking a bottle of wine to unwind. That body and that soul are not going to make it to the finish line in good shape.

The statistics speak volumes. With so many lawyers enduring chronic stress, depression, and anxiety, while self-medicating and not getting the help they need, our profession is not sustainable.

In the summer of 2016, the National Task Force on Lawyer Well-Being was formed. It consisted of representatives from the Commission on Lawyer Assistance Programs, the National Organization of Bar Counsel, the Association of Professional Responsibility Lawyers, the ABA Standing Committee on Professionalism, the ABA Center for Professional Responsibility, the ABA Young Lawyers Division, the ABA Law Practice Division: Attorney Well-Being Committee, the National Conference of Chief Justices, and the National Conference of Bar Examiners. They analyzed data for a year. They recognized a dire situation:

> The legal profession is already struggling. Our profession confronts a dwindling market share as the public turns to more accessible, affordable alternative legal service providers. We are at a crossroads. To maintain public confidence in the profession, to meet the need for innovation in how we deliver legal services, to increase access to justice, and to reduce the level of toxicity that has allowed mental health and substance use disorders to fester among our colleagues, we have to act now. Change will require a wide-eyed and candid assessment of our members' state of being, accompanied by courageous commitment to re-envisioning what it means to live the life of a lawyer.[6]

---

[6] National Task Force for Well-Being, *The Path to Lawyer Well-Being: Practical Recommendations for Positive Change* (American Bar Association, August 14, 2017), https://www.americanbar.org/content/dam/aba/images/abanews/ThePathToLawyerWellBeingReportRevFINAL.pdf.

The Task Force published a report, *The Path to Lawyer Well-Being: Practical Recommendations for Positive Change*, in August 2017.

A few months later, in February 2018, the American Bar Association's House of Delegates adopted a resolution that urged law schools, law firms, bar associations, lawyer regulatory agencies, and other agencies that employ lawyers to adopt measures to help lawyers struggling with substance abuse and mental health issues. The resolution incorporated the recommendations of the National Task Force on Lawyer Well-Being.

The Task Force's recommendations are focused on the following:

1. Identifying stakeholders and the role each of us can play in reducing the level of toxicity in our profession
2. Eliminating the stigma associated with help-seeking behaviors
3. Emphasizing that well-being is an indispensable part of a lawyer's duty of competence
4. Educating lawyers, judges, and law students on lawyer well-being issues
5. Taking small, incremental steps to change how law is practiced and how lawyers are regulated to instill greater well-being in the profession

Did you read that? Well-being is an "indispensable" part of your duty of competence as a lawyer. Ours is no longer a profession where wearing your beat-down spirit, your battered, neglected body and soul, and lamenting how much you work is an acceptable badge of honor. It's unacceptable, and it's directly contrary to your *legal duty of competence* as an attorney. In other words, you have an affirmative obligation to take care of yourself, to be well in mind, body, and spirit.

Let's start honoring our bodies, our minds, our spirits. Let's treat this body like it's the only vessel we ever get to move us through this lifetime. Because it is.

Input Management

Guru Jagat, the founder of RA MA Institute for Applied Yogic Science and Technology, a Kundalini yoga school with locations in Venice, California; Mallorca, Spain; and New York City; and author of the bestselling book *Invincible Living: The Power of Yoga, the Energy of Breath, and Other Tools for a Radiant Life*, is a global leader in creating and defining the new feminine matriarchal archetype, and we've learned a lot from all of her teachings, many of which flow from Yogi Bhajan.[7]

Guru Jagat says our systems are not equipped to deal with the mega amounts of input we get from our jobs, our families, and social media, and our systems are not equipped to deal with the output that is expected of us on a daily basis. All of the demands bombard our nervous system, and that's where we start feeling the brakes slamming on. We feel less engaged, less invested, less alert, more anxious, and overwhelmed.

If you stay on that path, where is there energy and room to achieve what you want and create the life you want? Where is there room for your fulfillment and satisfaction and happiness if you can't handle the daily input and output? We have to take command of the input. We choose to eliminate the majority of the input. When we go on Instagram and scroll through a feed, it doesn't make us feel better, even if we're following wellness sites. If we take a hot bath, get in the sauna, or meditate even for ten minutes, *that* makes us feel good. We can feel the change in our bodies and our minds, and it's a good change. So, for us, input management is key.

---

[7] Guru Jagat, *Invincible Living: The Power of Yoga, The Energy of Breath, and Other Tools for a Radiant Life* (HarperElixir, 2017).

Manage Your Output

Once you manage the input, you need to create the energy within yourself to handle the input and produce the necessary output—what we put out into the world. We build and manage our output energy through meditation practices; Kundalini yoga practices; chanting; Reiki energy healing; hot baths; infrared sauna sessions; massage therapy; and natal, transiting sky, and progressed chart readings. This is what works for us, but so many others work too. Prayer, attending a quiet church service, surfing, hiking, book clubs. People find meditation in all sorts of activities, including walking, baking, knitting, or even washing dishes. The important thing is to find something that quiets your soul and replenishes your spirit. Try different things and see what works for you.

A one-week challenge: Get a piece of paper and make two columns. In the first column, write down your input each day for a week—everything. That means email, websites, television shows, music on the radio, phone conversations, newspapers, all of it. At the end of the day, in the second column, next to each input, write how it made you feel. Better? Worse? Neutral? Did it increase your energy or take it away? Take back control over your input and see what a difference that makes in your energy, in your mood, in your life.

Living Intentionally

We believe in setting intentions—for our days, our weeks, our years, our lives. We believe intentions are powerful and we should harness and use them for our highest and best good. If we wake up and immediately give thanks for the day, express gratitude, and set the intention that this is going to be a happy day, that sticks with us. And it becomes more difficult for hiccups along the course of the day to derail our intentions. If, on the other hand, we don't set an intention for the day, every little thing that goes wrong casts a darker and darker cloud over the day, and we're suddenly living in the inescapable gloom of a bad day. But, objectively speaking, the day was the same. It was only our mindset that could have been different.

Take control of your mindset. Take control of the way you view your life and the circumstances you encounter. Feel gratitude for the little things and the big things. What are they? Write them down. Tune in. Be here. You get one shot at this life. Make it greater than you imagined.

Acting intentionally also means holding space for yourself. It means being compassionate and recognizing when you are asking too much of yourself or setting unrealistic expectations. Perfection is not only not possible, but it's not enjoyable. Living with intention means living with care and kindness, for others and for yourself.

Preparing for a Presentation

"What's the highest and best use of your time?" is a question that we ask ourselves and each other with respect to our law practices too. Here's an example.

We were approached to speak and present at a Fireside Chat put on by a division of Trial Guides, the publisher of this book. While we both had a lot of public speaking experience, it was the first time we had to prepare a presentation together from beginning to end. We wanted to make sure that the presentation was useful to all trial lawyers, that we gave those lawyers who wouldn't be trying cases the next week tools to use in their pretrial litigation, and we wanted to give a flavor of Trial By Woman and how we do things around here. We had a lot of ideas swirling in our heads, and we went back and forth by email, phone, and FaceTime, but the presentation hadn't clicked yet in the way we wanted it to. We were both busy at the time, preparing for trials, raising our kids, taking care of our homes, running our law practices. *But we knew we needed to call a time out and get some face-to-face time.* We held a meeting at the Ojai Valley Inn and Spa.

It was a Tuesday morning in March. The sun was pressing through the fog. We met at the outdoor restaurant in front of the huge oak tree with lanterns suspended from the old branches. We were wearing our favorite comfy clothes: leggings, sweaters, and boots, hair twisted up and necks wrapped in scarves. We collapsed into our chairs, ordered breakfast, and set about the business of clearing out whatever cobwebs were going to get in the way of our progress that day. One of us had a toddler with a rash and was waiting for a call from home to hear the doctor's report and felt angst-ridden about not being there with a kiddo in the doctor's office, and the other was headed for Seattle for work and was angst-ridden about her decision to leave her kids behind for a few days.

Here's the thing: our feelings about those heavy issues—the guilt we feel as moms sometimes—had to be resolved before we could be productive and creative. In other words, we had to take care of ourselves before we could accomplish what needed to be accomplished that day. And, instinctively, we knew that in advance, which is why we scheduled the meet at the Ojai Valley Inn. So, we had a heart-to-heart over breakfast, and then we did a forty-minute guided meditation. What was left after our heart-to-heart was cleared out with the meditation, and after that very small investment of time taking care of ourselves, we were outstandingly, remarkably productive and focused.

After the meditation, we went to the inn's patio with our paper outline and pens. In thirty minutes, we made unbelievable progress on our presentation. After a while, we got stuck. We knew we needed a change of scenery to get things moving. So, we moved, sat by the fire in the lounge for a few minutes and talked about ways to work through the parts we were stuck on, and—wouldn't you know it?—more ideas started flowing just because we moved our bodies and changed our scenery. We changed venues a lot of times that day, and we finished our presentation and had a product that we were proud of and that met all of our intentions.

The point is we weren't popping champagne, going to individual massages, or talking to other people lounging by the pool. Everything we did was together—meditation, massages, lunch—and when the ideas came, we wrote them down with paper and pen and talked them through. When we got stuck, we talked it through until the right ideas came. When we really got stuck, we physically moved our bodies to a new space, a new environment. This doesn't have to be in a hotel—you could do this in a park and a café.

There's a strongly held belief in our society, and in our industry, that you have to be in an office to get work done. Not true. Our best work—personally and professionally—happens when we're on long walks or hikes and when we're taking care of ourselves.

We both have offices, but we very rarely go there to do work. We can't figure out why people want to have offices downtown or in any urban environment. If you have to go to an office, the best place to have one is where you can get outside and go for a walk in nature when you need inspiration or when you're stuck. For us, there's too much input in an urban environment to allow space for any nurturing, creativity, or meaningful work. And we find when we bring clients to that type of environment, they are far more receptive to it than they are to a typical law office.

So, take some time to try some new things and see what resonates with you, with your heart, with your body.

Chapter Takeaways

- Taking care of your own well-being is an indispensable part of your duty of competence as a lawyer.
- Taking small, incremental steps to change how law is practiced and how lawyers are regulated can instill greater well-being in the profession.
- Practicing self-care sometimes means getting out of the office to figure out some thorny problem, and seeing if you can think more clearly in a different space.

20

On New Motherhood and Family

When Trial by Woman Becomes Trial by Mother

A Letter from Theresa, to the Mamas

When I was pregnant, there were books everywhere—books about what piece of fruit your baby is the same size as this week, books on what to definitely do when you're pregnant, books on what definitely *not* to do when you're pregnant, books on how to give birth, and books on how to take care of a newborn. There were books on every imaginable pregnancy and motherhood topic. But there were no books about being a pregnant trial lawyer or being a trial lawyer who is a mother. And, wow, would that have been helpful.

I felt really alone when I was pregnant and when I was first figuring out how to "do" motherhood as a trial lawyer. Sometimes, I still feel alone, and sometimes I still feel like I'm trying to figure it out.

When you're pregnant, everyone wants to give you advice. Advice about nursing and which kind of baby wraps or carriers are best was helpful and interesting. But what I would have loved would have been for someone to come up to me, take me by the hand, and say, "Come with me. Sit down. I'm going to tell you what it's like to be a trial lawyer and mother."

I'm holding your hand, and we're sitting down. There are things I want to share with you, my trial lawyer sister, that I wish someone had shared with me. Not everything would have been easier, but I would have felt a little more prepared and, more than anything, supported.

Being pregnant is amazing. The changes that are happening to your body, the way your baby is growing, is a miracle. The dreams that you have for this little human are exciting, and the love you feel is already beyond measure. Pregnancy is a time of tenderness, of softness, of nesting and nurturing and planning. All thoughts turn to family and to you in your new role as mother.

And then you walk into work in the morning. There it is. The male energy. It smacks you in the face, waking you up from your prenatally blissful state. You take it on every day. You get into the role you have to play to be a successful trial lawyer. That's what I did with my first child. I acted like I wasn't pregnant.

Something is due tomorrow, and I need to stay late? No problem. Everyone wants to power through this deposition and skip lunch? No complaints from me. We're in trial, and the next break isn't for forty-five minutes, and I have to pee? It's OK, I can wait. Congratulations? For what? Oh, right, I'm pregnant. I forgot. I never think about it. I'm a killer trial lawyer, so, that's all I'm thinking about.

I thought I was supposed to pretend I wasn't pregnant and ignore my baby when I was "being a trial lawyer."

Every single one of these things happened to me—several times—when I was pregnant with my daughter, Quinn. I made these choices.

I said and did these things. At the time, I thought I was being a great lawyer. I thought I was doing what I was supposed to do. I feel ashamed admitting it now. Not because I did anything wrong, but because I didn't know any better, and I didn't have anyone to tell me or show me what it could look like.

There was so much I didn't realize. I had already built my reputation. So have you. Pregnancy and motherhood don't erode your reputation. You don't have to fight harder when you're pregnant or when you're a mother. You can take your foot off the gas. And it's more than OK. It's a must.

You don't get to do this pregnancy again. It's your job to soak up every minute of it, to read all of the books, to laugh with your partner when your baby is the size of a squash, to let your partner rub your legs and make your dinner and draw your bath and gush over what an amazing mother you are going to be. This is the time for those things. You are no less of a trial lawyer for it.

I had a second shot at being a pregnant trial lawyer, with my son, Jackson. And what a different trip it was. It looked more like this:

- In a deposition: *We've been going for forty minutes, and I'd like to take a break please* [profuse apologies from opposing counsel for not offering me a break sooner, followed by asking me what time I would like to break for lunch and how long of a lunch break I would like to take].
- In scheduling with opposing counsel: *No, I'm not available for a deposition that day because I have a doctor's appointment* [followed by scheduling around all of my prenatal appointments without complaint or objection].
- In trial at sidebar: *Your Honor, I know it's not time for a scheduled break, but I need to take a break to use the restroom please* [followed by gracious allowance].

In all parts of life, we show people how to treat us. It's no different when we're pregnant trial lawyers. All of my overcompensating when

I was pregnant with Quinn was for me, because I was scared that I was somehow less. In reality, I was more. I was growing a human. And, because of that, I was a woman to be respected and revered. As soon as I respected and revered myself, so did everyone else. And, by the way, I still got calls from lawyers, including men, wanting to try cases with me even though I was pregnant.

So for you, my dear working mama-to-be, what follows here is my best advice. It's the advice I wish I had been given, and I hope it makes your journey all the more sweet.

Be Gentle with Yourself

The expectations we set for ourselves are the highest. Lower your expectations. Be gentle with yourself. Be kind. Be loving. See yourself and treat yourself as the miracle-growing vessel that you are. Your body is magical. It has all it needs to grow a human. It knows exactly what to do without you telling it. Come along for the ride. *Be there* for every delicious moment of this miraculous experience. Don't miss it.

What this looks like is different for everyone. For me, it was long baths, hypno-birthing therapy, birth meditations, taking the time to really nourish my body and my baby with food. And setting professional limits. I took the weekends off. I didn't "catch up" or "get ahead." I accomplished what I could accomplish during the week and did nothing on the weekends. No briefs, no emails. And during the week, I kept regular hours. I didn't work late. If I had a doctor's appointment, I missed work. Looking back, I have no idea what I "missed" at work when I was taking care of myself. Everything got done; so, if I had been working instead of taking care of myself, I would have been doing something that didn't need to get done.

I did not lose the respect of any of my peers for taking care of myself and my baby. In fact, I probably lost more respect when I wasn't taking care of myself and my baby.

When I was pregnant with Jackson, my client came in from out of state, and I took her to her deposition. It was the first time I met the defense lawyer in person. I was obviously pregnant. The defense lawyer was a kind gentleman who had high school aged kids.

At the end of the deposition, he looked at me and said, "I guess we won't be getting much done on this case in the next few months."

Because I heard his tone and felt his energy, I knew he didn't mean that the way it sounded. What he meant was, "Congratulations, I can see you're pregnant. I want you to know I'll be happy to work with you on scheduling to accommodate your maternity leave." This man, as lovely as he otherwise was, just didn't have the right words.

So, in response to, "I guess we won't be getting much done on this case in the next few months," I said, "That's right, I'll be on maternity leave from mid-June through September. If you expect something to come up during that time that needs to be handled, let me know before mid-June, and I'd be happy to work something out with you."

Take as Much Maternity Leave as You Possibly Can

Every moment of your child's life is special, but those first days, weeks, months are amazing and irreplaceable. This is a sacred time. It's a time of bonding, nourishment, and bliss. That little person who was in your belly for so long finally comes out. You meet her, and it's magical. The world changes, because you have changed. You are a mother. Your heart feels more than you ever thought it could. You are in awe of this little person you helped create and grow. You are beyond in love. You are fiercely protective. You would lay your life down for this baby of yours.

The feelings are big—bigger than anything you've ever felt. Suddenly, everything else comes into focus. Priorities are clarified. You recognize that some things you spent your emotional, physical, or intellectual capital on weren't important, and you let them go. You become a role model and a teacher. You are a guide in the most magnificent way.

You will be awake at hours you've rarely been awake. You will stare at your baby—her perfect lips, ears, fingers, and toes. Together, you'll create a rhythm for your new life together. You'll figure out together how and when to eat, sleep, bathe, and gaze lovingly at each other.

You are truly in a state of euphoria in these sacred, early days. Naturally, there comes a time when you are tired or your breasts hurt because you're nursing or you're sore from the delivery, whether it was vaginal or surgical. But even those feelings are imbued with love and adoration and excitement and pure magic.

I remember going to the doctor for my six-week checkup after each of my children and being told I was "cleared" to go back to work. I was fortunate to still have six more weeks ahead of me. After my daughter was born, I remember thinking, "I'm just getting the hang of breastfeeding and taking care of her and taking care of myself. There's no way I could leave her and work." After my son was born, I remember not feeling physically able to do an eight-plus-hours-per-day job if I had to. I was still very sore, still bleeding, and I was exhausted because I had a newborn and a two-year-old. After my first delivery, my mind wasn't ready to work at six weeks, and after my second delivery, my body wasn't ready to work at six weeks. As mothers, we have to honor both our minds and our bodies. Our minds and our bodies know what's right for us.

Make a specific plan to take as much time as you possibly can. Arrange for short-term disability, arrange for family leave, arrange to use your vacation days and sick days and flex days and PTO days. Arrange to stay home without pay if you can. I have a friend who worked extra before her baby came so that she had enough money to pay her bills during the portion of her maternity leave that was unpaid. I am grabbing you by the shoulders and looking into your eyes and urging you, please take at least three months off. And if it turns out you want to go back to work sooner, I'm sure you'll be welcomed with open arms.

Working too hard has become a bizarre badge of honor in our culture. When I ask a woman how she's doing, I almost always hear about how busy she is, how run-down she is, how she gives and gives to her job, her husband, and her children until she's empty. Is this how you want to live your life? Is this a good thing? When you pass on, do you want people to say about you, she worked herself to the bone; she rarely had any fun; she gave everything she had to her job and husband and kids; she was always tired and run-down and unhappy; and she didn't know how to, or didn't care enough, to take care of herself?

When I'm gone, I want people to say, this woman had an amazing life; she was an extraordinary mother who raised kind, loving, compassionate humans and good citizens, and she and her children loved each other unconditionally; she was a loyal and devoted wife and a true partner to her husband, yet she let him take care of her; she created a warm and an inviting home; she traveled the world with her family, sharing experiences that opened all of their minds to new thoughts and new possibilities; she was a cherished friend; and she was a mentor to many, offering thoughtful guidance and encouraging women and inspiring women to create greatness within their own lives.

For a long time, I thought my titles defined me. I'm a lawyer; I'm a daughter; I'm a wife; I'm a mother. The truth is our roles *do not* define us. How we connect with and relate to other humans within those roles is how we truly define ourselves in this world.

As mothers, we must lead by example. Decide what you want to model for your children. Decide what you want them to say when you pass on and start modeling that and living that today. It starts with the birth of your child. What role will you play? What life will you model? Will you be the woman who wanted to take a long maternity leave but assumed it couldn't happen in her job and didn't take the time to figure out how to make it happen? Will you be the woman who let a male or an institution tell her how much time was appropriate for her to take off to bond with her child? Or will you be the woman who says, the birth of my child is a critically important time in my life and my child's life, and here's how I'm going to handle it.

Take the time. Honor yourself and your child. Whatever you want is possible. You only have to believe it's possible. Create your life, and model for your child from the start.

Maternity Leave Means No Emails

I was diligent about this with my first maternity leave. I didn't check email while I was breastfeeding my daughter. When she slept in my arms, I just stared at her. I was 100 percent *present*, and it felt *good*. I fell off the wagon, so to speak, with my second maternity leave. Initially, I was multitasking—checking emails while I was breastfeeding and holding him while he slept. I had my own firm to run at that point, and I felt like I knew what I was doing in the newborn department; so, I figured I could do it all more efficiently this time around. But it didn't take long to figure out that, for me, it didn't feel right *at all*. I felt disconnected from my baby and myself as a new mother. I felt distracted. When I realized what was happening, I disconnected from work and from my email and got present. And that's how I spent the rest of my leave.

Yes, as a woman who runs her own firm, there were times during my leave that I had to carve out time to address things that came up. But those few times were at night, after both kids were asleep. And it was task-specific. I didn't check email, surf the internet, piddle around with small tasks to avoid doing what I had to do. I sat down, did what was absolutely needed to be done as efficiently as possible, turned off my computer, and went back to being on maternity leave. Being able to do that has actually improved my ability to work as a mother post-maternity leave.

Make a New-Mama Care Plan

Pregnant women are accommodated and revered in our society. As soon as the baby is delivered, however, it can feel like the mama is forgotten and all of the focus is on the baby. Even the new mama does this! But the new mama's well-being and care is more important than ever once baby arrives. This is the woman who must *create* the food that will nourish her baby. In order to produce milk, you have to nourish yourself. You can't neglect yourself. The best way to prevent that from happening is to make a plan in advance.

When I was a first-time mama, none of this was on my radar. For weeks, I had a house filled with family from out of town wanting to visit the baby and support us. The truth is, like most people, they focused on the baby and not so much the mama. Don't get me wrong, it was wonderful to have helping hands around the house and company and love. But the overwhelming feeling I had was isolation. I remember one evening, sitting on the sofa in the family room, and my husband had prepared another wonderful meal. My newborn, however, wanted to nurse and suckle for two hours straight beginning at dinnertime every night. I sat on the sofa with my baby, watching my husband and our family eat. I was starving—because I was exclusively breastfeeding, which requires a lot of calories. They wrapped up my plate and set it aside. But what I really needed was for someone to see what was happening night after night, bring the food over to me, and feed me if necessary. This is what the new mama needs. I'm sure my husband and family didn't intend to exclude me. The truth is I didn't know how to ask for what I needed. I needed to be taken care of because I was so drained from taking care of a brand-new baby for the better part of twenty-four hours a day. I was so concerned about taking care of my baby that I wasn't thinking about taking care of myself. In that moment, in that recovery time, I needed someone else to take care of me. I just didn't realize it.

There are services that deliver wholesome, nourishing foods to your front door. All you have to do is heat them up. You can stock your own pantry, fridge, and freezer with good foods before you go on leave. Whatever you do, make a plan in advance. You can't avoid being tired. You can't avoid your house being a little or a lot less tidy than normal. But you can avoid being hungry, and you can avoid putting junk into your body. What you eat becomes your baby's food. And what you eat fuels your body. The better the food, the better your body works.

Redesign Your Work

Some days I want to be a stay-at-home mom. Some days I want to be a lawyer. This is an ongoing battle I struggle with on a regular basis. I recognize that I'm privileged to have the choice. Privileged to be educated, to be successful, to have children.

Before I had my first child, I was working fifty to sixty hours per week. I put a lot of pressure on myself to be the best for my clients. The workload was manageable, and the hours were doable for that stage of my life.

I was newly married and planning for a family. And I planned to continue at that pace even after I had kids. It never crossed my mind that things might change—that I might want things to change. Or that I might not know what I want.

After a devastating miscarriage, everything changed. I couldn't envision working even forty hours per week, much less fifty, sixty, or more hours during trial. I couldn't imagine being away from home and away from a child every day. I knew I wanted to work, but I really didn't know what that was going to look like when my daughter would eventually arrive.

My life went off the rails after the miscarriage. I dove into work to bury the pain. I never properly healed my heart. It wasn't long before I quit my job, left my very generous salary and very generous bonuses, left my free health-care and free disability insurance, and plummeted into the unknown.

Courtney had been a friend for a year or two at that point. I looked up to her. She worked for herself. She worked on only a handful of cases at a time. I wanted to be able to have that lifestyle someday, but I didn't know how to get from where I was as an associate working full-time at a law firm to where she was. The truth is it never occurred to me that it was possible. Then, one day, Courtney said to me, "You know, you can do what I do if you want to. You're good enough to do it." That changed the world for me. To have her say I was good enough was everything. Because I didn't know I was. I still didn't know how I would get from Point A to Point B, but someone had told me it was possible.

So there I was, barely keeping the wheels on, when Courtney introduced me to Nick Rowley. He offered to create a job for me as the managing partner of his law firm's unstaffed San Diego office. He said there was one condition: "You have to have that baby you want."

By the time I was planning for my daughter's arrival, I had a flexible job that allowed me to work from home and make my own hours. It was everything I didn't know that I would need.

Listen to Yourself When Things Change

When my daughter was born, I had a home office. A nanny came into my house a few days a week. I nursed my daughter every two hours and popped out of the office to take a deep inhale of her delicious baby scent anytime I wanted. I took depositions by phone. Everything was going better than I could have imagined.

But as she got older, a feeling started growing inside of me. I didn't want our nanny to be the one to see her sit up for the first time, crawl for the first time, say her first word, or take her first step. I wanted—*needed*—for those moments to be *mine*.

That's when I asked myself this question: Do I even want to do this anymore? Do I want to work? I *loved* being a mom. And I was *really good* at it. I felt conflicted. Not just one side of me feels this way and the other side of me feels that way. It was more like my insides were being twisted and wrenched in this battle between working mom and stay-at-home mom.

I had a stay-at-home mom. My grandmother was a stay-at-home mom. My great-grandmother was a stay-at-home mom. That's what I saw and what I knew. I spent a lot of time with my grandparents. They were young and active, and they loved having me around. I had a swing set in their backyard. I had my own room at their house. I watched my grandmother cook, do laundry, clean the house, shop for groceries, go shopping with her friends, and generally take care of my grandfather, their house, and everything in it. My grandmother has eleven siblings. Almost all of them lived very close to her house. When people came over to visit, the women gathered around the kitchen table, and the men were shooed off to the den. Mothering, caretaking, homemaking was all I ever saw.

And it wasn't until my mid-thirties, when my daughter came, that the thought of being a full-time mother ever crossed my mind. But what about the prestigious undergraduate degree from the University of Virginia? And what about the law degree? And what about the fact that I passed the bar? And what about the fact that I was incredibly experienced and incredibly successful in the five short years I had been practicing? What about all of the awards I received as a lawyer? What about all of the accolades and professional accomplishments and plaques? Oh, the plaques.

Job and Accomplishments versus Family

My job defined me. My accomplishments defined me. I was always the smart one. I was the first person to go to college in my family. I was a *lawyer*. And that was *important*. I helped people. I did good things and big things and impressive things. And I would be walking away from all of that if I were *just a mom*. And now, here I was. Every hormone, every cell, every biological drive in my body was shouting, "Quit!!!! Be with your baby!!!!" But my mind fought back.

I learned a lot in that first year about being a working mother and, in particular, being a working mother trying cases. Courtney and I had our children around the same time. We were brand-new moms when we tried a huge brain injury case against a big corporation. My daughter was nine months, and her son was four months. It was a bifurcated trial where a fifteen-year-old on a bike without a helmet was hit in a crosswalk by a truck driver. The bike got all the way across the road and got halfway onto the sidewalk when the truck driver hit the bike's back wheel.

Courtney and I were both breastfeeding. We were given accommodations by the court. During breaks, the courtroom clerk would take us to another floor and open a vacant courtroom for us. We had nannies pushing our babies around the courthouse grounds for the morning. We would meet the nannies and babies in the vacant courtroom during the 10 a.m. break and nurse our babies. At noon, we would have lunch nearby with the nannies and babies. During the afternoon break, the court clerk would let us into the vacant courtroom again, this time to pump breast milk—our babies were at the hotel.

Not long into this three-week trial, the court clerk stopped letting us into the vacant courtroom. After waiting outside the locked courtroom a couple of times without the clerk showing up to let us in, we figured we no longer had that accommodation. So, Courtney and I nursed our babies and pumped in the toilet stalls of the public restrooms while we prepared for the next witnesses.

Ask for What You Need

What makes me feel shame is that I didn't have the courage to say anything. I didn't have the courage to stand up for myself. I didn't want to rock the boat or draw attention to myself. I was embarrassed to need an accommodation and was fine to act like I really didn't need an accommodation. I regret that choice. I wish I had done better for myself. I wish I'd had the strength to insist that what I deserved and needed be given back to me.

Later, that became a defining moment in my life. I realized that, in that moment, I was a little girl who wanted to be accepted and loved and not cause any problems. But I was also a mother who didn't stand up for herself and didn't stand up for her daughter. This is a story I'll tell my daughter as a teaching tool. You know when something is wrong. You know how it feels in your gut. Know that there is *nothing* wrong with speaking up for yourself. Know that it is your *obligation* to speak up for yourself. It's your job to take care of you.

The more experience I had with motherhood and being a working litigator, the more easily I was able to stand my ground. For example, I had a male attorney demand one evening by email that I take a deposition on a case that wasn't mine and that I wasn't at all familiar with. I clearly and directly explained that I would not being taking the deposition:

1. I did not have adequate time to prepare for the deposition.
2. I was a breastfeeding mother and, if I was going to be away from my child for any length of time, I needed to pump and store enough breast milk to feed my child in my absence and that it was not physically possible to produce an adequate milk supply on such short notice.

The attorney then understood and told me that I should feel free to ask if there was any way he could help me in the future.

Sometimes the pendulum swings back and forth for us rather quickly and strongly. That is how it has been for me with being a mother and working. I've learned that when you ask for what you really need, people are there to help you.

Our Childhoods and Our Adult Choices

My mom went to work full-time when I was in high school. She left in the morning before I left for school, and she came home late each night. I remember feeling lonely. I remember feeling a little lost. I remember missing her. I know that I had the opportunity to make poor choices when she wasn't around. And I know that I made many poor choices. Stupid choices sometimes.

As with anything else, our viewpoints are colored by our experiences. My viewpoint on motherhood and working is colored by my experience as someone who had a stay-at-home mom and then didn't have a stay-at-home mom. And my viewpoint is also colored by the fact that I am a working mom.

My solution has been to design my law firm, my practice, and my schedule to allow me to feel like a stay-at-home mom and still work. I have an office in my home. This is where I work. I don't go to my "real" office. If I have to take a deposition, I do it by phone. If I have a hearing, I attend by phone. My files are electronic. My mail is scanned and sent to me. Everything is automated so that I can focus on the task at hand—whether that's working or raising babies.

A number of years ago, I met a female defense attorney who works full-time in litigation and has young children. She said she loves her work and was candid about needing time away from her kids. She said she's a better mother because she works. She is happy, and the schedule and the childcare arrangement work for her. I know other lady lawyers with children who have to work full-time for financial reasons and would prefer to work part-time or not at all.

Years ago, I met a defense attorney at a high-profile San Diego firm who "job shares" with another attorney. Because of that arrangement, she was able to litigate cases and have time at home with her kids.

The choices I've made today are different from the choices I thought I would have made. And I don't know what choices I'll make in the future. I know that I struggle with this question, this issue, of how to mother and how to work. I know a lot of you struggle too. And it's OK.

Each woman chooses. That's the beauty of our country. Each mother chooses whether to work, how much to work, where to work, when to work. As women in this country, and in this profession, we are privileged. We have choices. We are not prisoners of circumstance. We are educated, professional, thoughtful women. And many of us are also mothers. Some of us choose to continue working. Some of us choose to stop working and be full-time mothers. Some of us create a middle ground.

Our choices don't make some mothers better than others and some mothers worse than others. They are just choices. And they are our choices to make.

Open your mind. Open your heart. Tune in. Connect with yourself. Envision your ideal situation. What do you really, really want? See it. Feel what it would feel like to be living that life. Then expect it. Create it with your mind, your thoughts, your energy, and the energy of the Universe. What you want is available to you.

It's OK to Set Boundaries That Work for You

Courtney and I are trial lawyers. We litigate cases. Everything having to do with a case before, during, and even after trials, that's us. That's what we do.

What happens when a trial lawyer doesn't want to try cases? Identity crisis. Am I still a trial lawyer? Does it matter? I'm still a lawyer. But I'm not a trial lawyer. Right? Or is it like when you're in Los Angeles, and your waiter tells you he's an actor. You ask him what he's been in, and he hasn't been in anything. He's not an actor. He wants to be an actor. Am I no longer a trial lawyer if I don't want to try cases?

That was the identity crisis I had after I had my second child. After a lot of back-and-forth in my own head, I told Courtney and her husband, Nick, "Until further notice, I don't want to try cases. I'll work up the cases, take the depositions; I'll do everything except try the cases. I don't want to be in court all day for weeks on end, working late, and be away from my two-year-old and newborn. I need to be with my babies right now." And God bless them, they supported me 100 percent. And so it went for about a year.

Around that time, a case I had worked on for a couple of years was set for trial. I was afraid to try the case by myself and wasn't sure if I even wanted to get back into the courtroom. Was I still a trial lawyer? Could I still do it? Did I want to be away from my kids during a grueling trial schedule? I talked it through with Nick Rowley, and he encouraged me to get back in the saddle and said he would come down and do all the heavy lifting. The jury awarded a $6.5 million verdict.

That was what I needed to reignite my passion for trial. Shortly after that, I had another case set for trial. At that point, I was excited and ready to go. My friend, Keith Bruno, and I tried the case together. In the middle of that trial, we were offered a substantial settlement that was a phenomenal result for our client.

What we want may change. Our boundaries may change. And all of that is OK. It's our job to identify what we want, set our boundaries, and be flexible enough to change when our needs and the needs of our families change.

Practical Stuff for Lawyer Mamas

We have been in trial while pregnant. We've been in trial with babies. We don't have it all figured out, but we've found some things that help.

Pumping

I wish I had started pumping while I was on maternity leave. There was so much *milk*! By the time my milk supply adjusted to my baby's demand, there was only as much milk as the baby needed. That meant that storing extra milk for days when I had to be away was next to impossible. With my second child, I started pumping milk right away and freezing it. By the time I had to leave him for a half day or a day, I had plenty of milk stored.

Work Schedules

Make your schedule work for you. Just because you had a certain schedule before your baby was born doesn't mean you have to keep the same schedule. Work longer hours fewer days per week. Work short days. Work part-time. Work for yourself. Whatever you need, it can be done. But it begins with you identifying what you need and making it happen.

Childcare

Childcare is a deeply personal choice. Some prefer to have care providers in their homes. Some prefer live-in care. Some prefer day-care facilities. Some prefer in-home care at a caregiver's home. Experiment. See what works for you. The key is being open until you find the right fit. We have friends in New York that use share nannies to cut down on costs. There are a lot more options now than there were ten, five, even two years ago for working mothers. We have a long way to go, but know that there is more available to you if you are willing to honor yourself and your needs.

Courtney:

> The state of maternity leave in America is archaic and must change. Eighty-eight percent of women in America do not have paid access to maternity leave. Half of new mothers are not even eligible for the Family Medical Leave Act. As women business owners and leaders, we are the ones who can change this—and create a better future for our children and our society. We do this by demanding paid leave for ourselves and securing it for those around us. Whether we are in a position of power or not, we have to lead from wherever we are, and part of leadership is recognizing that our voice is powerful enough to speak for those who cannot speak for themselves—mothers, babies, and otherwise.

Chapter Takeaways

- Go easy on yourself. You won't get a chance to do this pregnancy again, and your career can work around you and your needs.
- Take as much maternity leave as you possibly can, in whatever way you can manage it. Your baby is only this tiny once. Both you and your baby need this time.
- Set the boundaries you need when you get back to work, and reimagine your life in whatever new way you need it to work.

On Health and Healing

An Interview with Michele Hakakha, MD, and Michael R. Sanchez, MD

This interview is with Dr. Michele Hakakha, board-certified ob-gyn, and Dr. Michael R. Sanchez, attending physician at Cedars Sinai, Obstetric Anesthesia. We spoke on April 16, 2018.

We are sitting in Michele's beautiful, light-filled living room in her home in Los Angeles. We became friends after she delivered my first son. Born and raised on the island of Maui, her spirit remains open and warm. She is truly one of my favorite people to be around, but I think I didn't truly start getting to know her until I saw her in the operating room. Her grace in the midst of absolute intensity—her ability to exude competence and authority while simultaneously putting everyone in the room at ease—has been an inspiration to me, personally and professionally. She runs a high-profile private practice in Beverly Hills, California. She is a surgeon, a mother, a friend, and a game changer in her field. She is a badass. She is wearing a gorgeous blue Ulla Johnson dress and a pair of red strappy flats. The Gray Malin photography on the wall is a reminder of her love of ocean and sand. We both have a glass of wine, and her dog, Duffy, is sitting on her lap.

Michael, Michele's friend and colleague, is a board-certified OB anesthesiologist working at Cedars Sinai in Los Angeles. He has been at the epicenter of women's health for the majority of his career. He and Michele have been good friends throughout the course of their careers and had a meeting planned tonight to go over their recent trip to set up a medical clinic in Guatemala. He has just walked through the door, in scrubs, and has fixed himself a big bowl of salad. He was not expecting to get roped into our conversation, so of course, we invited him to join us. I'm grateful he did. I think you'll find them both, as I do, delightful.

Courtney: So, I have here a world-class anesthesiologist, a renowned and beautiful ob-gyn, and a glass of wine. If this isn't a party... I'm so excited to be here with you both. Michele, you are from Maui. Tell us about the girl barefoot on the beach in Maui who ends up running her own kick-ass practice.

Michele: My father was a dentist. He wanted me to practice with him, but I felt like I had another calling. Since I was twelve years old, I wanted to do OB. I had hands-on experience when I was twelve. I went into Maui Memorial Hospital with my dad's best friend, and he let me deliver a baby with his hands around me, and I fell in love. I was bringing another spirit into the world from another world.

Courtney: Let's talk about what you're excited about right now in health care for women.

Michele: I'm excited about the fact that there are many options for women who historically have felt like—how real can I get right now?

Courtney: Real real.

Michele: I think the thing that's changing the most is women's sexuality as they get older. Right, so historically it's been, like, you're going through menopause; you don't need to have sex anymore. It hurts. It's uncomfortable. So, close up shop. But now we have so many things that can help with that, and you don't have to sit there and suffer through it, and you have to realize that men want to have sex until they're seventy-five, eight-five, and so on, and so do we.

For a long time, I think women said, "You know what? I'm done having kids, and I don't have to enjoy having sex, and I don't have to be happy anymore." And that was what was expected 'cause there were so many, no offense, male physicians who said, "You have to suck it up. Take one for the team. Have sex, don't enjoy it." That's not how it has to be anymore. We have so many options with hormones and creams and lasers.

You don't have to, you don't have to forfeit having babies to work, to not be a good mother, to not be a good lover, to not be a good . . . You can have everything.

Michael: I think it's hard for women now because in so many households the women, the moms, the women have to work to support the family. I think a lot of the nurses we work with have to work hard to make ends meet. They have families and work. I don't think they get to work out. I don't think they get to take care of themselves. I think it's burnout. It's hard working twelve-hour shifts—doctors too.

Courtney: You see burnout?

Michael: Yes.

Courtney: What are our options if we are burnt out? Let's say, let's say we are focusing on our careers, and we are post-thirty-five mothers. Are there options for libido, for enjoyment, for sanity, and for balance—are there options? Is there life after kids? After business? After the workday?

Michele: I think ultimately we have to take just one hour. Take one hour a day and go exercise, go do meditation, go do yoga . . .

Michael: Do something for yourself. Take time for yourself.

Michele: But you feel guilty taking time for yourself.

Courtney: Well, for me, you help with that guilt. When I have a physician telling me to take care of myself, I feel a little less guilty at least. Hopefully, whoever's reading this knows it's doctor's orders and that's the bump in confidence they need to take care of themselves.

Michele: Yes! And that looks like different things for different people. You have to find that alone time. That looks like yoga . . . running. That looks like meditation. Yes, reading. That looks like hiking. That looks like whatever it takes for you to have at least one hour out of twenty-four hours. Your dog sitting on your lap. Um, it, it really is whatever that is for you. Is that shopping? Is that walking? Is that traveling? Is that visiting your family?

You need to not put yourself at the bottom because we all do that. We put our kids first and our husbands first and our work first, and we say, "I'm fine, I'm fine, I'm fine." You need to take time for yourself always, at least one hour a day. It won't make a difference in your income or your family's—it's about sustainability. It's going make a difference in how you are as a person and how you reflect as a mother, as a spouse, as everything else.

Courtney: Dr. Mike, why do you think women have a hard time doing this, and do you think there is a way that men can help?

Michael: With women taking care of themselves? I think as men we almost have to give them permission.

Courtney: That's so true.

Michele: Wow. I mean, that's the best statement.

Michael: Like, it's OK the house is a mess. It's OK if the kids are going crazy . . . They need that time. I think as a husband, spouse, or partner, you have to understand that and then just say, "It's OK, I've got the kids now" or "I will go do the grocery shopping" or "I will cook dinner and you go."

Courtney: What's the result of that?

Michael: I think it'd be a happier relationship. If you give the time for your spouse and what they need to do, they'll come back in a much happier place.

Michele: Yes. Because we feel like we have to have everything perfect all the time.

Courtney: What happens when a woman is depleted? What happens to the family?

Michele: The entire machine breaks down. I had a good talk with a woman who's an ob-gyn at Cedars, and I said, "I have a patient in labor. I have a kid who's supposed to go to tennis. I have another one who's supposed to go to a reading class. He's at work, and I am running this whole thing. My practice, my kids, I don't know who's picking up who. I don't know who's making dinner." She said to me, "The woman runs everything. If one screw falls outta place, the whole machine breaks down." And she's right. There are times when

I'm trying to function as a doctor, as a mother, as a wife, and I can't do it all. I can't, and it's so stressful for me.

Courtney: When women like you speak up like this—with honesty, with compassion—it helps all of us. I truly believe that. I think there has been a lot of great movement in the last decade as far as wellness goes. As far as taking care of women goes. And encouraging all of us to take care of ourselves. But I think we have a long way to go. It's sad, a lot of this still goes overlooked.

Is that something you've seen in medicine? Women being overlooked? Their comfort, their safety?

Michele: (to Michael) You have brought so many techniques to Cedars to make women be more comfortable. No one else has done what you have done.

Michael: Epidurals, I think, are an example—I think part of that would stem back earlier when they had issues with insurance reimbursements. Insurers felt that women could have babies without epidurals, and it was fine, and it wasn't until insurance companies and ACOG said, "You know what? Women, if they request epidurals, they should be able to have pain relief and the insurance companies should pay for it." So that was not too long ago when we didn't have reimbursement for epidurals. Being able to have epidurals not only provides pain relief but provides a safety net in case of emergency.

Courtney: There is stigma around these issues. I guess it starts with whether we choose even to have babies, how we have them if we do, and so on. Do these stigmas come up in your treatment with your patients, Michele?

Michele: Of course. I think it's really important that women make choices that are right for them, their lives, and their bodies. When we encourage women to do what's right for them, our health-care system changes accordingly. What matters most is the health and safety of the mother and the baby.

Courtney: And you have a tremendous amount of experience keeping women and babies safe. Your track record is amazing. Do you think that has anything to do with your being a woman yourself?

Michele: Yes.

Michael: Yes.

Courtney: Let's talk about med school—being a woman in med school. A smart, capable, very beautiful woman in med school. Was it hard?

Michele: Yes. It was hard because I felt like every time I did something that was great based on grades or accomplishments, it was chalked up to, "You might've slept with someone" or "Somehow someone gave this to you because of the way you look" versus what you actually earned.

I worked very hard. Maybe sometimes harder to prove that I belonged there.

You have to be almost twice as smart. Twice as good. You have to be more driven, because if you're not, it doesn't work because everyone expects you to be a housewife or thinks you got helped along because of the way you look or because of your sex. And that's real when you walk into the operating room and have to prove yourself.

Courtney: How does that translate into your career? You got out and went out on your own, so you are running a practice, a business—and you are the only OB in your practice. You are present for all of your patients' births, you are a mother of two young amazing girls, you are in surgery multiple times a week, you are plugged in to different organizations, you have that group of girlfriends I adore . . . Who are you?

Michele: I do a good job, you know? I care about what I do. I care about my patients so much. And I'm a control freak. I don't want anyone else managing my patients. I think what's hard is managing the being a woman and being sensual, being into fashion and makeup, being a mother and everything else, and managing that while also being a tough doctor in the OR and, and . . .

Courtney: What about for you, Michele? Do women have to work harder than men for you to trust them—their competence?

Michele: Hmm. (pause) Sometimes nurses do.

Courtney: I think sometimes women are hard on other women. That's true in what I do. When I see a woman's name on the pleadings, I think, "Oh dear, here we go. This is going to be difficult." I don't like that about myself, but it's true.

Michele: Yes.

Courtney: So, one of the other things I'm seeing out there is that women are running successful businesses, starting their own practices, working longer, and getting coupled up or having babies later. Is that another aspect of your practice?

Michele: Yeah, I think fertility is a big issue right now because we are—waiting longer to have kids. People are married, and they're divorced, and they have another family. They are getting advanced degrees. And I think women need to know that there are a lot of options. That there are a lot of great advances that are happening that make it so we can have families later, if that is our choice. But we can also have families and be successful. That it's all OK.

Michael: I see that too. There's this pressure to have families early. I mean, I work with residents. There are many times residents will be pregnant—women residents are pregnant—but they don't want to say anything. They won't say anything about it because they don't want people to judge them or pass them over because they're pregnant. You know, so you're, not only are you pregnant, you're tired. I can't imagine being pregnant and tired and then having the demanding hours of residency, and then trying to hide it all.

Courtney: My gosh.

Michele: I remember studying for my board exams. That entire dining room table was covered in books. I had a one-year-old at home. I was still breastfeeding. I had to fly to Texas to sit in front of three old men who were quizzing me about years of doing what I do. I mean, no offense, but I don't think men could do what we do.

Michael: We can't—I can't even do what you do now.

Michele: Run a practice. Have children. Run a household. It's extremely demanding.

Courtney: What advice are you giving your patients about this? You work with extremely high-functioning, high-demand women. What are you doing to help them protect their longevity, their health, their sanity?

Michele: Well, I think I'm talking to them about everything. It's looking at the whole picture. I'm not talking to them just about their vaginal issues. I am talking to them about their sanity, their emotions. I'm talking to them about PMS, and I talk to them about myself. About everything I've been through, and what I have learned and feared and struggled with—that's what's amazing about me being a woman and being in women's health care. If I was a urologist, I don't know that I would be able to equate to the same issues. I've been through puberty and miscarriages and pregnancies and periods—and everything that I talk to people about every day, and so I bring a lot of my real-world experience to what I tell them about, you know, and I think that's really helpful. People really appreciate me telling them what I've been through.

Courtney: It's one of the most special things you have done for me, that's for sure—aside from delivering my two kids. You have said things to me that have healed me in ways you'll never know . . . Speaking of healing, the two of you were involved with a group from Cedars that went to Guatemala to treat women and children and perform surgery . . . Dr. Mike, this was your seventh trip.

Michael: This year we helped women in a different fashion because we had our first prenatal clinic and lay midwife training. There, women die from common causes that we can treat here. They die from things that don't commonly happen here. They die from bleeding, high blood pressure, preeclampsia, so we help teach the lay midwives to prevent that.

Courtney: Michele, you're so visibly reenergized. What about you drove you to go in the first place? What did you bring back with you?

Michele: I was blessed with wonderful parents who believed in education and who had the means to help me achieve a medical degree. After many years in private practice taking care of very privileged women, I felt something missing. I needed to remind myself why I went into medicine, why I do what I do every day and every night.

Practicing medicine in a remote village in the mountains of Guatemala was practicing medicine at its most basic level. It separated me from all of the external factors we deal with while trying to practice medicine in the United States: insurance, billing, overhead, lawsuits, Yelp reviews, et cetera. We operated on women who had severe gynecologic needs and literally transformed their lives. They no longer had to walk around with their uteruses hanging out between their legs. They no longer had to leak urine constantly. They could resume work and sexual relations with their husbands. They complained very little, needed very little pain medication, and were so very thankful.

It's humbling and it's rewarding. It's the best thing I've done in a long time. It reminded me to reinforce within my daughters that one of the best things you can do with your life is to give back. To take the gifts, talents, and training that we have been blessed with and use those things to do something to help someone else. There is no better gift you can give.

22

Tips for Law Students

A law school education is invaluable and, of course, required, but we graduate without much guidance on how to navigate the first years of practice. Where do we fit in? We're not the law clerk anymore. But we also don't know how to make any meaningful contribution to the firm or the practice. Or worse, we think we're making a meaningful contribution, but we're really not! Most of us have substantial debt from law school, and maybe we're not even sure that we're in the right area of practice. We may have just taken the first job we could get that would pay the bills. And, after putting in the hours to graduate from law school and pass the bar, most of us aren't champs at self-care.

In 2014, the American Bar Association Board of Governors commissioned the Survey of Law Student Well-Being, which was designed to track alcohol, drug use, and mental health issues in law students. More than 3,300 law students at fifteen law schools participated in the survey. Here's what they found:

- More than one in four law students reported binge drinking within the prior two weeks of the survey.
- One out of seven students reported they had used prescription drugs without a prescription in the past year.
- The use of marijuana and cocaine increased substantially since similar research was done in 1991, with the use of cocaine doubling.
- More than one out of six students had depression and nearly one out of four had anxiety.
- Forty-two percent of respondents said they needed help for mental health issues, but only about half of them actually received counseling.

This is not an ideal place to start when you're entering an industry that is replete with drug and alcohol abuse and mental health problems. We have to do better. And we can. Read this book. It's for you. Understand that wellness and well-being are part of your duties as a lawyer. Get yourself healthy and well now, and keep yourself healthy and well when you enter practice.

Tips for Law Students

Here are our top tips for law students.

Clerk as Often as Possible

Clerk as often as possible in as many different offices and for as many different agencies as possible. That's how you figure out what type of law you want to practice and what your day-to-day work life will most likely look like in a particular area of practice. Some schools have Innocence Projects you can volunteer on to get a taste of criminal work as early as your second semester of law school. Local prosecutor's offices almost always hire law clerks who are still in school. Many of them hire from their pool of clerks. Private law firms also hire law students.

Many law schools have visiting or adjunct professors who are practicing attorneys. Take a class with a practicing lawyer. If you like him or her, approach him or her about working as a law clerk for a semester. Join a trial team, especially one coached by a practicing trial attorney. If you aim for one clerkship per semester, you'll have a chance to get on the front lines of many different types of practice areas and get a good sense of where you want to be.

Clerk Where You Want to Work

Relationships are everything. Clerk where you want to work. It's hard for law school graduates to get jobs. There are lots of applicants and lots of resumes floating around. Having been hiring attorneys ourselves, we can say that resumes don't get people hired. Relationships get people hired. Working as a law clerk (without pay if necessary) is the way to get your foot in the door and demonstrate that you will be an indispensable member of the firm.

Get in there. Do what you're asked. And then, do more than what you're asked. Become the go-to person to get things done, whether that's running to the courthouse to file papers before the clerk's office closes, getting a package to FedEx before the cutoff, or helping carry boxes to court. Instead of thinking about how the firm and its lawyers and staff can help you, start asking how you can help *them*. Be there as often as you can. Be kind. Be curious. Work hard. Have fun. If it's a good fit, you'll have a job offer.

A note about our experience: neither of us have worked in a very large firm. We stayed away from that path because we always heard that the law clerks and young lawyers were separated from the lawyers doing the real work, and we'd been told in interviews that we'd never see the inside of a courtroom unless we met our annual billable hours and then did pro bono work. We wanted to be the ones doing the real work, and we wanted to be in court; so, we scratched the big names off of our lists. Also, large firms tend to have formal interview and hiring processes for clerks. Small and midsize firms tend to be more flexible.

Ask Questions

Ask questions. Partners and law firm owners don't expect you to know everything, but you are expected to get your assigned tasks right. In the first few weeks at a law firm or in a public defender's office, it can feel like people are speaking another language. That's normal. Ask for clarification if you need it, and don't be afraid to ask more than once. And when you ask questions, try to do it in person. Instead of shooting an email off to coworkers a few yards away, get up and walk to them. Human interaction will enhance the quality of your relationships.

Understand the Whole Picture

Try to understand the whole picture. When we were new lawyers, much of the work we were assigned was piecemeal. For example, we were asked to write a statement of facts to attach to a motion for summary judgment or to respond to a certain part of discovery. We would do the work, but without context. You will be exponentially more effective if you get your hands on the whole motion, the rest of the discovery, the rest of the file. Read it, ask questions, understand how and where what you are contributing fits into the whole. By doing this, you will escalate your learning and experience, and the quality of your work will skyrocket.

Seek Out Feedback

Seek out feedback. In our experience and from what we hear from young lawyers, when you're first starting out, it's hard to gauge whether you are doing a good job. Often, the people you are working with are very busy and distracted with their own work. We encourage you to speak up. If there is a lawyer overseeing your work, take her for coffee and ask direct questions. Where are you doing well, and where do you need to improve?

Keep Your Debt as Low as You Can

Keep your law school debt as low as possible. Get roommates, live at home, get a side job. Yes, lawyers can make a lot of money, but not all lawyers do. Even if you do make a lot of money, a law school payment of $1,000 per month would take a pretty big bite out of your budget. Equally important, you don't want to be forced to take a higher-paying job that won't get you the experience you want, just so you can make your loan payment. Many public defender and prosecutor jobs start out with lower than average pay, and it takes several years to increase to a competitive wage. If you want to try cases, you want to be able to keep government jobs like that on your list. So, keep your debt low to keep your job options open.

Think Like a Business Owner

Remember that the practice of law is also a business, so start thinking like a business owner now. Even if you end up joining a firm, you will advance more quickly if you understand what it takes to contribute to the business. Learn what it takes to bring in business, take interest in the financial aspect of the law firms where you clerk, take business classes and training online, and swap out summer reading for books on business.

Check out these books:

- anything by Adam Grant[1]
- *The E-Myth Revisited* by Michael Gerber[2]
- podcasts by Timothy Ferriss[3]
- *Fire Starter Sessions* by Danielle LaPorte[4]

Start Caring for Yourself Now

Take care of your mind, body, and spirit now so it's second nature when you start working. All of the self-care we talk about in this book is relevant to all women—not just lawyers. You need a well-structured and fortified baseline of energy and self-care to thrive. It's so much easier to start that practice now and carry it with you into your practice than to scramble once you're in the thick of it and be clamoring for some relief.

Think Ahead about Life Goals

Think about how you want your personal life to fit into your practice and vice versa. What do you want your life to look like? How much do you want to work? Do you want to work for yourself or someone else? Now figure out how you are going to get there, what you have to do,

---

[1] http://www.adamgrant.net

[2] Michael Gerber, T*he E-Myth Revisited: Why Most Small Businesses Don't Work and What to Do About It* (New York: HarperCollins, 2001).

[3] https://tim.blog/podcast/

[4] Danielle LaPorte, *The Firestarter Sessions: A Soulful and Practical Guide to Creating Success on Your Own Terms* (New York: Harmony Books, 2012).

and how much time it will take. Make your plan and work on it every single day. You probably don't have the answers to all of those questions yet, and that's OK. But start asking yourself these questions and see what answers you come up with. And then ask again periodically. See if anything changes as you clerk and watch other women practice. And remember, your answers may change in the midst of your practice. And that's OK.

As a law student, you have the power to change our profession. By implementing the growth, self-care, and trial skills we teach in this book, you'll not only improve your life, but you'll improve your law school experience, and you'll take part in shifting the culture of our profession. No longer will sexism be acceptable. No longer will women lawyers feel like second-class citizens. No longer will we stay in jobs we don't want or take supporting roles. Women will be revered in the law and recognized for the skills that make us uniquely suited to be trial lawyers. Get ready to take your place in the profession.

Chapter Takeaways

- Law school is a high-pressure environment. It is the perfect time to learn how to take care of your body and mind.
- There are so many exciting options in the law, we recommend sampling different clerkships where you will build the relationships that will support your career.
- Don't let law school debt drive your career decisions. Work hard and be smart to keep yours in check by budgeting, controlling your expenses, and making a plan.
- Think and plan now about the kind of life you want to have as a lawyer.

PART SIX

Being a Woman in the Courtroom

Being a Woman in the Courtroom

It would be nice if we didn't have to write this section of the book, but we do. We have to talk about a woman's appearance in court and appropriate behavior in court. Fortunately, only one of these is complicated. A woman's appearance—hair, clothes, makeup, shoes, nails, purses—it's all more complicated than a man's. There's a lot of gray out there. Very little that is black-and-white. Yes, we wish we could wear wigs and robes like they do in the United Kingdom. It would be so much easier. No planning a trial wardrobe. No worrying about colors and cut and style and what image we're portraying. But the reality is we need to talk about these things and get to a place where we all feel comfortable. We don't claim to have all the answers. We can tell you what works for us and what doesn't, and hopefully, this conversation will spark many others and inspire you to embrace what works for you and what reflects the level of respect and decorum owed to our judicial system.

23

Dressing the Part

Probably the question that we're asked most often by other women lawyers is, "What do I wear?" How do you decide what to wear to a deposition versus what to wear to trial? What is appropriate? What if I don't like what the other women lawyers are wearing? Am I allowed to be myself?

We wish we could tell them that it doesn't matter, but the truth is this: what we wear, as women, matters. At this time on the planet, this is something we still have to grapple with. Hopefully less so when our daughters become adults and maybe not at all when their daughters do. But for now, we have to think about how we present ourselves, and a large part of that, for women, is what we wear.

When we are dressed appropriately, yet comfortably, our ability to do our job is exponentially greater. How we dress can affect our confidence, our presentation, our energy levels, our self-esteem, and the way in which we connect with others. There have been times where what we wore, in part, created the confidence we needed to do our jobs and do them well. A large part of our job is to create and maintain the energy in the courtroom, with our client, with our colleagues, and in our families. Our clothes reflect how we want to show up in the world. We have to be aware of what we're communicating to other people with what we're wearing.

People notice what women wear. In Western civilization we have been socially conditioned to judge women by their appearances. We can't tell you how many times male and female judges, defense lawyers, court reporters, jurors, lawyers on our own team, you name it—they have all commented on what we were wearing at some point in any given trial. More important to what we do as a trial lawyer, every conversation we've had with a jury post-verdict has included on some level, some comment or question about our clothes, shoes, bag, hair, and so on. We have rarely—probably never is the truth—heard similar comments about the male attorneys and associates on our team. Well, except, of course, Courtney's husband and his cowboy boots, but we're pretty sure that's part of the reason why he wears them.

To this point, the struggle over what to wear isn't unique to women. Although suits may have been meant for men, it doesn't mean that men automatically know what to wear in the courtroom setting. What we wear as a society has become significantly less formal in the last fifty years. Decorum is not as universal nor as uniform as it once was. We used to dress up more. For church, for flights (go find some amazing old photos of 1960s air travel), for school, or even for Sunday supper. These trends have relaxed, and we—all of us—have been left with a certain level of ambiguity about what's appropriate.

Courtney:

> When we started writing this book, this was a subject Theresa and I disagreed about. I'm hesitant to talk about the subject of what women wear at all. I feel like doing so makes me complicit in something I am very passionately against—marginalizing women and emphasizing appearance in a way that can be limiting or cause women to feel they have to change

themselves. In my view it detracts, significantly, from the real work we should be doing. And yet, I wouldn't be being brutally honest if I didn't admit that dressing and appearance play a significant role in my professional life, and that it's something I have struggled with and continue to struggle with.

I have lost track of how many times I have gotten myself dressed and then questioned and debated what I am wearing until I got all the way to the courthouse, all the way through the day, back in the judge's chambers, out at lunch, sometimes through whatever work meetings or dinners I go to—all the way through the end of the night. What a waste of energy. But I know I'm not alone. I have tried it all. I have worked so hard to cover myself up, to dress down, to look older, then to look younger, to look thinner then to look like I wasn't so thin. I've taken lessons on how to blow-dry my own hair (that wasn't something that was emphasized in my hippie upbringing), and then I have spent hours trying to make my ponytail look "casual." I have shoved my swollen pregnant feet into the highest heels right before a closing argument (huge mistake), and I have worn my husbands' jacket over my gasoline-soaked pantsuit that reeked (you can imagine) through my entire long and complicated direct of an expert witness (long story). What will make them respect me? Listen to me? Like me?

If you have ever struggled with what to wear, you aren't alone, at all. We don't have any hard-and-fast rules for you, but like everything in this book, we can give you some tips and pointers and pragmatic suggestions that we have accumulated over the years.

Judging Appearances: Why We Do It

When we first meet someone, our brains are naturally prone to judge each other's appearance. We are hardwired from our primal days to use our subconscious brain to fill in missing details so that we can quickly assess whether what we are looking at is a threat. This mechanism is still a part of who we are and how our brains behave. We all know from experience: first impressions stick.

> One reason our brains persist in using stereotypes, experts say, is that often they give us broadly accurate information, even if all the details don't line up . . . When people don't fit our preconceived notions, we tend to ignore the contradictions, until they are too dramatic to overlook.[1]

It is our job as leaders, as lawyers, as women, to understand that appearances matter and to be mindful of how we present ourselves in the world.

It Starts a Long Time before the Beginning

When we walk into the courthouse, what is the first thing the jurors see? Is our face all screwed up as we slam the two dollars down on the counter for our coffee? Are we rushing down the halls wobbling around on too-high heels with our fancy, pretty purses swinging like wrecking

---

[1] Pam Belluck, "Yes Looks Do Matter," *New York Times* (April 24, 2009).

balls? Are we approachable? Do we look like we had a team of artists design our Kabuki masks for the day?

Just like we have to be aware of how we present to the world, our job in the courtroom is to be cognizant of the *appearance* of our trial. We consider how our client appears to the jurors, whether we are going to sit four lawyers in suits at counsel table or whether we are going to sit up there alone, whether we are going to have the client's sister with the tattoo on her neck and the cigarette in her hand come and testify today, whether we are going to criticize our tech guy who forgot the cables right here in front of everyone or keep our cool and maintain awareness of our surroundings.

We tell our clients and witnesses that the trial begins when they get in the car at their home that morning. They don't know who is driving next to them on the freeway, who's waiting for the same parking space, who is standing on the courthouse steps as they walk up, who is in the hallways, and so on. The same goes for us.

Free to Move

We have to be free to move. Trial, for us, is like running a marathon. But it's not only trial—sometimes just going to the office to take a deposition or have a team meeting can require a lot of movement and endurance. In and out of the courtroom, we need to move. Why? Dynamic movement is essential to connection.

What we wear has to support that dynamic movement. That means everything from the underwear to the shoes.

But what is appropriate, or comfortable, and what looks good and feels good can be different for different women. Anytime we stretch ourselves and our cells in a way that is not authentic, it shows. Most times we are the last to know. And that includes clothes.

On Being Sexy

Fashion is a powerful communication tool. When we dress, we have to decide what it is that we are trying to communicate. Sometimes it feels like any attention is good attention. Sexy definitely gets you attention. Sometimes in a mediation, we put on the shoes with the red soles and march in there like we own the place. And sometimes we end up owning the place when we leave. That's something we would never do in trial. Different audience. Different goal. Different intention. There is a time and a place for everything. There's something terribly alluring about someone who isn't showing it all, at least not all at once. Think about the sari. Or an Audrey Hepburn neckline. Delicious. The confidence of the woman who doesn't show it all can be intoxicating. Bottom line: the courtroom is not a place for vixens, unless you are OK being seen as one and understand that making that choice limits your power.

It is entirely possible to be beautiful, sexy, and interesting without showing skin, being inappropriate, or wearing labels.

Our appearance, behavior, or possessions should not take attention away from our cases or clients. Be yourself, but leave sexy for the bedroom.

Shoes

Courtney:

I stick with mid to low heels after kids. I have a high-heel collection I am pretty proud of—but when it comes to trial, those tend to stay in their boxes. Look, I have been known to live it up when I know it's a half day and I'm not doing any of the witnesses. I'm five feet eleven, and with really high heels, I look like an Amazon warrior. Halfway into a four-week trial, sometimes you need a few hours as an Amazon warrior princess. But overall, when it comes to shoes, I have to be able to move. Do you need a hard-and-fast rule? Look at your ankles. If you can't keep your ankles steady as you walk, your heels are too high. Either get more practice or swap them out for something you can manage.

The research shows that heels and skirts remain the power suit for female professionals. That does not mean we have to wear these things to be successful, but that they remain part of the expectations of the world around us. It is OK to go outside of those expectations, but know that that is what you are doing and do so mindfully.

Theresa wears really high heels in court, and she can walk in them like a boss. I wear kitten heels or Gucci loafers because they feel better for me at this stage in my life.

Theresa:

I'm five feet four. People think I'm at least five feet seven because I always wear heels. I think I'm as tall as Courtney and am always shocked to see photos of us side by side. On the rare occasion that I've stepped out of my heels, I'm almost sure to get a gasp, followed by, "Oh my God, you're so short!" in a tone that suggests I've shocked and tricked them somehow—especially my male colleagues. I started practicing walking in a pair of my mom's patent leather black heels when I was in elementary school. When I was a television news reporter, I would run down the street in heels, trek through fields in heels, stand in the pouring rain in heels, stand in a snowstorm in heels. You name it, I did it in heels. Put me in flats, and I will trip over my own feet. I do better in heels and feel most comfortable in heels.

Makeup

We know quite a few professional and successful women lawyers who have never and will never wear makeup, and it suits them perfectly. Again, it's what makes you look and feel comfortable.

However, a number of studies show that women who wear makeup are considered to be more professional and are taken more seriously than women who don't. This is something to consider, especially when it tends to be women who are harsher on other women. Luckily, the trend to wear less or even no makeup seems to be growing.

Generally, we're not going to tell anyone to add more makeup. But if you are hiding behind an inch of foundation and eyeliner, you are putting something, physically and energetically, between you and the world, and that's something you have to think about. We encourage you to think about why you are piling on so much makeup and what impact that has on your self-esteem and how you are perceived by people around you. Also, the more time you spend with makeup, the less time you spend thinking about your day, what you want to accomplish, setting your intention for the great things you are going to do. Your male counterpart is certainly using that time differently.

To be clear: we're not saying our way is the right way. Makeup is personal and also makes women feel strong and pretty. But have some awareness of what you are putting on your face and how much of it and why you're doing it. Our experience with a lot of makeup has been the same, repeatedly, over the years: when we get super dolled up, we're treated like dolls.

Our personal preference for makeup is clean and light. We are children of the eighties and love blush. Luckily the people in our lives (mostly) wipe our faces as we're walking out the front door before we embarrass ourselves. When you see us together, just know that no one was there to tone down our blush. It was the opposite. Neither of us wear lipstick because it disappears and then we look dead again, so if we do anything at all, it's a gloss. Courtney likes a tinted moisturizer because she thinks she looks like she's on vacation—sometimes cover up for late-night freak-out break-outs—and mascara. Theresa tosses in a line of eyeliner and some dabs of under-eye concealer because her skin is see-through. A few weeks into a long trial, Courtney breaks out the under-eye highlighter—the good stuff. We do what makes us feel fresh and pretty while mixing trial and toddlers.

Clean Beauty

Using natural products is very important to both of us. In the United States, makeup companies are not required by law to be transparent about their formulations. The industry is unregulated and doesn't have any chemical policies. As a result, companies are allowed to put just about any type of chemical into personal care products, including carcinogens. The average American woman, who uses roughly a dozen beauty products a day, is ingesting hundreds of chemicals every day that are associated—even in low doses—with cancer, birth defects, respiratory problems, and learning disabilities.

Luckily, women are pushing to change all of this and a lot of companies are responding and creating safe, nontoxic products, without those harmful chemicals, that work just as well as the old formulas. EWG.org is a website that shows you what is in the products you use. Some of the brands we like are ILIA, Juice Beauty, Beautycounter, and Courtney's favorite, RMS.

Hair

Courtney:

Personal hygiene is important. Clean, manageable hair is a lot easier to deal with than sticky spray-can hair. However, I see a lot of women who have great hair all the time. Theresa is one of them. If you know how to do it and you like doing it, by all means go for it. For me, I keep my hair simple mainly because that's all I know how to do. As a child, my hair experience generally consisted of getting it curled by my mother every year for Halloween, the result of which were second- and third-degree burns on my ears. A lot of jurors have told me they like my ponytail, but I think they are just being nice.

I think you have a little more space to play with hair. Some people do really cool things, and it's something that allows you to express yourself with less recourse than when it's your clothes or shoes. I started getting gray hair after I had my first baby. Like, the day after I had him. I freaked out and still cover my grays, but I tire of the maintenance. I'm too vain to stop now, but I don't see myself doing this much longer. I see a lot more women these days who don't dye their hair. When I see a young, healthy woman who does not dye her hair, I light up inside.

Bottom line with hair: do what you enjoy and what doesn't distract you, but overall if you don't stress about it, no one else will.

Theresa:

I paid Courtney to say I have good hair. My hair is half-Mermaid: wavy in some places and straight in others and only looks good in its natural state underwater. So, I blow it dry every day. Sometimes I wear it down. Sometimes I wear it back. Above all, I aim for professional, respectable, and not distracting in court. And I have a big forehead and look weird if I don't arrange the hair around the forehead somehow.

What to Wear

Our job is to carry energy and give off energy. Clothes reflect how you want to show up and what energy you bring to whatever you are doing. We can use our clothes and appearance to project and create confidence.

Of course, what you wear changes depending on where you are. What you wear to a job interview might not be the same thing you wear to mediation compared to a deposition or even just a normal day at work. We've run from dropping off our kids to show up at a deposition in running pants so that we could go to the gym afterward. We've dressed in designer duds and fancy heels to go to certain mediations. You have to ask yourself, who is your audience and how do you want to present yourself?

Courtney:

> When I got out of law school, I was twenty-three years old. I had zero professional experience. I worked my way through college and law school as a server and bartender. Before that I was a lifeguard in Ventura County, and I don't like to wear shoes. I looked for older, successful women to model, but came up rather short. The advice I received, from women lawyers but also from male judges, sometimes in the form of an order, was sharp and didn't resonate with me. Always wear a skirt suit and pumps. If you wear a pantsuit, keep the pumps. If you want to get wild, they make those suits in red and purple. The women I saw either wore unflattering, drab suits or low-cut, Ally McBeal-style miniskirts, neither which appealed to me. So I navigated my way through my first few years on my own.
>
> I've tried covering myself up so that I could "blend in" with my male trial team, and I have tried getting noticed by drawing

attention to my outfit. (Neither worked out well.) I've tried no makeup, dull hair, and gray suits to see if I could eliminate myself completely. I've shown up in low-cut blouses because I bought them, never tried them on, and had to go with whatever was left in my suitcase. I've tried cute little suits with fishtail hems, masculine full pantsuits with high necklines, professional cut dresses, cotton black dresses, Jackie O sweater sets, and even turtlenecks (skip that one). I splurged on some flats that had a symbol on top, thinking I would impress everyone, and when I got to court, my trial partner (now husband) ripped the symbol off of both shoes after I walked through security, so there was a big chunk of dried glue on my black shoes for the duration of the month-long trial. Needless to say, when it comes to what to wear, I have tried it all.

My personal rules are as follows: I have to be able to move, the clothes need to fit, and I have to feel good in them. I tend to shy away from black. I am in the business of selling hope and prefer not to do it dressed like an undertaker. Also, when I was younger, black tended to make me look a little less daytime and a little more cocktail waitress. I prefer monochromes—mostly grays and navy. I think patterns are great but not when you look like a tablecloth. Clean lines, minimalist, and monochrome tend to be chic and classy but also professional.

Blazers are great. I think you can dress up and professionalize pretty much any combination with a blazer. My go-to work outfit out of the courtroom is jeans, T-shirt, and blazer. It has classic French allure and it's easy. Also, when a blazer fits well, it doesn't matter where it came from or how much it costs.

I love sweaters. I always bring a sweater in my trial purse because they crank the air conditioning, and when I'm nervous, I shake anyway. If I'm feeling dull, a sweater under my blazer with a pantsuit makes me feel a little more chic. I like that, when I have a sweater, I can take off my blazer and feel a little less restricted.

Dresses are actually my favorite. I think there are some gorgeous, flattering, simple dresses being made these days, and I love them because it means I only have to decide on one thing, which is really helpful as I am not very good at clothes. Obviously I have serious limits—can I bend over to plug in my computer (why are all courtroom plugs on the floor?); do I look like I'm going to work at the (cool university) library and not the nightclub? I'm not a fan of cleavage, and thanks to my second kid who sucked them away, that's something I don't have to worry about anymore, but come on—again, are you looking for the attention? If so, then maybe reconsider and look for it somewhere else later.

Pants are also great. Pants with a cardigan is a nice look as long as it's not too casual. I have been told by some over the years that we need to "look like schlubs" so that we can trick the jurors into thinking we're the underdog. I worked with a very well-known trial lawyer who went so far as to handwrite his captions for his exhibit binders on lined paper to do this. Straight up: it was embarrassing and fake. My opinion: if you try to look like a loser, the world has no problem treating you that way. Have respect for yourself, the jurors, your clients, and how hard you worked to get here by not hiding who you are.

Ashley Parris, a kick-ass lawyer mom and good friend, says that times are changing. Americans tend to value wealth as a sign of leadership and credibility. If you look at our politics, entertainment, and advertising, she isn't wrong. I like my Theory suits, and they aren't cheap, but I tend to leave my diamond tiara at home. You're not going to get a *Paper Bag Princess* skit from me—I've never been good at tricking people into thinking I'm something I'm not.[2]

---

[2] If you haven't read it, find a copy of Robert Munsch's *The Paper Bag Princess* (New York: Annick Press, 1980), and give it away to any little girl in your life.

The Fit

How your clothes fit matters. Why do men look so good into their eighties, even with pot bellies and saggy rumps? Because they get their suits custom-made. Spending a little more on a well-made suit or a pair of pants that fit well will serve you in spades. Discomfort is a distraction—we are working to avoid those. As a personal preference, we tend to go a little looser rather than tighter. When clothes are tight, they tend to pinch and draw attention to the least flattering bits of the skin. Confining the body in weird ways is ugly.

When we are less confined, we tend to move better, feel better, and therefore look better. The body is beautiful when you let it be. If you don't know what I'm talking about, you haven't spent enough time at nude hot springs. There is nothing more beautiful and reassuring than those seventy- and eighty-year-old women walking free and unbounded, skin pink from the warm water, the picture of embodiment.

Courtney:

I have it easy. I'm naturally slim. I'm tall. I'm very lucky for a lot of gifts that I was given that I have no control over. I also work hard at it—really hard. I eat clean, I run, I do a lot of yoga, I get up and outside on days when I would rather binge Netflix. But I believe this is true for all women of all shapes—when you try to stuff yourself into some shape, that's where your energy is going—into the stuffing, into the contorting, not into what you are doing. There is nothing more empowering than loving and embracing your body. I didn't understand this until I tried a case about three months after I had my first baby. My body was in a completely different shape. My boobs weren't where they belonged, my bum didn't fit into my pants, and, well, none of my clothes fit. I was embarrassed to be in my maternity clothes, which had pilled and gone slack in all the wrong places, but I was too uncomfortable to shove myself into my normal clothes. I went out and I bought Spanx—those sucky tight pantyhose things that hold in your belly and shape your bum—and a pair of heels, to give me a little boost. In the morning when I looked in the mirror, I felt like my body and legs looked much better—I felt less insecure. But by the end of the afternoon, my stomach was in knots from not breathing right all day, the elastic cutting into my gut, and my feet were screaming. I was in such a rush to get out of the courtroom that I agreed to whatever jury instructions the defense was proposing. I wasn't even listening.

The case I was trying was difficult, and I needed to move around, let alone breathe—I knew this wasn't going to work. The next morning I decided the hell with it and put on my loafers. They were cute, but of course, loafers have their limits. They were roomy. Squishy. Gave me a pep in my step. I put on my maternity clothes that fit snug but with enough give to let me bend and reach and write on the board. Before I left, I ate a full and nourishing breakfast so that I felt loved and energized for my opening. And guess what? You know what.

Look, our bodies, like our moods, our circumstances, our cases, change all the time. There is no one prescription for what to wear or how to wear it. Thank goodness! We would be autobots! However, it's important to have some driving ethos so that we don't spend our time and energy second-guessing ourselves instead of focusing on the tasks at hand.

Our What-to-Wear Rules

Here are our top what-to-wear rules for in and out of the courtroom:

- You need to be able to move.
- You need to be able to breathe.
- Your clothes need to fit.
- You need to like it, at least a little.
- You need to keep the focus on the case and the client, not what you're wearing.

Accessories

For both of us, accessories are talismans. Everything we wear means something to us and gives us strength and power. We rarely change them. But, sometimes, when we're especially nervous or superstitious, we pile them on. This is never a good thing. Coco Chanel said it best, "Before you leave the house, look at yourself in the mirror and take one thing off."

Wear your accessories for you, but keep it cool, Betty. If you are wearing something because you hope it will get you attention, take it off. If you are deciding between a string of pearls and a giant collar of bright blue bobbles that ding when you walk, well, then we would side with Nancy Reagan there and suggest the pearls. We have been told over the years that we can't wear nice bangles or that we should take off all gold jewelry and diamonds so that we look like schlubs. We're not schlubs. We work hard and love the things and have earned things, and they are beautiful. However, just because you have it doesn't mean you need to wear it. Less is always more. We all own some pretty nice things that don't belong in the courtroom.

Pregnant in the Courtroom

Courtney:

I sat on the plane next to an actress who told me that, when she was pregnant with her fifth child, she was filming a show where she was afraid that if they found out she was pregnant they would fire her. So, she simply hid it. She ate less, sucked in her belly, wore compression underwear, and dressed in dark clothes. She went on a pretty famous late-night show, and no one could tell she was six months pregnant. I can't imagine how terrible that must have felt, physically and otherwise. We have a lot of work to do still when it comes to pregnancy, maternity, and work.

I have tried at least three or four high-profile, high-damages cases pregnant. Generally, I start strong in a nice suit or dress and finish in something a step above sweatpants. I don't wear makeup when I'm pregnant because it makes me itchy, and I prefer dresses because they are stretchy. We love Ingrid and Isabel. Hatch (no relation to Theresa) is pretty fancy but gorgeous. I think that when you are pregnant you can pretty much wear anything as long as you put a blazer on it. I think you have to give yourself your best shot. You're already starting behind the starting block; you're tired, irritated, and hungry. Get yourself a stretchy dress and put a blazer over it. All my jurors have loved that I was pregnant. I think it's rather entertaining to watch a giant woman squeezing in and out of counsel table and then waddling to and from the bathroom all day. Do whatever you have to do to find some comfort, a little grace, and as much simplicity as you can manage.

The Trial Bag

We like nice sturdy bags that can hold our laptops, notepads, and all of our junk. We know rolly bags are better for us and that we should use one, but we're still tote girls. No labels, no insignia, just simple.

Courtney:

In my bag, aside from the pens and sticky notes and obligatory necessities of being a lawyer, I always have something to read, usually a New Yorker or a Harper's, something to spray my face with at breaks, face oil, and tons of water. I drink water like it's my job. If you slam twenty Red Bulls, it will show in your face, your body, your mind, and your frazzled aura. Don't do it. Theresa always brings snacks; on days where we are busy, she grabs kids' snacks. We have been known to share Squeezies in the hallway while we are prepping our witnesses. I also pack things that give me joy. I have a lip gloss that smells like roses, a small copper Ganesha figurine, two pairs of headphones, and flip-flops so I can shut it out and go walking at lunch. Pack for yourself like you would pack for a lover. It's cheesy, but leave treats and goodies that will make your day, your life, better. A lot of courtrooms and offices we are in have artificial lighting and recirculated air. Sometimes a special goody in your bag can make all the difference for making it through the day successfully and with grace. I pack my bag the night before and lay out my clothes like a fifth grader because it works and it gives me more time for me in the morning—drinking coffee, snuggling with kids, meditating, going for a hike.

Chapter Takeaways

- As lawyers and leaders, we need to be aware of how we present ourselves, in and out of the courtroom.
- The most important thing when it comes to dressing is that you are comfortable and confident.
- Spend a little extra on tailoring and have clothes fitted to your shape.

24

Minding Your Behavior

Lawyers are leaders. We lead by example, in the courtroom and out of the courtroom. But how do we effectively lead when we are interrupted or marginalized in the courtroom?

Women, Interrupted

Interruptions are considered rude because they break into a person's speech and thus hinder a person's expression, and most people agree that they do not enjoy being interrupted.[1] Psychologists, linguists, and behaviorists have found, however, that there is more to interruptions than simple rudeness. Viewed through a psychological or sociological lens, interruptions are a "violation of a current speaker's right to complete a turn."[2] Research suggests that interruptions are attempts by speakers to maximize their power positions in group settings through assertions of dominance.[3]

Dating as far back as the early 1970s, the majority of the behavioral research on gender and interruptions indicates that men interrupt women more often than women interrupt men.[4] In 1975, Professors Don Zimmerman and Candace West studied public conversations between mixed-gendered groups and found that men were responsible

---

[1] As seen by the numerous articles that have been written on ways to prevent being interrupted. *See* Judith Martin, "Do Not Pardon the Interruption," *Washington Post: Arts & Living* (Aug. 28, 2005), http://www.washingtonpost.com/wp-dyn/content/article/2005/08/27/AR2005082701151.html; *See also,* e.g., Claire Cohen, "Tired of Being Interrupted at Work? Here's How to Stop Anyone Talking Over You," *Telegraph: Women's Business* (Mar. 18, 2015), http://www.telegraph.co.uk/women/womens-business/11479811/Work-advice-How-to-stopanyone-interrupting-you-in-meetings.html (offering practical recommendations to minimize interruptions); and Connie Dieken, "Enough. Stop Interrupting Me!," *Huffington Post: The Blog* (Dec. 16, 2012), https://www.huffingtonpost.com/connie-dieken/enough-stop-interrupting-_b_1968857.html (explaining reasons for interruptions as well as offering practical preventative and response tactics).

[2] Don H. Zimmerman and Candace West, "Sex Roles, Interruptions and Silences in Conversations," in *Language and Sex: Difference and Dominance*, eds. Barrie Thorne and Nancy Henley (Stanford: Stanford University Press, 1975) 105, 123.

[3] Julia A. Goldberg, "Interrupting the Discourse on Interruptions: An Analysis in Terms of Relationally Neutral, Power and Rapport-Oriented Acts," *Journal of Pragmatics* 14, no, 6 (1990): 883–903 https://doi.org/10.1016/0378-2166(90)90045-F (classifying interruptions as being power-driven or neutral displays of rapport).

[4] Zimmerman and West, "Sex Roles, Interruptions and Silences in Conversations," 117.

for forty-six of forty-eight interruptions.[5] In 2014, Professor Adrienne Hancock and Benjamin Rubin found that women are interrupted at a higher rate than men.[6] Hancock and Rubin monitored eight trained male and female communication partners in a controlled setting and observed eighty three-minute conversations among participants while transcribing and coding various behaviors, such as interruptions, hedging, self-references, and justifiers.[7] Interestingly, the speaker's gender did not produce significant changes in language, but participants of both genders used more dependent clauses when speaking with women, and when a participant was speaking with a woman, he or she was more likely to interrupt than when the same person was speaking with a man.[8] This finding was consistent for both male and female interrupters: both genders interrupt women more than men.

In another 2014 study, Kieran Snyder observed similar behaviors between men and women in a professional setting—a tech company.[9] Over a four-week period, Snyder observed and tallied interruptions during business meetings that ranged from four to fifteen participants, with the typical gender breakdown being 60 percent male and 40 percent female.[10] Snyder noted 314 interruptions over 900 minutes of conversations and found that men interrupt more often than women (212 to 102 interruptions).[11]

---

[5] Zimmerman and West, "Sex Roles, Interruptions and Silences in Conversations," 116.

[6] Adrienne B. Hancock and Benjamin A. Rubin, "Influence of Communication Partner's Gender on Language," *Journal of Language and Social Psychology* 34, no. 1 (January, 2015): 46–64, https://doi.org/10.1177/0261927X14533197

[7] *Id.*

[8] *Id.*

[9] Kieran Snyder, "How to Get Ahead as a Woman in Tech: Interrupt Men," *Slate* (July, 23, 2014) http://www.slate.com/blogs/lexicon_valley/2014/07/23/study_men_interrupt_women_more_in_tech_workplaces_but_high_ranking_women.html.

[10] *Id.*

[11] *Id.*

Men were nearly three times as likely to interrupt women as they were to interrupt other men.[12] Women were also far more likely to interrupt other women than they were to interrupt men.[13] This last point includes a striking number: 89 of the 102 interruptions by women were of other women; only 13 of the 314 total interruptions were women interrupting men.[14] Thus, as Snyder points out, "[t]hat is less than once per hour, in a climate where interruptions occur an average of once every two minutes and fifty-one seconds."[15] Across research methods and environments, the findings remain consistent: women are interrupted more than men.

In their 1975 study, Don Zimmerman and Candace West at University of California Santa Barbara found that there is a gender-based hierarchy in conversations. In other words, men dominated conversations in a way that was similar to the way that adults interrupt and speak over subservient children. The study found that men assert a right to control topics and do so without repercussion. Men do not view women as equal partners in conversation, the study found. While the study didn't say that this is always the case, it pointed out that the macro concept applies in an least one microcosm, which, in the case of the study, was a community college environment.

Most women trial lawyers are not surprised by this data and have experienced similar incidents of male-dominated conversation, oral argument, and blatant interruption commonly in their practice as trial lawyers.

Forty-two years later, another study hit even closer to home for female trial lawyers.[16]

---

[12] *Id.*

[13] *Id.*

[14] *Id.*

[15] *Id.*

[16] Tonja Jacobi and Dylan Schweers, "Justice, Interrupted: The Effect of Gender, Ideology and Seniority at Supreme Court Oral Arguments," *Virginia Law Review* 103 (October 24, 2017), Northwestern Law and Economics Research Paper Series, no. 17-03, available at SSRN: https://ssrn.com/abstract=2933016.

The study evaluated a publicly available database of Roberts Court oral arguments as well as transcripts of the 1990, 2002, and 2015 terms, and analyzed the extent to which the justices interrupted one another and how lawyers interrupted justices, contrary to the rules of the Court. The study found that female justices were interrupted at highly disproportionate rates by the male justices and by male lawyers.

The study found that, on average, women justices were interrupted at about three times the rate as male justices. In 1990, Justice Sandra Day O'Connor was interrupted 2.9 times more than the average male justice. In 2002, female justices were interrupted 2.9 times more often than male justices. And in 2015, female justices were interrupted 3.9 times more often than male justices.

What's more, men are less likely to recognize when they've interrupted someone, and, even more challenging, they're less likely to acknowledge interrupting a woman than interrupting a man. Men are 33 percent more likely to recognize when they have interrupted another man than when they have interrupted a woman.

Making matters worse, women are nearly 30 percent more likely to defer to a man than another man is, and women are 69 percent more likely to defer to another women than a man is.

Mansplaining

The concept of *mansplaining* really took off when author Rebecca Solnit described not only how a patronizing man interrupted her to explain something to her, but also was explaining her own book to her.[17] However, according to the study on interruptions at the Supreme Court level, this mansplaining phenomenon has been around for decades and shows up clearly in the U.S. Supreme Court transcripts, even

---

[17] Rebecca Solnit, "Men Who Explain Things," *L.A. Times* (April 13, 2008).

when women have reached "the highest pinnacle possible in one of the highest-status professions," as the study put it.

The Workaround

Interestingly, the Supreme Court study looked at seniority and interruptions. Researchers found that seniority didn't prevent women from being interrupted. But the longer a female justice was on the Court, the more time she had to learn how to limit interruptions. Looking back to the time the first female justice, Sandra Day O'Connor, was appointed to the Court, the researchers saw clear changes in the way that all four female justices changed the way they speak and ask questions. Researchers found that the justices shifted from a typically female, less assertive style of asking questions to a more typically male, direct and aggressive style of asking questions to avoid being interrupted.

The study refers to work by Professor Janet Ainsworth, who found that there is a marked difference between the way men and women speak. According to Ainsworth, women's speech is indirect and polite with declarative sentences, interrogatory questions, and conditional verb usage, while men's speech is assertive and direct with imperative sentences.[18] An example of indirect speech is using words like *could*, *might*, *would*, as in "Would you please write me that demurrer this week?" The direct way to ask the same question cuts out the conditional verb. "Please write me that demurrer by the end of the week."

Historically, men asserted themselves through language because they had no fear of offending, while women's communication was based on surviving and flourishing without having control of economics and

---

[18] Janet E. Ainsworth, "In a Different Register: The Pragmatics of Powerlessness in Police Interrogation," *The Yale Law Journal* 103, no. 2 (November, 1993): 259, 263; Faye Crosby and Linda Nyquist, "The Female Register: An Empirical Study of Lakoff's Hypotheses," *Language in Society* 6, no. 3 (December, 1977): 313–315, 317.

the like.[19] It is common as women to undermine ourselves with words and phrases. Many women start their sentences with "I think . . ." and apologize before asking a question, "Sorry but, I was wondering . . ." How to fix it? Cut it out. Just make the statement. Ask the question. Do it with warmth but do it with confidence.

We don't purport to have *the* solution. But we offer these studies to open our collective minds to the realities of what women are facing in the courtrooms and in life, and to look at ways that other women in positions of power and influence have addressed the problem so that we can better express ourselves without fear of judgment or disapproval.

Chapter Takeaways

- The examples we set affect the people around us; it's time to rise to the challenge and raise the bar with our actions and behavior.
- How we treat other women directly impacts how we and all women are treated.

---

[19] Shari Kendall, "Mother's Place in Language and Woman's Place," in *Language and Woman's Place: Text and Commentaries*, ed. Mary Bucholtz (Oxford University Press, 2004), 202, 206 (analyzing female-specific language as evidence of institutionalized gender roles).

25

Calling Men to Action

Courtney Rowley

This is a very important time in history. It is a time for a brutally honest review of who we have been and, importantly, who we will be. Supporting, promoting, and standing up for the rights of one class of humans benefits everyone. Actions speak louder than words. In order for women to truly realize and experience professional equality, men need to be on board. More and more men, successful men, are realizing the importance of this and are mentoring, promoting, and encouraging women.

We will become a society where men and women respect one another and work together in ways that complement and amplify one another. The question is how soon, and who is going to get left behind. We still have places in the world where women are not allowed to read, where there is female circumcision and endemic rape. We bring up these extreme and very ugly truths to point out that some men, not just historically, but right now, this minute, suppress, abuse, and mistreat millions of women. The horrors that afflict women in the world and the lack of equality that exists in our own country will change when men decide to care about women's issues as much as women do. In that regard, the time is now to effect change on a global scale. Your support and active involvement is so important. Promoting women in the legal profession here in the United States, the country with the best justice system in the world, will have an impact on the rest of the world. We believe that it begins here in the United States.

This chapter is a resource for men who are willing to promote, work with, and most importantly, actively care about women as professionals and colleagues. We have met some great men who are breaking the mold of the traditional law firm, who are looking for resources and insights on how to create dynamic, diverse, supportive, and creative environments for women. We aren't talking about helping women work from home, work less, or otherwise exit the workplace as a form of accommodation, though there may be times when these things make sense. We are talking about men who work with and for women who want to step into the future successfully, prosperously, and strategically. This chapter is for men and women who truly care and see the benefit of the equality we are fighting for.

The legal cultures are shifting. The most successful law firms, year after year, are the ones that have women in leadership positions.

Science, studies, and simple common sense tell us that the voices of men, especially white men—have had the greatest power and influence throughout history. The use of your voices, and more importantly the examples you set with your actions on behalf of women, will have a monumental impact on what we—your spouses, daughters, and granddaughters—are fighting for.

How and Where to Begin

As a man, there are so many forums where you have dominance and privilege over women. Every one of them is a place where you have the power to affirmatively effect change that will make the world a better place for women. But in order to even begin, it is essential that you see and acknowledge the inequality and injustice that exists. This lack of equality actually harms everybody.

We need you to listen and feel what it is that we feel. Ask the women in your life for their brutal honesty on the topic of equality and lack thereof. Ask them for examples of experiences they have had in their life where they were treated differently or less-than because they were women. Please listen. Don't apologize, don't interrupt, just listen, and truly imagine what it is to be in our skin. There is such a great power in listening to, reversing roles, and thereby validating the experience of another human. We talk about this in chapter 14, "Jury Selection by Woman." As human beings, we all want to be heard. If a woman tells you she was hurt, listen. Validate her. Empathize. Speak up when a woman (or anyone) is mistreated. If you are in a group where a man is talking about something that is disrespectful or harmful to women, speak up.

Nicole Stamp, who wrote an open letter to men after #MeToo went viral, suggested the phrase, "That's not cool." The idea is to have a response to disrespectful behavior by other men instead of letting it go without comment. Having the courage to use your voice can change the culture of how men speak about and thereby treat women. Period.

Change the Way You Talk

Stop the misogynist insults. *Bitch. Cunt. Slut.* Help us eliminate them from the vernacular completely. If you hear something, say something. If it's you who wants to insult someone, focus on the behavior, not the gender. Those words have too much negative connotation built up over too much time and no longer serve our world.

If you make a mistake? Own it. Apologize, correct, and move on.

This is pretty obvious, but no pet names at work. No *sweetie*, *honey*, *babe*, or *dear*. No matter how long you've worked together or known one another. You are powerful. What you say about someone has tremendous impact on how women are considered by others.

Amplify other women's voices at work, in print (refer to writings by women), and in the world. "That's what Theresa said." "Courtney has a point." "Actually, Bob, I think that was Jenna's idea." As explained in chapter 7, when people amplify the work of others, it spreads respect and positive expectations in a culture. When it comes from a man, it can carry a lot of weight. Acknowledging one woman's work can shift how women are considered throughout your firm, your courthouse, your county.

Introduce women to clients. Get them in front of referral lawyers. Introduce them to advertisers. Get them involved in every aspect of the law firm, courthouse, or nonprofit that you can. The idea is to expose women to as many areas of the practice as you can, fostering a more dynamic and creative workforce but also pushing women into areas they might have been reluctant to volunteer for. Women are significantly less likely than men to volunteer to try new areas of work, and your actions and behavior can change that.

When you do introduce women to a client, at a meeting, at an event, at an awards ceremony, do it without talking about how they look. "This is our little Amy. Isn't she gorgeous?" We believe there is a place and time for compliments, but if it is in the context of work, keep them work related. "This is Amy. She's a fantastic researcher and is very interested in medical malpractice. I want her to sit in on this meeting, Dr. Matthews, to help us prepare." If you're unsure about complimenting a woman, use this rule: compliment those things she *does*, not her appearance. Compliment her work ethic, her intelligence, or her public speaking ability, not her clothes, her body, or her hair.

Watch the dynamics at meetings, especially those meetings you lead. How often are women speaking up? Do male voices dominate? Are women being interrupted? Go out of your way to solicit opinions from women and anyone who is not speaking up. You will be surprised at how many great ideas are going unsaid.

Bottom line: demanding respectful conversation about women in your workplace and with your friends not only elevates how women are treated at work but also changes how women are treated in the world.

Socializing at Work

I used to think that working late, having dinners and drinks, or even getting a drink after work were necessary parts of being in this profession. When I was twenty-five, I went to the Trial Lawyer's College in Dubois, Wyoming. I was the youngest student to ever attend. A year later, I was the youngest staff member to be invited there. It was a tremendous honor, and it launched me in a completely different direction. I went on a hike with Nick Rowley, a young, up-and-coming trial lawyer. He told me, "Skip the line." As we pounded up boulders and heaved air, breathless in the altitude, he laid out a plan. He told me to go home and go try cases. Any case, every case. He told me to knock on doors and tell everyone I know that I wanted to try cases. Once I did that, he would send me some of his. And that's what I did. I did nothing but try cases, nonstop, for years. This meant I got a lot of experience. But it also meant that I had to form relationships with the people giving me those cases: men.

I was very young when I started doing this. I was flying all over the place working with some of the top trial lawyers in the country. And for the most part, it was an amazing experience. But many times, I found myself in situations I didn't want to be in, at dinners that made me uncomfortable, smiling back at compliments that made me feel small and confused. I tried to morph myself into what I thought was expected of me. I had a collegiate sports background, so I could be "one of the guys." I went to school in Wales, so I could "drink." I was young and energetic, so I could be "bubbly." I accepted that drinking and eating alone, with men, was something I had to do in order to get and try cases.

Now, I feel differently, and I wish I'd had somebody to tell me what I am telling you. Drinking and eating can be part of the profession, part of working with people and making connections, but there are many ways to socialize consciously and professionally, in a way that is comfortable and appropriate for everyone involved.

Office parties don't have to be held at night. If they are, don't just *invite* employees to bring spouses and significant others, *encourage* it. These days, for the most part, I don't drink in public or go to parties without my husband. That's both a luxury and a personal choice. If my husband can't go, I bring a sibling or a parent, or I don't stay very long. If you are unmarried, or happily coupled with a person who doesn't have the luxury (or desire) to attend all of your work functions, then know that it is your choice, always, and that if it doesn't feel right, don't do it. That goes to whether you eat the thing, drink the thing, or even attend the thing in the first place.

When you can, cut out the late-night dinners. Dinner in the Midwest is at 5:30 or 6:00. Respect the fact that nighttime is private time and that people need to get home to their families, their homes, their lives.

If do you have a later dinner, do it in a group. Be aware that one-on-one dinners can easily become intimate. If you have to have a one-on-one meal, can you do breakfast or lunch in a well-lit public place? If you do have dinner, do it consciously and with the intention of keeping it work-focused in form and substance.

If you are working late, which happens in our field, again, be intentional and use your judgement. We all have to eat, of course. But we all also know that dinner with a colleague is different from a date. If there is any confusion, go old-school: What would this look like to your spouse? To her spouse? To any passerby? If it looks like a date, if it feels like a date, take the initiative and do something about it.

If you are traveling, separate hotels is a good idea. If not separate hotels, then ask to put the hotel rooms on separate floors. As the mentor, you have that power, so use it. If you don't have that power, have the courage to talk to those who do.

Facebook C.E.O. Sheryl Sandberg has said to men who mentor women, "If you don't feel comfortable having dinner alone with a woman, then don't have dinner with men."[1] Whatever you do, do it across the board for men and women. Either all travel or no travel, all dinner or no dinner. Keep it equal and set that example.

Let's Talk about Consent

According to an *ABC News-Washington Post* poll, over 33 million U.S. women have been sexually harassed and 14 million have been abused in work-related incidents. What is *consent*? Not "go for it until you hear a no." Not a "lack of no." When frightened or challenged, many women seize and freeze, or they will put on a fake smile until they can leave. Consent is a clear yes.

Men and women together at work might be attracted sexually. We all know it happens. But ask yourself a few questions before you

---

[1] Gary Langer, "Unwanted Sexual Advances, Not Just a Hollywood Weinstein Story Poll Finds" *ABC News* (October 17, 2017) https://abcnews.go.com/Politics/unwanted-sexual-advances-hollywood-weinstein-story-poll/story?id=50521721.

proceed. Where do you both rank on the company totem pole? Is she subordinate to you? Does she rely on your opinion for a raise or promotion? Or are the roles reversed—do you rely on her opinion for a raise or promotion? Is she from another firm with a fee-sharing agreement? Does that fact play into either your or her side of the attraction you feel? Any relationship with a financial component is a bad idea.

Tread extremely carefully. Unless you feel like this might be your future spouse, go elsewhere to find a girlfriend or a one-night stand. The heart wants what the heart wants. But the pants want what the pants want too. Unless this really is the heart, look somewhere else.

How do you know if it is the heart? If this woman is so important to you that you could see yourself quitting this job and starting over at a new firm just to have a future with her—maybe you've found your new life partner. If not, walk away. Seriously. Walk. The. Fuck. Away.

What If Others Are Behaving Badly?

Sincerity lends itself to decency. If you see something that looks abusive, say something. But it doesn't have to get as far as *abusive* to warrant a discussion. Does it look like someone's behaving badly, or there's a power imbalance? Is anyone being coerced? Say something, even if it's uncomfortable. We have avoided too many uncomfortable conversations for too long. We are all navigating uncharted waters, and we are going to have to work together to make this new path. Be the good guy. Speak up. Say something.

Mentoring Women and Young Lawyers

Most successful people I know will say that part of why they are where they are today is because they had a mentor. In our profession, men outnumber women. When we are talking about experienced lawyers, men outnumber women significantly. Men in higher positions of power can give us invaluable insights, can make key introductions, and can provide much-needed support in this difficult and often lonely profession. I have had phenomenal mentoring from men.

However, the #MeToo movement has changed the climate, and some men have said to us that they feel afraid to mentor women, because they're afraid to step wrong. But to only mentor men would be a massive setback for women. I can't overstate the importance of seeing myself as important, valuable, and intelligent in the eyes of mentors, people whom I look up to and who have valuable experience in my field. This is called mirroring. The incredible value to a younger lawyer of seeing herself valued, respected, and encouraged by a senior colleague is priceless. There aren't enough senior women lawyers available to be mentors, so we need you to step up.

As children and as parents, we know how valuable mirroring is when it comes to self-esteem, confidence, and self-worth.

I think about this often as I parent our young girls—we have three. I easily compliment their dress or their hair, but I have to be deliberate and remember to compliment their intelligence or creativity. A few months ago, we had our good friend John Choate staying with us while we were trying a case in downtown LA. He has a young daughter of his own. One morning, while we were drinking coffee, my two-year-old daughter wandered into the kitchen with sleepy eyes and bed head. John's face lit up with a big smile as he shouted out enthusiastically, "Good morning! Are you going to build a robot today?" He immediately looked past her appearance and saw the potential in what she could do.

That said, there are a few guidelines for being a mentor to a younger woman lawyer:

- If you have a history, say no.
- If you have an attraction to her, say no.
- If you develop an attraction to her, stop. Just stop.
- Meet in public.
- Keep it focused—majority on professional growth. Chitchat, family, and other niceties in moderation can foster empathy and connection, but in excess can border on intimacy.

Emotional Affairs

The workplace is ground zero for emotional affairs. An emotional affair is when an emotional line is crossed, and has nothing to do with whether there is a physical relationship. An emotional affair can occur *whether or not* there is dissatisfaction in a marriage. Therapist and best-selling author Esther Perel, renowned for her research and new perspectives on relationships, gave a TED talk in 2015 where she explains that people who engage in intimate relationships outside the marriage aren't always looking for a new partner. She says that "it isn't so much that we're looking for another person, as much as we are looking for another self. . . . As Marcel Proust said, 'it's our imagination that is responsible for love, not the other person.'"[2]

---

[2] Esther Perel, "Rethinking Infidelity… A Talk for Anyone Who Has Ever Loved," March 2015, filmed at TED2015, video, https://www.ted.com/talks/esther_perel_rethinking_infidelity_a_talk_for_anyone_who_has_ever_loved.

Encourage Work-Life Balance

Encourage work-life balance by modeling it yourself. Take leave for important family events. Take paternity leave and encourage others to do the same. Men who pick up their kids from school or leave for a child's events are usually applauded for being "great dads" while moms who do the same things are simply expected to do so and their commitment to work is often questioned. Dismantle that double standard with your actions and words.

Chapter Takeaways

- Change the way you talk about women, and get rid of degrading terms from your speech.
- Keep work socializing during the daytime, or include spouses.
- Mentor young women lawyers, but keep it professional and in public places. Make sure it doesn't feel like a date.
- Encourage both women and men to have work-life balance.

Epilogue

At the Vancouver Peace Summit in September 2009, the Dalai Lama said he is a feminist, and he predicted that Western women will save the world. It's been widely reported that the Dalai Lama has said on many occasions that he believes women are more compassionate and have a nurturing instinct, and that he wants to see more women in charge of national defense because they are more likely to empathize with those who suffer during conflicts. The Dalai Lama has been quoted as saying:

> [W]e need more effort to promote basic human values—human compassion, human affection. And in that respect, females have more sensitivity for others' pain and suffering.[1]

---

[1] Amy O'Brian, "'We Need More Effort to Promote Basic Human Values': Dalai Lama," *Vancouver Sun* (September, 9, 2009), http://www.vancouversun.com/news/peace-summit/real+change+must+start+with+individuals+dalai+lama+tells+summit/2039661/story.html.

As women, it is time for us to embrace our roles as mothers, wives, nurturers, caregivers, and protectors and to honor our innate skills of empathy, compassion, and love for others. The world is shifting away from the patriarchy and toward the matriarchy, and it is our time to step into that world with grace. Our world needs the healing that women can provide, in and out of our homes. As trial lawyers, we're in a unique position to empathize, convey compassion, and help the wounded heal. We can be the universal mother archetype to ourselves, to our families, to our clients, and to the world. But we can only do it if we take care of ourselves first. We can only do it if we establish ourselves as leaders in the new world of the practice of law, where well-being is an obligation, a priority, where it becomes a way of life and a new way of practicing law. We can only do it if we reject running ourselves into the ground as a badge of honor. We can only do it if we respect and honor our bodies, minds, and spirits, and expect others to do the same. We must lead by example—a new example.

Let's fast-forward twenty years to a time when our daughters may choose to become trial lawyers. Or not. Whatever field they choose, what it will look like for them depends on the example we set and the changes we make today.

It's morning. She wakes with the sun streaming light through the windows. She is not rattled by a blaring alarm. She stretches, swings her legs over the side of the bed, and pads over to her yoga mat, warm from the morning sun. She spends ten minutes in two Yin yoga poses, balancing her adrenal glands and preparing her body gently for the day. She meditates for twenty minutes. She moves to the kitchen, drinks a cleansing tonic of lemon and water, takes a long walk outside, mentally planning her day and setting her intentions. She feeds her body and then sets about her tasks for the day. When she hits a rut, gets stuck, loses focus, she stops, takes a break and exercises. She eats a nourishing lunch. She handles her afternoon deposition by phone and then heads out to meet with other women trial lawyers. They come together to help one another, to lift one another up. In the courtroom, she is given time to speak, without interruption. She is respected. She is valued and followed as a leader. And she continues to carry the torch of women trial lawyer leaders: speaking the truth, carrying herself with grace, honoring her mind, body, and spirit, and those of others.

This is what we know will happen, and knowing this future is coming is our call to action, now. We all are trial by woman.

Appendix A

A Checklist to Increase Your Success in and out of the Courtroom

We put this little section together so you can give yourself a quick refresher on the most salient advice and calls to action in the book. This is your checklist or to-do list. Copy it in your own handwriting so it really sinks in, and put it somewhere you'll see it every day, especially the days you need a pep talk. It's the CliffsNotes to the book!

- **Get Trial Perspective.** The number one way to increase your value and the value of your cases is to use a Trial Perspective approach. How will what you are working on now play out at the end of the case—in front of a jury?
- **Invest in yourself.** We are in a technological age where the world is at our fingertips, and we have access to knowledge in a way that we never have had before. Where are you weak? Get strong.
- **Get focused.** As soon as you get a case, print out the jury instructions. Write your mini-opening. Keep editing and clarifying as your case develops.
- **Build momentum.** Take the initiative and go hard and fast into case development. Set the depositions. Go to the scene. Get affidavits. Call the witnesses in your case. Who drives the bus? Mama drives the bus.
- **Get feedback.** Develop your case, practice public speaking, and gain confidence with focus groups. Want to know how your work is being received? How you are being perceived? Ask.

- **Just jump.** You deserve prosperity and success. You are more talented and capable than you will ever know. Slow the boat and look at what you're doing—really look. Are you making decisions from a place of strength and consideration? Or fear? Are you using all you were given, or are you making the motions and taking a backseat while time moves along without you? How is your heart? What does it need from you? From this life?
- **Get community.** Women thrive when we work together, nourish one another, support one another. When we tend and befriend, we lower our cortisol and elevate our consciousness. Build and develop a network of women who raise you up.
- **Don't just self-care, CARE:** Wellness isn't a luxury; it's the way we replenish ourselves so that we can create the love and energy we were put on this earth to give. Put your oxygen mask on before you help others. Make a conscious effort to live with intention and feed your soul.
- **Raise the vibration.** Whether you are a woman or a man, you play a significant role in what our civilization will look like in the next five or ten years, and how we write the history of the legal profession. What can you do to strengthen and encourage the people around you? Where have you fallen short, and what can you do to do it better next time? How can you be of service to those around you? Lawyers are leaders, baby. Be the light. Guide the way.

Appendix B

Fee-Sharing Agreement

The following is one example of a fee-sharing agreement we've used in California, one of the states where we both practice. Check your state rules for required language in your jurisdiction.

ASSOCIATE ATTORNEY AUTHORIZATION AND FEE-SHARING AGREEMENT

This disclosure is being made pursuant to California Rules of Professional Conduct, Rule Conduct 2-200.

I understand and agree that the following division of fees will be made in my personal injury case arising from a _____ incident.

The attorney's fees earned in the case will be divided as follows:

50 % of attorney's fee to _____

50 % of attorney's fee to _____

I understand that this division of attorney's fees does not affect the amount of my recovery. I understand that the total fee charged by all lawyers is not increased solely because of the division of fees set forth above and is not unconscionable as that term is defined in rule 4-200.

Dated:

Signed: _____
               Client

Appendix C

Motion to Request Adequate Time for Voir Dire

This is a sample of the motion that we use to request adequate time from the judge for voir dire and a mini-opening, for the state of California. We file this motion or a similar one in every case we try, in every jurisdiction.

SUPERIOR COURT OF THE STATE OF CALIFORNIA
FOR THE COUNTY OF XXX

XXX, an individual,	) CASE NO.:
Plaintiffs,	) PLAINTIFF'S Motion *in limine* to
vs.	) preclude any preset time
XXX,	) limitations on voir dire and to
Defendants.	) permit a mini-opening statement
	) PURSUANT TO CODE OF CIVIL
	) PROCEDURE § 222.5

TO THE COURT, ALL PARTIES, AND THEIR COUNSEL OF RECORD:

Plaintiff respectfully moves the Court *in limine* for an order to preclude any preset time limitations on voir dire pursuant to Code of Civil Procedure § 222.5. Plaintiff further requests a 3-5 minute mini-opening statement, which must be granted by this Court as a result of amendments to Code of Civil Procedure § 222.5, which took effect on January 1, 2018. This motion is based on this notice and memorandum of points and authorities; the pleadings, records, and files in this action; and on such other evidence as may be presented at the hearing.

MEMORANDUM OF POINTS OF AUTHORITIES

A. Trial Courts Shall Not Establish Arbitrary Time Limits for Voir Dire or Establish a Blanket Policy of a Time Limit for Voir Dire

Plaintiff asks that this Court not preestablish a time limit on voir dire. Plaintiff's counsel has no intention of wasting time, covering irrelevant subject matter, or otherwise delaying the voir dire process. Rather, it is critically important that all counsel have the opportunity to engage in a full, complete, and probing examination of all potential jurors to ensure that no potential jurors with inherent biases or prejudices for or against either party are selected as members of the jury panel.

Jury selection is a dynamic process. The subject matter raised by the venire and the amount of time necessary to thoroughly explore issues of bias and prejudice vary not only from case to case but from venire to venire. Thus, to be given a predetermined amount of time within which to conduct questioning of jurors for bias ignores the inherently dynamic nature of jury selection. A predetermined time limitation on voir dire makes it impossible for the parties to benefit from what the Legislature intended of the voir dire process: that potential jurors be liberally questioned to explore potential biases and prejudices.

Code of Civil Procedure § 222.5 states in relevant part:

> (a) To select a fair and impartial jury in a civil jury trial, the trial judge shall conduct an initial examination of prospective jurors.
>
> (b)(1) Upon completion of the trial judge's initial examination, counsel for each party shall have the right to examine, by oral and direct questioning, any of the prospective jurors in order to enable counsel to intelligently exercise both peremptory challenges and challenges for cause. The scope of the examination conducted by counsel shall be within reasonable limits prescribed by the trial judge in the judge's sound discretion subject to the provisions of this chapter. During any examination conducted by counsel for the parties, the trial judge shall permit liberal and probing examination calculated to discover bias or prejudice with regard to the circumstances of the particular case before the court. The fact that a topic has been included in the trial judge's examination shall not preclude appropriate follow up questioning in the same area by counsel. The trial judge shall permit counsel to conduct voir dire examination without requiring prior submission of the questions unless a particular counsel engages in improper questioning.
>
> **(2) The trial judge shall not impose specific unreasonable or arbitrary time limits or establish an inflexible time limit policy for voir dire.**

Cal. Civ. Proc. Code § 222.5 (emphasis added)

Thus, Plaintiff requests that no predetermined time limitation be established for voir dire.

B. Plaintiff Hereby Requests a Brief 3- to 5-Minute Mini-Opening Statement Prior to Voir Dire, Which Must Be Allowed Pursuant to CCP § 222.5(d).

Amendments to Code of Civil Procedure § 222.5 that took effect on January 1, 2018, require the court to allow a mini-opening statement prior to voir dire at the request of any party:

> (d) Upon the request of a party, the trial judge shall allow a brief opening statement by counsel for each party prior to the commencement of the oral questioning phase of the voir dire process.

CCP § 222.5(d) (emphasis added)

Plaintiff hereby requests a 3- to 5-minute mini-opening statement, which, by law, must be granted.

Conclusion

Pursuant to Code of Civil Procedure § 222.5, Plaintiff respectfully requests that this Court allow liberal voir dire without preset time limitations and permit a 3- to 5-minute mini-opening statement prior to voir dire.

Appendix D

Juror Questionnaire

1. Please state:
    a. Your full name: _____
    b. Age: ____ Gender: _____ Place of Birth: _____
    c. Place(s) you were raised: _____
    _____

    d. Present marital status:
    Single and never married ____
    Divorced and was married for ____ years
    Separated and was married for ____ years
    Widowed and was married for ____ years
    Married currently for ____ years
    Living with partner for ____ years
    Engaged to be married ____

    If you have been married more than once, please state the length of each marriage: _____
    _____

2. If you have children or step-children, please list the following:

Age & Sex	Level of Education	Occupation, if adult	City of residence	Who child lives with

For adult children or step-children, please state occupation(s) of partners or spouses: _____
_____

3. The city of your present residence: _____
   a. Length of residence in the city: _____
   b. General area in which you reside: _____
   c. Other cities you have lived in, in this state: _____
   _____
   d. Other states you have lived in, in this country: _____
   _____
   e. Other countries you have lived in: _____
   _____

4. Please describe your educational background:
   a. Completed high school: Yes ___ No ___
      G.E.D.? Yes ___ No ___
      If not, state last grade completed: _____
   b. Attended trade, technical, or business school: Yes ___ No ___
      School attended, type of study, and certificates received: _____
      _____
      _____
   c. Attended college and/or graduate school: Yes ___ No ___
      School attended, type of study, and degree received:
      _____

5. Please state your present and past occupations beginning with the most current. If you are retired, indicate your occupations before retirement. Indicate whether each job was full-time (FT) or part-time (PT). If you are disabled, please note whether this is temporary or permanent, and state the date(s) you went on disability:

Name of Business	Dates Employed	City	Title	Job Description

    a. Have you supervised other people at your present or past place of employment? Yes ___ No ___
    If so, please describe, including number of persons supervised:

_____
_____

6. Are you, or have you ever been, in business for yourself?
    Yes ___ No ___
    If "Yes", please explain, including type of business(es), when owned/operated, and the number of employees:

_____
_____

7. Has any family member or close friend ever been in business for himself/herself?
    Yes ___ No ___
    If "Yes", please explain, including type of business (es), when owned/operated, and the number of employees:

_____
_____

8. Please state the present and past occupations of your mate or spouse, beginning with the most current. If he/she is retired, indicate his/her occupations before retirement. Indicate whether each job was full-time (FT) or part-time (PT). If your mate or spouse is disabled, please note whether this is temporary or permanent, and state the date(s) he/she went on disability:

Name of Business	Dates Employed	City	Title	Job Description

9. Please state the occupations (past, if retired or deceased) of your parents and/or step-parents:

   _____
   _____

10. What clubs or organizations do you and/or your spouse or partner belong to?

    _____
    _____

11. Please describe any special skills you may have, or are developing, non-work as well as work-related:

    _____
    _____

    a. Please state what you consider your areas of expertise: _____
    _____

12. If you or any family member or close friend has ever studied and/or worked in the field of law, please describe:

    _____
    _____

13. If you or any family member or close friend has ever studied and/or worked in the field of law enforcement (of any type), please describe:

    _____
    _____

14. If you or any family member or close friend has ever studied and/or worked in the field of medicine, please describe:
   _____
   _____

15. If you or any family member or close friend has ever studied and/or worked in the field of insurance, please describe:
   _____
   _____

16. If you or any family member or close friend has ever studied and/or worked in the field of risk management, please describe:
   _____
   _____

17. If you or any family member or close friend has ever studied and/or worked in the field of accident reconstruction, please describe:
   _____
   _____

18. If you or any family member or close friend has ever studied and/or worked in the field transportation, please describe:
   _____
   _____

19. If you have ever sought the services of any lawyer for any purpose, please explain:
   _____
   _____

   a. If you have ever been to court for any reason other than jury duty, please describe the circumstances:
      _____
      _____

20. If you have ever had any direct contact with law enforcement officers, e.g. filing complaints, answering questions, being stopped, being detained, reporting a crime, please describe the circumstances:

_____
_____

21. Have you or anyone close to you ever sued (or filed a claim against) any person and/or business or entity? Yes ___ No ___
    If so, what was the case about?

    _____
    _____

    What was the outcome?

    _____
    _____

22. Have you or anyone close to you ever been sued by anyone? Yes ___ No ___
    If so, what was the case about?

    _____
    _____

    What was the outcome?

    _____
    _____

23. Have you or anyone close to you ever owned a business that was sued or that had any type of claim brought against it or its employees? Yes ___ No ___
    If so, what was the case about?

    _____
    _____

    What was the outcome?

    _____
    _____

24. Have you or anyone close to you ever given a deposition and/or testified in any proceeding? Yes __ No __
If so, please explain:
_____
_____

25. Do you have a valid driver's license? Yes __ No __.
If "No", have you ever had a valid driver's license? Yes __ No __
What states? _____

   a. What types of vehicles are you qualified to drive?
   _____
   _____

26. If you do not drive a motor vehicle, please state the reason:
_____
_____

27. What types of vehicles or machinery are you experienced in driving?
_____
_____

   a. Please describe the vehicles driven by your immediate family; including you:
   _____
   _____

   b. Please describe the vehicles driven by your immediate family as part of their work, if any; including you:
   _____
   _____

   c. Have you or anyone close to you been involved in a serious accident of any kind while driving on the job? Yes __ No __
   _____
   _____

If "Yes", please explain:
_____
_____

28. If driving is, or has been, part of the job responsibilities of yourself or anyone close to you, please state the nature of employment:
_____
_____

29. Please describe in detail any serious motor vehicle accidents you have had:
_____
_____

   a. Please do the same for relatives and close friends:
   _____
   _____

   b. If anyone close to you has ever been injured, been disabled, or has died as a result of traumatic injuries from a motor vehicle accident, please describe:
   _____
   _____

30. Please describe in detail any injury accidents (not just vehicle-related) you have caused:
_____
_____

   a. Please do the same for relatives and close friends:
   _____
   _____

31. If you have ever caused anyone to die, be injured, or be disabled as a result of traumatic injuries, please describe:
   _____
   _____

32. Have you ever belonged to any organization that has as its goal the promotion or enforcement of any specific law? Yes ___ No ___
   If so, please describe:
   _____
   _____

   a. Please list any current causes that you approve of/support:
   _____
   _____

33. Have you ever belonged to any organization that has as its goal the abolishment of any specific law? Yes ___ No ___

   a. Please list any current causes that you disapprove of/oppose:
   _____
   _____

34. Do you feel that you can be fair and impartial to both sides, should you sit as a juror to hear this lawsuit? Yes ___ No ___ Not sure ___
   Please explain your answer:
   _____
   _____

35. Do you believe that you can and will listen to the evidence presented by both sides in this lawsuit, accept the jury instructions given by the Court, and engage actively in the deliberation process with your fellow jurors? Yes __ No __ Not sure __
Please explain your answer:
_____
_____

36. Do you speak Spanish? Yes __ No __

37. What feelings, if any, do you have about people who speak only Spanish, and not English?
_____
_____

38. Are you an immigrant? Yes __ No __

39. What feelings, if any, do you have about people who immigrated to the United States from Mexico?
_____
_____

40. Do you have any beliefs that might prevent you from serving as a juror on this case? Yes __ No __
If "Yes", please explain:
_____
_____

41. Is there any information not asked in this questionnaire you feel the Court should know about you? Yes __ No __
If so, what is that information?
_____
_____

42. What purpose do you think lawyers serve in our society?
_____
_____

43. Do you believe that accidents and injuries are just a part of life and should not be the subject of a lawsuit? Yes ___ No ___
Please explain your answer:
_____
_____

44. If you or a loved one were seriously injured or killed because of the fault of someone else, would you consider bringing a lawsuit? Yes ___ No ___
Please explain your answer:
_____
_____

45. How do you feel about awarding money damages to compensate a family member for the loss of financial support that they would have in later years received from the person who was killed in an accident?
Strongly Agree ___ Somewhat Agree ___ Somewhat Disagree ___ Strongly Disagree ___
Please explain your answer:
_____
_____

46. How do you feel about awarding money damages to compensate a family member for the loss of love, companionship, comfort, care, and affection that they would have received from the person who was killed in an accident?
Strongly Agree ___ Somewhat Agree ___ Somewhat Disagree ___ Strongly Disagree ___
Please explain your answer:
_____
_____

47. How do you feel about awarding money damages to compensate a seriously injured person for his medical expenses, loss of income, and pain suffering?
    Strongly Agree ___ Somewhat Agree ___ Somewhat Disagree ___ Strongly Disagree ___
    Please explain your answer:
    _____
    _____

48. Do you support caps or limits on the amount of money juries can award in a civil case? Yes ___ No ___
    Please explain your answer:
    _____
    _____

49. Some people are opposed to the idea of lawsuits brought for financial compensation over the death of a family member because the money will not bring the person back. Do you:
    Strongly Agree ___ Somewhat Agree ___ Somewhat Disagree ___ Strongly Disagree ___
    Please explain your answer:
    _____
    _____

50. Some people are opposed to the idea of lawsuits brought for financial compensation over the injuries of a person. Do you:
    Strongly Agree ___ Somewhat Agree ___ Somewhat Disagree ___ Strongly Disagree ___
    Please explain your answer:
    _____
    _____

51. Do you have any hesitations about making a multi-million dollar award if the evidence supports such an award? Yes ___ No ___
Please explain your answer:

_____
_____

52. As you sit here now, do you already have a limit in mind that you could never go over in awarding damages, no matter what the evidence was? Yes ___ No ___
Please explain your answer:

_____
_____

I certify, under penalty of perjury, that the foregoing is true and correct, and that I have received no assistance from any other person in completing this questionnaire. Executed in the County of _____.

Print name: _____ Signature: _____ Date: _____

About the Authors

(Courtney Rowley & Theresa Bowen Hatch, photo by Jaime Baird)

Courtney Rowley

Trial work has been my passion since I was a young teenager on the Oxnard High School mock trial team. I attended USC as an undergraduate and studied at Aberysthwyth in Wales. During law school at Loyola, I was on the Byrne Team and after winning the National Trial Advocacy Competition I was asked to come work for one of the top civil trial law firms in the country. I quickly learned that in order to truly get jury trial experience I would have to leave that very prestigious law firm. Against the advice of pretty much everybody, I left and never looked back. Slowly but surely, I built my own practice and reputation and have had the honor of litigating and trying cases all across the country.

I have represented many people who have been wrongfully or over zealously accused of crimes but my primary focus has been on helping injury victims and families overcome the hurdles of exercising their fundamental rights to the jury trial method of achieving justice in cases of discrimination, medical malpractice, brain injury, wrongful death, and catastrophic injuries. All the cases I have civilly prosecuted, to the tune of many hundreds of millions of dollars in victories, have involved insurance companies or governmental entities who have pools of money reserved and set aside to pay out on claims. In other words, I have never taken a penny from an individual civil defendant.

I teach and speak across the country to help preserve and develop the jury trial method. I have practiced and taught at the Gerry Spence Trial Lawyers College in Dubois, Wyoming, where I met my husband, Nicholas Rowley. Nick and I have worked as a trial team for over a decade.

I am a mother, avid reader, traveler/explorer, and yogi. There is nothing I love more than discovering new places and being outside connected to nature. Currently, I have two toddlers so I also eat a lot of vitamins and have a new ability to nap in the most absurd places. We live between Ojai, California and Decorah, Iowa. Together with Nick we have ten kids, ranging in age from naked baby to junior high schooler to college student to adult. Our eldest is currently serving as a combat corpsman in the United States Navy assigned to a Marine Corps unit, following the footsteps of his father who served in the US Air Force and Army.

I stand with many women and those who have come before us. The struggles, determination, creativity and enduring courage of women have made it possible for me to be where I am today and do what it is I seek to pull us further and inspire others. My gratitude grows the older I get. But for the most part, I have worked in a world consisting mostly of men being in charge, under their rules in their systems. I have grown up in a world that does not truly respect and honor women as equals. I have smiled in the face of discrimination more times than I could ever count and bent and shaped myself to be accepted and fit the expectations of these systems more than I wanted to admit, especially to myself.

As a woman, I have run the gamut of trying to balance life, from trying cases pregnant to being too overwhelmed and exhausted to care about practicing law. I am constantly recalibrating myself, redesigning what time and energy means for me and the ones I love. I still sometimes feel that I am just getting started.

Throughout my career, I would have loved to have had a guide, a mentor, someone I could trust, who could tell me how to traverse the terra incognita of being a female in a male dominated profession. I was so blessed to meet my best friend and law partner, Theresa Hatch. Together, we prop one another up and have been cheering and picking each other up for almost a decade. We hope that this book can be a guide for you, whether you are a woman or a man in the legal profession, or any profession, who is looking for some support and encouragement as you navigate the modern world.

There is a lot of power in knowing we are not alone. There are a lot of powerful, sometimes hilarious, stories in this book from creative, awake, courageous women. We have been sitting down and sharing meals with women and men who are excited and engaged in breaking away from the exclusion and subjugation of the past.

We certainly don't have all of the answers, but we are working very hard and are ready to shift the narrative. Together, we certainly can, I know it!

Theresa Bowen Hatch

Trial work is my second career, although it's now lasted so long that it's hard to remember when I was an on-air television news reporter and journalist. It seems I've always taken awhile to find the path that's the right fit for me. I went to three different colleges before graduating from the University of Virginia, worked for several different news organizations as a reporter and writer, went to two different law schools before graduating cum laude from the University of Baltimore School of Law as a two-time fellow of the Stephen L. Snyder Center for Litigation Skills, and didn't find and marry my perfect match in love and life until I was thirty-five.

The common thread in my work and pursuit of those paths, though, has always been a love of storytelling and shedding light on injustices. That passion was born at the Associated Press, grew during my years in television where I learned how to tell a story with almost nothing but images, and endures in my work as a lawyer. These cases that we're so privileged to work are the stories of people's lives.

I am a storyteller, a businesswoman, an entrepreneur, an avid runner and yogi, a lover of real estate and home design, a collector of crystal, and, above all, a wife and mother. My time with my family is precious, and over the years, I've experimented with many different ways of running my law practice around my family. Mostly, I work from my home office, rather than my "work" office, with an open door and kiddos toddling in an out throughout the day showing me pictures they've drawn, crawling under the desk, or climbing up onto my lap for a bear hug and a smooch.

My goal is to live more than I work, to keep the work from feeling like work, and to be someone and do something that helps people every day. Every day looks different. But every day is real, and every day is a gift.

In my career, I've been mentored by, and worked with, some of the best trial lawyers in the country—all of them men. Over and over, I found that the trial skills I learned from them—what they did in trial and how they tried their cases—didn't work for me as a woman. It took me a long time to learn that I'm best when I'm being me and not trying to be them. That's a lesson that I first learned as a student at Gerry Spence's Trial Lawyer's College and something I'm still practicing every day.

My dear friend, Courtney Rowley, and I founded Trial by Woman together, when we realized that the mentorship, support, guidance, cheerleading, inspiration, respect, and pure "we're in this togetherness" that we had in each other was something that most other women trial lawyers we knew didn't have. We started as friends and became business partners. We work cases together, try cases together, travel together, play with our kids together, recommend books to one another, challenge each other, go down the rabbit hole together, and have held hands through the biggest events life has had in store for us thus far—personally and professionally.

We want for you what we have in each other. That's why we're creating this community. Because, together, we are all Trial by Woman.